On The Election Of Grace

Or Of The Will Of God In Regard To Men. That Is A Short Exposition And Introduction Concerning The Highest Ground, Showing How Man May Attain To Divine Knowledge. Further, How The Passages Of Scripture Are To Be Understood That Treat Of Fallen Corrupt Adam And Of The New Birth From Christ.

Theosophic Questions
or
A General View Of Divine Revelation

Showing What God, Nature And Creature, As Well As Heaven, Hell And The World, Together With All Creatures, Are. From Whence All Things In Nature Have Had Their Origin, And Why God Has Created Them, And What They Are Useful or Profitable For. And In Particular Regarding Man, What Adam And Christ Is. Begun to be answered (but not completed) out of a right true theosophic ground in the year 1624.

Jacob Boehme

ISBN 1-56459-146-8

'I looked above, and saw in all of space but One;
Looked down, and saw in the foaming waves but One;
O heart, whether thou swimmest in floods or glowest in heat,
Flood and glow is but one; be it thine to be pure;
For where love awaketh, then dieth
The I, the dark despot of life.'

JELÁLEDDÍN.

From Hegel's *Philosophy of Art*,
translated by Professor Hastie.

CONTENTS

BIOGRAPHICAL SKETCH

ON THE ELECTION OF GRACE

THEOSOPHIC QUESTIONS

SKETCH OF THE
LIFE OF JACOB BÖHME

BY

DR. HERMANN ADOLPH FECHNER

TRANSLATED FROM THE GERMAN

INTRODUCTORY NOTE

THE want of information regarding the life of the theosophist, Jacob Böhme, may be easily explained. On the one hand, his existence was poor in external facts, because, like most of his spiritual brethren, he lived in a secluded way, removed from public concerns and affairs; and only the rough interference of alien forces was able to bring about his passive rise to eminence in his lifetime. On the other hand, his adherents and friends, in the same interest of inwardness (which considers the turbulent multiplicity of the world, not as material to be worked at, but as belonging to another and strange country), desired to know in letters, not his fortunes, but the experiences of his spiritual life and the kind of knowledge given by his mystical faculty. So indifferent were even important parts of his external life to the devotion to truth in his friends, that not only did they trouble themselves little about matter-of-factness and accuracy, but also under their eyes and pens, in their memory and narrative, such portions of his life unconsciously became an embellished fable. They had never questioned the master closely about his outward lot. After his death, indeed, they attached importance to the preservation of his writings, but not to the clarifying and correct delineation of his history. A third contingency even reduced the already essentially meagre sources. In the troubles and disturbances of the Thirty Years' War, few of his fellow-citizens felt themselves moved to record with accuracy the civil occurrences of their native town, political events having a more pressing claim upon the attention of the annalists, though even in this branch a certain meagreness and deficiency during the period of the war is unmistakable. Finally, the persecution of Böhme's followers and their dispersion to Holland was doubtless the occasion of the extant epistolary records, with incidental notices of circumstances in Böhme's life, being almost all scattered and lost.

THE LIFE OF JACOB BÖHME

1. *The civil life of Jacob Böhme.*

JACOB BÖHME was born in 1575 at Alt-Seidenberg, a village near the little town of Seidenberg in the Oberlausitz, immediately on the Bohemian frontier. The day of his birth and christening cannot now be determined, as the church-registers of Seidenberg only begin with the year 1630. He was the son of respected and well-to-do country-people, the descendant of a family which, to infer from its name (which may with the same right, according to the documentary evidence, be written Behme, Behem, Bheme, Böhm, Böhmer, Behmer and Bohem), and still more from the nearness of the Bohemian frontier, had its origin in Bohemia. As early as 1416 in the municipal records of Görlitz there is mention of a Hannes Böhme in Seidenberg, who doubtless was one of the theosophist's ancestors. Jacob was the fourth child of his father Jacob and his mother Ursula. His brothers and sisters were named Ursula, George, Michael and Martin. Old Jacob later married again, and the issue from this second marriage was three daughters, namely: Elizabeth, who married a certain Martin Schubert in Bellmannsdorf; Dorothy, afterwards the wife of Matthew Brandt at Görlitz; and Mary, who at the death of the father (which took place in 1619) was still a minor. On the 7th of February 1607, he had, on account of his second wife, come to an understanding with his children in regard to matters relating to their inheritance. Ambrose, the grandfather of Jacob Böhme, had had seven children: Hans, Merten, Ambrose, Ann, Margaret, Jacob (the father of the theosophist) and Dorothy. If Frankenberg[1] intends to make Böhme's family poor starvelings, such

[1] The authority most used for the life of Böhme, and the source richest in contents, is unquestionably the biography of Abraham von Frankenberg. He wrote it in Latin in 1637, and Henry Prunius translated it into German. It is, however, somewhat scanty in information, which, moreover, is to be

testimony rests upon a complete error. Of the grandfather, Ambrose, it is known that he was a respected man in the village, and filled the office of judge's Associate (*Gerichtschöppe*). He died in 1563. According to the custom of the country his farm passed to the youngest son, Jacob, who bought it off from the other heirs for six hundred marks at Martinmas 1563. For the same sum, Michael, the brother of the theosophist, acquired it in the year 1619 after the father's death, who (like the grandfather) had been judge's Associate, and also from 1568 lay-elder.

Unfortunately, exact information regarding the boyhood and youth of Jacob Böhme is almost entirely awanting. Only idle fictions of Frankenberg, which do not hold their ground against criticism, attempt to fill up the gap of these years. Jacob was sent by his parents to the town-school at Seidenberg, where he received comparatively good school teaching from the excellent rector, Johann Leder of Schmiedeberg. At that period such instruction was an educational advantage over most of the members of his stock, and this he owed to his being intended early for the artisan class. His weakness and sickliness from childhood made him unfit to engage in agriculture; although, as the youngest son, he would have been the rightful inheritor of the paternal farm. From the career thus early assigned to him by his parents, as well as from his bodily constitution, may be recognized the origin of that mysticism which later on flourished to perfection, and of the strong impulse towards thought and speculation. The office of teaching was then regarded entirely as a department and auxiliary of theology, and the Holy Scripture, by command of the theologian Government, had to be held as the basis of sacred and profane science. And if going to a school of this period had not yet more particularly given occasion to Böhme (with his natural tendency to inward absorption) for the deep religious development of

used with great caution. The author is well known by his propensity to believe all that is marvellous and to make use of it uncritically, to fashion the simplest facts into mysterious and magical enigmas, and to see everywhere spirits, spectres and spells. His writings abound in confused and absurdly artificial formulae and signs, which among the mystics of that period were made vehicles of occult powers and sciences.

his mind, yet the statement of Frankenberg, that even when a boy he was assiduous in his attendance at Church, and was quiet and God-fearing, may make the early taking of that direction intelligible. The father, moreover, according to a tradition, is said to have adhered to mystical doctrines; and the report is most credible, for in his position as lay-elder he might well feel himself led to speak much on religious matters in the family as well as in the congregation—just as if he belonged to the clergy himself—and above all to attach importance to a God-fearing disposition in his own house. Frankenberg goes too far when he adds that the logomachy of the theological schools was already odious to the boy, seeing he will in childhood hardly have come into such controversial circles; and neither his judgment thereon could be mature, nor could even an accidentally correct judgment be ascribed to him by way of commendation, which after all was the motive of the writer in adding this piece of intelligence. But it was very natural if the sedentary mode of life in the school, the continual preaching of theological teachers on repentance and faith, the assiduous church-going and the deepened perusal of the Bible,—it was natural if all this gave to a mind (which, in view of the weakness of his body, it was easy to excite) an obscure and darkly confused trend of reflection; and implanted in his breast a restless desire, which took root in an unfathomable depth, leading to a rapturous dwelling upon a goal, whose clearness was lost through the predominance of the world of feeling, and through the prevailing deficiency of the school education, which least of all was fitted to train speculative minds. His school education was defective as compared with the vast field which he attempted to win from the sphere of metaphysics. What a boy of fourteen years, destined to follow a handicraft, had learned in the school of a very small place, could never extend so far as to convey to him the terminology and logic necessary for the intelligibleness of a completely superseded philosophy, in such a way that, equipped with a higher culture, he might have occupied a recognized place in the learned literary world. He remained a theosophist, and did not become a philosophic thinker.

The chief thing that he carried away from his school in regard to learning were some scraps of Latin, which afterwards he turned to account in all directions, so as to become intelligible as well as unintelligible. But most of these expressions, which are brought in so frequently to the astonishment of the reader, are of theosophic origin and the result of later associations. So much, however, is evident, that a miracle did not, as the superstitious chroniclers claim, instil as by a stroke of magic the art of writing into the already grown-up theosophist. On the contrary, even his father knew how to wield the pen. And if the facility of a writer of our century still lay very far removed from the pen of the son, yet the large number of works and the scribbling diffuse style show that for him the difficulties of writing were a long way from outweighing the pleasure of intellectual production.

Now, while undoubted germs of Böhme's later development may be discovered among the intimations respecting his boyhood, it is to be regretted that, with the exception of the most scanty notices, all the trustworthy and genuine sources pertaining to the years of apprenticeship and travel leave us in the lurch. And it is so much the more to be regretted, as it is just in these years, when it is usual for every individual to adopt decidedly the later bent of his mind and character, that Böhme's nature also received the first firm impress. The turning to theosophy, to the mystical view of nature accompanied with ethical colouring, was certainly conditioned by outer influences, by intercourse or opposition, by attracting or repelling forces.

In his fourteenth year (1589) Jacob entered upon his apprenticeship to a shoemaker at Seidenberg, and in 1599 he became a master of the craft at Görlitz. On the 10th of May 1599 he married Katherine Kuntzschmann, the daughter of a master butcher of Görlitz. For more than twenty-five years, till the time of his death, Böhme lived with his wife in a happy and undisturbed union, which was blessed with six children. The sponsors of the children were all of burgher stock ; a fact pointing to Böhme having moved almost wholly in the narrow plebeian circles of the people of his own rank during the period of the exercise of his trade. On the other hand, there is no mention of the names of the sponsors in his Epistles, which date from a later period. The protectors, adherents and friends of the theosophist belonged for the most part to the nobility and the learned professions. His subsequent activity in the workshop of the mind had removed him from the common circles of the petty citizen-class which earlier he had been used to, and which in that age had sunk low. This activity introduced him to new acquaintances who shared his views and his longing, unhampered by the trammels of a mechanic calling and a mechanic sentiment. His old friends withdrew from him when attempts to incite on the part of the clergy sought to throw upon Böhme, who was said to be in relation with diabolic powers, the gloomy light of a heretic and a sorcerer.

Faithfully and diligently Jacob Böhme long continued to follow his trade. Indeed within a few years he had saved so much that in 1610 he was able to buy himself a house. Along with a mastership in the craft he had also acquired a cobbler's stall, but he sold it in 1613, when for the sake of writing he dropped his trade entirely. His newly-gained friends furnished him with assistance, so that he might devote himself with greater freedom from disturbance to his intellectual sphere of activity. Nevertheless the poor thinker often fell into pressing privation and want, as this assistance doubtless only reached him irregularly, and in relation to the needs of the father of a family was of little account. Just as little could the 470 marks obtained by the sale of his cobbler's stall long suffice for his maintenance. Even though the unity and the harmony of his internal state with the external relationships of life afforded him more satisfaction than a comfortable existence, which, by disregarding his impulse towards solving the inner contradiction, he might have obtained and supplemented by his trade; yet his cares at times drew from him plaints which his spiritual energy could not stifle. Thus in 1619 he writes: 'But I know at present no other means [than worldly occupations] to support the earthly body, along with wife and children. Therefore I will make zealous endeavour, and put the heavenly before all things so far as lies in my power' (Epistle 4). Accordingingly he found himself compelled now and again to have recourse to another branch of industry, so that he could sometimes complain that he was overwhelmed with too much worldly business (Epistle 1). By this he meant not merely care and anxiety in providing for the transmission of his writings, which he took upon himself at request. For some years he carried on a trade in woollen gloves, which he bought up from the peasants of the surrounding country, and took to market to Prague annually in the autumn. Further, at times he had recourse again to the cobbler's trade. It was on one of these business trips that Jacob Böhme saw the entry of the new king of Bohemia (Frederick v., Count Palatine) into Prague.

The Thirty Years' War, whose weight, just at the beginning, pressed heavily upon Bohemia and its dependencies, did not exempt our theosophist from its evils. Particularly in consequence of Frederick's accession to the throne in Prague, and his ill success, a host of public calamities tumbled upon the six cities of Upper Lusatia. The Elector John George I. of Saxony, in alliance with the Emperor Ferdinand, ordered Lusatia to be recovered from the Margrave John George of Jagerndorf (generalissimo at that time to Frederick v.) by the Burgrave Karl Hannibal of Dohna, who erected to himself in Silesia a bloody monument of his cruelty. Bautzen was compelled to surrender after a rigorous siege; it experienced all the horrors in the form of an obdurate and unmerciful foe. Görlitz also had to yield, and received a garrison of Saxon and imperial troops. Hoë von Hoënegg was preaching then in Bautzen cathedral in support of his master, the Elector, and the only orthodox Lutheran religion, which then was shamelessly ogling Catholicism and its champions, or the *Ecclesia militans*. As early as 1619 the Emperor Ferdinand had suffered barbarous Polish marauding parties to be sent into his rebellious territories by the Prince Bishop of Warsaw. These gangs of robbers, known and feared at that time under the name of Cossacks, and consisting of congregated riffraff, fleeced the inhabitants with inhuman cruelty, and swarmed through Silesia, Moravia and Bohemia, in order to restore the authority of the emperor and the only saving Church. For several years they continued to press heavily upon the eastern part of the empire, as fresh predatory bands were continually allured by gain and the word of the emperor. Jacob Böhme speaks of these ravages thus: 'For something of the great misery and horrible plundering, murdering and unheard of devilishness in Christendom which the Cossacks while passing through Silesia have worked among our neighbours, is perhaps known to you' (Epistle 34).

When Böhme was in Dresden in the spring of 1624, he witnessed such another public festivity as the entry of the Palatine Frederick into Prague. The emperor had just concluded peace with Bethlen Gabor. Everybody was jubilant; but from the first those better informed could not expect a long continuance of this state of things. In the sixty-second Epistle he says: 'Dresden is at present a city of rejoicing, as Prague was a short time ago, and affords a brilliant spectacle. From Hungary it is reported almost certainly that peace has been concluded between the emperor and Bethlen Gabor, but advices run differently.'

Böhme was small of stature, fallen away, and of a sorry appearance. It is probable that his constitution, weakly in itself, suffered moreover from the sedentary mode of life, from exhausting excitation of mind and nervous excitement. His temples were prominent, his nose aquiline, his eyes blue, his beard short and thin, his voice weak but of most pleasing sound in discourse. It is thus that Frankenberg describes the exterior of the man, of whom no further description exists. The pictures met with here and there are not authentic portraits.

The leaning towards contemplative mysticism must be designated as the fundamental trait of the whole character of Jacob Böhme. From this point of view all his distinguishing peculiarities—his virtues, his weaknesses, his externalisms that appear paradoxical—become intelligible. This fundamental trait of his character was intensely and profoundly religious. The impulse towards reflection and speculation was deeply rooted in this religious tone of mind. He sought for God everywhere. The inmost core of all religion, namely, the ethical relationship of man, was the secret which he attempted to wrest from heaven. In this attempt his entire self was merged. The centre, the source of the whole of things, drew all his yearnings and fibres, and therefrom his reflection proceeded. From that position he viewed all resolves, which were approved by mature consideration, as emanations of his religious consciousness. Gentleness and inwardness gave to the religious feature the outwardly attractive colouring peculiar to the contemplative mystics. As the Deity was in his heart, and the conviction given by the strong soul could alone afford him experience of his regeneration, of the Divine fact of inward sanctification (which to obtain from without was impossible to him, as the authority of his ego suffered not the intrusion of a foreign will into its sanctuary), he accordingly held the external forms of the visible church to be merely an accessory thing for the salvation of the Christian. Ceremonial worship, as soon as the true Christianity was beheld in it, formalistic faith and logomachy, as at that time was agreeable to the orthodox theologians and regarded as a most important part of divine worship, was an abomination to him. Thus on one occasion he exclaims: 'O thou antichristian world, what hast thou worked with thy ceremonies, that thou hast put them in the place of God! The Councils have only been directed to this point, that thou mightest be master of silver and gold, and of men's souls and consciences! It were better to have no ceremonies, but merely the practice of the express command of God' (*Threefold Life*, xi. 56). 'Dear Christendom has been led out of all the apostolic orders or virtues into human ordinances, and in seeming holiness the kingdom of Christ has been made a kingdom of pomp and show in connection with baptism and the Lord's Supper. Men have added ceremonies. O had they but kept the right faith and understanding' (*Threefold Life*, xiii. 28).

The inward mode of apprehension of the Christian doctrine was in the case of Böhme a strict requirement, for the sake of which he gave up all other goods. Impulse towards inner truth had spurred him on to laborious intellectual efforts; and when the Holy Scriptures, the foundation of his spiritual property, and which he reverenced highly, exhibited obscurities and contradictions to themselves and to sound reason, the impulse towards inner truth did not cause him to shrink from bringing them before the tribunal of his own conviction, which had attained to manifest clearness. Very different from those orthodox pastors and their devout flock, void of thought and will, who believed that they found just in contradiction, in absurdity and in the blind reciting of obscure formulae, the blessed mystery of Christianity, or rather of Lutheranism. In this connection Böhme declaims against external apprehension of the forgiveness of sin thus: 'Behold, thou poor wounded soul, thou standest and prayest: O God, forgive me my sins, let thy anger subside, and receive me into grace. And that is quite right; but thou understandest not how God receiveth the poor sinner. Thou supposest it is as when thou comest before thy sovereign prince, and hast forfeited thy life, and beseechest him, and he forgiveth thee thy misdeed by favour, and so thou art quit and free. But thy sins convict thee to thy face, and thy heart accuseth thee that thou art still obnoxious to punishment. Consider! in this way thou comest likewise before God, and thus many hypocrites are made. Thou thinkest that God by His essence and spirit can take thy sins away from thee. If it were so, then God would have to put Himself in motion on account of every individual that invokes Him, and would have to throw away his sins from him. Knowest thou not what the Scriptures say, that all our works shall follow us? God has put Himself in motion from eternity no more than twice, namely, in the creation of the world and the incarnation of Christ. When God forgiveth thy sin, He taketh nothing from thee, neither doth He descend from heaven into thee; for He was from eternity in thy soul, but in His own principle. Thy soul is gone out from God, from His principle, out of the holy will of the Majesty into wrath. In the wrath thou wert in eternal death; and the man Christ, who is God and man, has made a way through death and wrath to the Majesty of God. Thou must turn round, and enter by this path into the Majesty' (*Threefold Life*, xi. 61, 62). Certainly one of the finest and loftiest passages relating to this problem.

With penetrating criticism Böhme himself attacks the tenor or import of Scripture when it is in conflict with science; an intellectual height which belonged not exactly to the character of his age, in which Kepler got recognition only as a gold-maker. Thus in *Aurora*, xx. 2, on occasion of the explanation of Gen. i. 6, 7, 8, he says: 'This description shows yet again that the dear man Moses was not the author of it, for it is written in an unthinking and simple way, though it has nevertheless an excellent meaning.' Further (*Aurora*, xix. 79): 'The scribe Moses writes: God divided the light from the darkness, and called the light day and the darkness night. Then of the evening and morning was made the first day. As the expression *evening and morning* runs contrary to philosophy and reason, it is to be held that Moses was not the author of it, for evening and morning did not exist before the time of the sun.'

The people of the letter call him a heretic. Worship of the word without independent conviction, and hence also belief in authority, are odious to him. 'Heretics are such people as are born of Reason. where words only are exchanged, and words are explained by words, where the mind never experiences what the power and meaning of the word is' (*Apol. Tilk.*, i. 111). 'Now, although Reason bawls: Give us the Scripture and the letter! yet the external letter alone is not sufficient for real knowledge. The living letter, which is God's expressed word and being, must be disclosed and read in man himself' (*Sign. Rer.*, Pref. 4).

Böhme was decried by his enemies, the orthodox Lutherans, as a heretic and atheist. It is true that the dead formularies of religious belief were not at all hours in his mouth, and on that account zealots cast suspicion upon him. And yet he was with his heart a Protestant, although he attacked unsparingly the defects of Lutheranism. Catholicism in his view is Antichrist.

Böhme kept to the outer Lutheran rites of worship; and though he despised ceremonies without inwardness, yet he disdained not form as a symbol of the spiritual state. Even the mystic felt the need of producing expressions and marks of the inner life in the sphere of externality. But he always preserved pure the principle of tolerance, which the mystics have of old set up so boldly and defended so courageously. It was only towards intolerance itself and towards the wrangling of the clergy that he knew no indulgence. One of the finest passages is found in the *Incarnation of Christ*, I. xiii. 3: 'You contend about religion, and yet there is no contention in religion: there are diversity of gifts, but one and the same spirit speaketh. As a tree has manifold branches, and the fruit has a manifold form, not being just like one another; or as the earth bears diverse herbs and flowers, the earth being the one mother: so is it with those who speak by God's spirit; each of them speaks out of the wonder of his gifts. But their tree or their field, upon which they rest, is Christ in God. And you, binders of spirit, will not suffer this. You insist on stopping the mouth of your Christ, whom yet you yourselves teach unknown with the earthly tongue, and insist on binding him to your law. O, the true church of Christ has no law! Christ is the temple where we must enter. The heap of stones does not make a new man. But the temple of Christ, where God's spirit teaches, awakens the half-dead image, so that it begins to bud.'

Just as Jacob Böhme in his early years had to bear scorn and mockery from his comrades, because he separated himself from them, led a solitary life, and was assiduous in his attendance at church, so did he continue to accustom himself to live always more and more in the inwardness of his world of feeling. Keeping watch on self makes the inner eye and ear delicate, and again, it makes every mental fact a matter of the heart. Hence his bearing towards others was gentle, modest and humble,—very rare virtues in those days of the most undisguised egoism. For in what else at that time did the ossified Philistinism consist, but in the narrow illiberal assertion of the personal ego, without being inspired by any social or theoretic idea of the whole with disregard for individuality? He respected the convictions of other individual subjects, if they were really inward, just as he himself did not wish to be disturbed in his own. On the other hand, as he knew nothing but his own inner self, this was expressed in a love of truth, in a directness and naïveté, which are everywhere conspicuous in his writings, and characterize his view of the world without. How often the reader finds him in most zealous colloquy with the devil, how often he converses with his own poor soul, and how simple-heartedly he tells what took place in the deepest ground of his soul! Once he addresses the evil Principle thus: 'Hearken Lucifer! Who is to blame for the fact that thou hast become a devil? Is it God, as thou lyingly sayest? *O No!* Thou thyself art to blame. The fountain-spirits in thy body, which thou thyself art, have brought forth such a son to thee. Thou canst not say that God hath kindled the Salitter out of which he made thee; but thy fountain-spirits have done so, when thou wert already a prince and king in God. Therefore when thou sayest that God hath created thee thus, or without sufficient reason hath spewed thee out of thy place, thou art a liar and a murderer. For the whole heavenly host bears witness against thee, that thou hast prepared for thyself the fierce fiery quality. If it be not true, then go before the face of God and justify thyself. But thou seest it well without that, and needest not to behold it. Wouldest thou not rather have a friendly kiss from the Son of God, that thou mightest be refreshed? If thou art right, then just look upon Him once, and perhaps thou wilt become sound' (*Aurora*, xiii. 49).

This naïveté sometimes rises even to poetry: 'If all trees were scribes and all branches pens, and if all hills were books and all waters ink, they could not give a sufficient description of the sorrow and misery which Lucifer with his angels has brought into his place' (*Aurora*, xvi. 26). It sounds equally naïve when he is incensed against the anatomists and men-flayers, or against the lawyers and their abettors.

Quite in this vein was his polemic against the attacks of other writers, which in the beginning was carried on in an extremely good-tempered way. He believed that everyone must be as true to his inner self and the world without as he himself was. With the most touching mildness he exhorts his opponents to gentleness. But when, as in his controversy with the Primarius, he is opposed by naked malice, and all his conciliatory exhortations are rejected with scorn, then anger gets the better of him, as the man true to nature. At this point he stoutly returns the blows received, and exposes the weaknesses of his opponent. 'It is a great shame,' he is addressing the Pastor-Primarius Richter, 'that you cause such untruth to be printed to the reproach of another. At your house would probably be found large flasks and glasses of spirits. But that the Primarius says I am fond of swilling foreign wines and spirits, this he infers from his own case, and thinks it is with another as with himself. O no! we poor folk have not wherewithal to pay for them; we must be content with a draught of beer, as we can produce it. But the Primarius must be supplied with foreign wines, though other people have to put up with smaller beverage. Spanish wines cause us sometimes to lose the Primarius. Further, it is evident by the wine-blossoms upon his face that he drinks strong wines much more than I do, for I have no such signs as he has. He drinks more foreign wines in a week than I do in a whole year. But I understand very well where the rub is: He knows that I through divine providence have often been commanded to go to great lords and nobles. Hence he imagines that, when we meet, we sit together and drink to excess, as he is wont to do among his company.' Now, when his opponent had been worsted, and he himself had obtained a recognition of his own worth, then in his heart that was overflowing with jubilation he could not refuse himself a triumph, which was as far removed from malicious joy as from over-tender, weak and characterless sentiment. Thus he writes from Dresden to Dr. Kober: 'If the Primarius at Görlitz have any complaint to make against me, he might present it here to the Electoral Council, and discontinue his poisonous calumnies in the Council at Görlitz. Here I would abide the decision of the law, and would set forth his lies to his face, which he has poured out in a venomous way regarding me before the congregation and in the pasquil.'

In this connection we have Böhme wholly as a child of his time. In the Apology directed against the Primarius the polemic comes out most sharply, though his other writings contain declamations on the universal corruption, which are filled with vigorous expressions, in language that appears obscene at the present day. The Revelation of John and certain books of the Old Testament could not but furnish material. There remains a rudeness that characterizes the age, and which admits not of natural growth in excuse. Moral and intellectual barbarism was the common evil, and lent to language that crude colouring. The power and originality of Luther and Hutten had once given it authorization. Such authorization now ceased to exist, for the spirit had gone to the devil and the *caput mortuum* had remained. Böhme so far forms an honourable exception, inasmuch as, apart from moderation and mystical mildness, he allowed only his undisguised feeling to speak, and exhibited therein character and simplicity; whereas in the case of others an openly displayed demoralization made its appearance.

The modesty and humility of which Böhme never divested himself,—neither when nobles and learned men disdained not to seek out the poor shoemaker in his dwelling, nor when the Electoral Court let him have its approbation,—recognized in fact the bounds of a strict morality. He never shrank from confessing the truth frankly and candidly. Want and persecution were able to draw sighs from him, but the noble pride of self-consciousness never left him. In privation and want he showed nobility of soul. Honestly throughout his life he gave proof of what he expresses in his written defence against Richter, namely, that it was not his custom to flatter the rich with a view to presents and gifts.

Such a nature must, quite consistently, have felt entirely in place in the bosom of the close familiarity of domestic life. There his heart built itself a temple. But when he passed into the manifoldness of public life, his eyes were easily dazzled. His view of his relation to the Saxon Court and of the outcome of the whole occurrence in Dresden, shows him as a man who was formed indeed for warm friendship, for true spiritual intercourse among narrow circles; but who, among courtiers and church dignitaries versed in the ways of the world, believed implicitly what was meant to be merely a form of politeness without truth, and would to his own eye, had it looked with keener glance, have been transformed into feint and show.

For a similar reason his political combinations, so far as the turbulent and pressing events of the day led him to make them, were at times startling. In the fourth Epistle he writes to Christian Bernhard thus: 'I admonish you to give heed as to whether the time of the great expedition be not at hand, upon the mountains of Israel in Babel; especially in regard to the Transylvanian, who will obtain aid from the Turks, and easily reach the river Rhine. I account, however, that the election of a right German Emperor must yet be delayed a little. Meanwhile there will follow great war and strife, as well as destruction of many cities, strongholds and powerful countries.'

On the whole the presentiment was fulfilled as to what is said concerning Bethlen Gabor and the Turks. The election of the Emperor belongs to the sphere of the fantastic.

But when his judgment related to the sphere in which he had full life and movement, Böhme reveals a sound sense, an impartial attitude, which avoids fanaticism as happily as it does indifferentism. He perceives correctly the impure motives and the unworthiness of the military leaders: 'All that for which men at present contend and fight, and destroy country and people, is only an empty husk without fruit, and belongs to the fiery world for separation. There is no true understanding in any party. They all quarrel about the name and will of God, and no party will do His will. They have in view nothing but their own glory and carnal pleasures. If they were true Christians, they would have no dispute or quarrel' (Epistle 46).

Jacob Böhme is a genuine German character, like Eckhart, Suso, Tauler, and above all Luther; faithfully preserving his God in his heart, and faithfully fighting for Him outwardly. His was one of those dreaming, brooding, God-intimate natures, whom the impulse to search out truth lays hold of and profoundly agitates within themselves, in their whole ego ; and gives not rest and repose till they have fathomed the process of reconciliation by intuition and feeling. Sunk in themselves they behold God, and since God is all, they behold the world in God. Thus already in this world they live in another world, and undauntedly and courageously proclaim the truth as more particularly revealed to them.

2. *The spiritual life of Jacob Böhme, and his intercourse with his adherents.*

The early-followed visionary bent of his whole mind prevented Jacob Böhme from viewing his own states with an objectively pure attention. Weak health afforded all too great an opportunity for the play of phantasy. Its activity became so vigorous and extensive, that thoughts mixed up with glowing images—to others they seemed feverish—of the imagination lifted him even into superhuman, enraptured states, in which all his sensuous supports and everything earthly in his surroundings disappeared, and in which he gave himself up unreservedly to that supersensible sphere of sense, to that spiritual world of manifestation, and lost himself entirely in the object of his musing.

It is neither necessary nor possible by means of criticism to reject the report of such states. Frankenberg can lay no claim to documentary credibility, and yet there remains to his communications an historical core, which is sufficient, when compared with the theosophist's own words, to recognize the peculiar character of Böhme's states. Frankenberg relates (professedly on Böhme's own statement) that even when an apprentice he had a manifestation that was more than earthly, which however to our eyes bears a natural stamp. We are told that when he was alone in the shop, a man wished to buy a pair of shoes from him. Only after a long delay, because he had no authority to do business, did he agree to it. Then the stranger withdrew a little from the shop, stood still, and called out in a loud voice: 'Jacob, come forth!' He took him by the hand, looked at him with a penetrating gaze and said in a prophetic tone: 'Jacob, thou art little, but thou shalt become great and another man, so that the world shall marvel at thee. Therefore, be pious, fear God and honour His word. In particular, read in the Holy Scripture, where thou obtainest consolation and instruction; for thou wilt have to suffer much want, poverty and persecution. But be of good cheer and continue steadfast, for God loveth thee and is gracious unto thee.'—The narrative records nothing that is more than human, but it gives evidence of the capacity of the youthful Böhme to receive as earnest exhortation any encouragement towards further reflection and towards the inwardness of the affective life. The modest behaviour of the youth, his figure, his features (which certainly announced early the significance of his future), doubtless drew the attention of men of feeling and culture; as indeed the peculiar fire of the eye in exceptional individuals often reveals the power of mind by an indescribable dominating and enthralling of those about them.

The statement that his master turned him out of doors, 'because he could not suffer such a house-prophet,' is also credible. It is at all times the fate of the unfortunate man of high endowments, to whom his right standpoint amid the billows of life is denied, to be favoured with scorn and persecution by the profane, who recognize not the traces of genius. Thus the sound, sane mind, undiscovered by a guiding provident hand, could not but be stunted and turn into barbaristic side paths; not a rare phenomenon in that age, in which belief in the extraordinary had perished through simple ridicule of what was not understood, and the people were estranged from all higher conception of life.

The spiritual development of Böhme presents three constituent elements. Two of these were conditioned mainly by impressions and influences from without; the third, however, as the valuable kernel, struggled forth with difficulty through barbarisms. The two former elements are found in the currents of nature-philosophy, specific theosophy and mystical theology, continuations respectively of Paracelsus, Weigel and Schwenkfeldt. Their inward connection through the central point of self-suppression constitutes the distinctive character of Böhme's doctrine.

The contemplation of the ethical discord between evil and good rent asunder his inner life. The demand for unity drove him to violent efforts, which he himself movingly describes as a fearful struggle. His ego would have unity, and rested not until the whole world had been forced into the one idea of God by the immense but uncultivated power of his own mind. Nature and the human soul, as direct revelations of contradiction, were the objects of his contemplation. Having arrived at experience of the ethical consciousness along with intuition of the inward eye, he swims in the ocean of mystical blessedness: 'After finding within me a violent opposition, namely, the prompting in flesh and blood and the mighty conflict between the woman's and the serpent's seed, I set myself once for all so unyieldingly in combat against the serpent's seed and my own corrupt nature, though with the assistance of God, that I believed I should overcome and break that inborn evil will and tendency, and unite myself to the love of God in Christ, to hide myself in the heart of God from the terrible tempest of the wrath of God and the fierceness of the devil, in order that God's Spirit might govern, impel and lead me. I resolved, moreover, to count myself as dead in my innate form, till God's Spirit obtained a form in me, and I laid hold of Him, in order that I might lead my life through and in Him. Further, I proposed to myself to will nothing, save what I apprehended in His light and will. He was to be my will and my doing. Which indeed was not possible for me to effect, and yet I stood in an earnest purpose, and in very earnest combat and warfare against myself. And what has then come about, none may well know but God and my own soul; for I would sooner put my life to utmost hazard than desist. Thus did I strive by God's assistance a good while for the knight's garland, which I afterwards with the breaking open of the gates of the deep in the centre of Nature attained with very great joy, as there dawned upon my soul a wonderful light, which was foreign to the wild nature. And therein I first apprehended what God and man were, and what God had to do with man, which I never understood before. Neither did I ever seek in such a way but as a child that hangs to its mother and longs after her. In like manner my soul longed after this light, and yet with no knowledge beforehand of what should or would befall me, but only as a child.' [1]

How from the ethical impulse towards internal unity his ego reached the contemplation of nature, and how also in this sphere a similar spiritual unity became a necessity to

[1] *Apol. Tilk.*, 21-26.

him, he describes in the *Aurora* as follows: 'But when this [the contradiction which the popular view of Nature and the dispensation of Providence presents] had given me many a hard blow, doubtless from the Spirit, which had a longing towards me, I fell at last into a severe melancholy and sadness when I contemplated the great deep of the world, also the sun and stars, the clouds, rain and snow, and considered in my mind the whole creation of this world, in which I found in all things evil and good, love and wrath; both in the irrational creatures, viz. in wood, stones, earth and elements, as well as in men and beasts. I considered, moreover, the little spark proper to man, what he might be esteemed in the eyes of God in comparison with those great works of the heavens and the earth. But as I found that in all things there was evil and good, both in the elements and in the creatures, and that it fared as well in this world with the wicked as with the righteous, also that barbarous peoples occupied the best countries and that good fortune assisted them still more than the religious and devout, I became very melancholy and greatly troubled, and no Scripture could comfort me, though the Scriptures were well known to me. At the same time the devil certainly will not have been idle, as he often inculcated into me heathen thoughts, which I will here keep silent on. But when in this tribulation my spirit (for I understood little or nothing what it was) elevated itself earnestly to God by a great assault, my whole heart and soul, together with all my thoughts and will being included therein, to wrestle without ceasing with the love and mercy of God, and not give over unless he blessed me, that is, unless he enlightened me with his holy Spirit, so that I might understand his will and be freed from my sadness; then did the spirit break through. But when in my applied zeal I made so fierce an onslaught against God and all the gates of hell, as if there existed in me still more power, being ready to hazard my life upon it (which certainly had not been possible to me without the assistance of the Spirit of God), straightway after some hard assaults my spirit broke through the gates of hell even to the inmost birth of the Deity, and was there embraced with love, as a bridegroom embraces his dear bride.

But what kind of triumphing there was in the spirit, I cannot express either in speech or writing. Neither can it be compared with anything, save with that where life is born in the midst of death, and it is to be likened to resurrection from the dead. In this light my spirit immediately saw through all things, and recognized God in all creatures, in herbs and grass, who He is and how He is, and what His will is. And forthwith in this light my will waxed with a great impulse to describe the being of God' (*Aurora*, xix. 5-13).

Thus did Böhme's world of thoughts continue to struggle amid fantastically mystical conceptions. Now and then a dawning light broke through the nebulous night of the spirit. From time to time it opened out, like the flower of a plant (Epistle 12). But it was twelve years before day broke forth. Then there fell upon him as it were a sudden shower, and, as he says, what that lights upon, it hits. Thus it was with him, so that he wrote down whatever he could apprehend, to bring it into external form. And as a sign of his light inwardly breaking through, he called the fruit of his long striving, *Aurora*, his first work. According to him it was destined to announce the day, but the sun never shone for him brightly and clearly; clouds and storm covered up the full light of day. Lightning-flashes gleamed forth indeed frequently, but the *Philosophus teutonicus* remained in the sphere of mysticism and reached no speculative clearness. What he felt and empirically was sensible of, was reserved for others of his nation to erect into the mature system of thought of a sure-footed philosophy.

The internal sun shone for him often and for a considerable period, but not always steadfastly. When it concealed itself, he understood not even his own work. The rapture connected with this mysticism, its prolific moments, he knows not how to compare more fittingly than with the relationship of the bridegroom to the bride, a relationship that comes still more decidedly into prominence among Catholic mystics, as in the case of his follower, Angelus Silesius. Such visions are not the exclusive property of mystics; the difference only is that they do not appear in poets and thinkers in their first, unreflected, almost sensual form. Böhme lived not in the age of the *Aufklärung*. What wonder, therefore, if that which was merely the fruit of laborious reflection seemed to him to be the immediate gift of God, and which, being without logical exactness, internal perception with powerful spiritual fetters strove to hold together collectively.

The people of his native town, however, thought differently about these ecstatic states. Calumny and fictitious additions to a real historical basis came to form a legend, which is repeated in almost the same words in almost all the chronicles that make any mention of Böhme, and runs thus: 'Jacob Böhme, the cobbler at Görlitz, was for many years the principal enthusiast. He often had his *raptus* and ecstasies, in which he sat down in a corner and wrote day and night, though at other times he could neither write nor read; moreover he brought large books to his house. When these his writings were sent to certain universities for examination, they were constructed in such a manner that (as the vulgar declare) the academic theologians and professors were unable to refute them; or (as I believe) on account of the abominable blasphemies which they found therein, they would not regard them further or reply to them.'

The immediateness of intellectual, productive perception led him indeed into transcendental excesses, which appear very frequently in mystics. Mysticism is conviction of the immanence of God in the human subject. A step further and the mystic is convinced that he shares the omniscience of God, so that he can read the future. Hence the prophecies of Jacob Böhme, which are still used by his adherents among the people of his own country, partly in the same way as any other superstition, with a view to interpretation of the future. If they are useless for this purpose, they testify so much the more clearly to the fact that Böhme was not the meritorious instrument in the hand of a mysterious external power, but has himself the most pertinent share in his creations. Occasionally the prophesyings bear wholly the stamp of the indefinite Apocalyptic prophecy of a future judgment, an end of the world, and the last things. This was for the prophet a wide and open field, which conformed entirely to Böhme's system. This field he reaped thoroughly, just as even to-day idealists plunge into a prognostication of the future in accordance with cosmic periods. In the system of Böhme the third principle, or the world, divides into the first and second principles, the Evil and the Good. Each of these will be given up to its own nature: the one to continual torment and longing after the other, and the Good to the immediacy of blessedness. 'When the time of the external literal constellation is at an end, the built tower, viz. the outer man, falls down, together with his opinions; and everything breaks to pieces, even down to the one soul, which then stands bare and naked before God.'[1]—'Besides, I hear a howling and great lamentation, that all thy servants cry woe upon thee, because thou plaguest them. Moreover, thou hast forgotten my noble seed, and not sown it; but hast sown thy wild seed, for promoting thy great gluttony and magnificence. Lo, I have spewed thee out towards Babel into the winepress of my wrath, and there I will press thee. And I will plant my lily-twig in my rose-garden which yields me fruit that my soul longs for, and of it shall my sick Adam eat, that he may become strong and enter into his Paradise.'[2]

Babel and Antichrist signify the external church, all that is not mystico-religious, the secular mode of life, the dry framework in place of the spiritual content, the Catholic hierarchy, Lutheran fanaticism. He predicts their early overthrow, as the present afforded his mind so little satisfaction in support of the truth of the inward Protestant principle. But as regards time and actual fact he wisely confines himself to indefinite expressions, which may be understood both in a symbolical and in an actual reference. In the writing addressed to Kaym he states that he has no knowledge regarding the millennium; that Scripture contradicts itself when men seek to interpret it. He knows indeed that the time is nigh, but the year and day he does not know, and therefore leaves it to God, otherwise he would be found a liar before Him. Prophecies are of no importance to him, and of no service to the world. In the eternal inner Sabbath of the new birth is the salvation of the world.

[1] *Myst. Magn.*, xxxvi. 56. [2] *Three Principles*, xx. 43.

But when Böhme, nevertheless, entered upon particulars, he very often had the misfortune to misunderstand the in-breathing God. Thus, the day before his end he predicted it erroneously for the third day. Yet, in consequence of indefiniteness of form, the prophecy regarding the death of the Primarius Richter did come true: 'Seeing you call me a prophet,—with evil intent, however, and for a reproach,—I shall tell you what the Lord has given me to know, namely, that the time is born in which God will require an account of your dispute about the cup of Christ, and punish you for it. That which you now fear, and yet repent not, that will come upon you.' [1]

As the prophecies came from moments of violent agitation of mind, they are delivered in a language which, on account of its poetry, is of more importance than the whole subject-matter. It heralds the note of Angelus Silesius and the Moravian song-writing, but without their dallying and languishing. Soft and tender, at other times again deep and sublime, it reminds us of the oriental freshness of the Old Testament poems. Thus there is a peculiar charm in the words which stand at the end of *Signatura rerum*: 'For a lily blossoms upon hill and dale in all the ends of the earth. He that seeketh findeth. Amen.'

The surprise occasioned by the vision-like internal beholding was so great, that Böhme, if he did not forget his long struggle and reflection, at least did not think of them in connection with the sudden mystical light. The fruit of study presented itself to him as Divine inspiration. And as he (after the manner of the learned men of that time) likewise understood by study compilation and sophistical quibbling, to which the spirit of a free creativeness was wanting, it was very natural that he should strictly distinguish his spiritual immediately produced principle from school philosophy, and should represent himself as a child that has received its unconscious knowledge from the power of hearing God. This unconscious element of immediate production (which marks him out from other minds, and is largely to blame for his obscurity and confusion) he apprehends quite

[1] *Apol. Richt.*, 26.

correctly in the statement, that his knowledge does not make him blessed, for he knows it not. It is not his, but God's Spirit knows it in him. He attracts him thereby to Himself; when He withdraws, then he knows nothing.[1]—He says that God has revealed to him more than he sought or understood. His knowledge rests not upon opinions, but upon a living intuition and feeling, for which he requires no doctor from the school of this world.[2] He calls himself a simple plain man, who has his knowledge and high knowing not from art and reason; great art he has never sought. In the twelfth Epistle he says: 'I can write of myself no otherwise than of a child that knows and understands nothing, neither has ever learnt, save what the Lord chooses to know in me.' Again, how completely, in consequence of indwellingness, the Spirit of the Lord became identical with his spirit, is evident when he says: 'Seeing then it is my work, which is impelled by my spirit, I will write it down for a memorial in such a way as I know it in my mind, and in the way in which I have attained to it; and I will set down nothing of another, which I have not myself experienced, lest I be found a liar before God.'[3]

Now, when Böhme so frequently maintains that he does not get his writings and science from man, we may give him entire credence in so far as his works are reproduced directly from his mind; but not to the extent that he has read no other writers, and that their views cannot be recognized in his doctrine. On the contrary, such views of others are often to be found again in him in a very undigested form. Thus incomprehensibility and failure are glaringly apparent in the mode of viewing the Paracelsian theosophy. He himself confesses that he has read the works of many masters, and searched through them, hoping thereby to find pearls relating to the ground of man. But he has not been able to find them, and after them his soul longed. Moreover, he says that he understands the opinions of the astrologers, and has read a few lines in their treatises, and knows well how they describe the course of the sun and stars; neither does he

[1] *Apol. Tilk.*, i. 587. [2] *Apol. Tilk.*, i. 301, ii. 53.
[3] *Three Principles*, xxiv. 1.

despise this, but holds it for the most part to be good and right.

In the twelfth Epistle he gives his judgment on the tenets of Paracelsus, Schwenkfeld, Weigel and Weihrauch. He himself opposes Stiefel and Meth in special controversial writings, and brings forward their opinions verbatim. Yet, even without this open public assurance, it would remain undoubted that Böhme diligently and from early youth read not only the Bible, which he often quotes and in a striking way, and which constitutes the characteristic feature of his views, but also zealously studied Paracelsus, Weigel, Schwenkfeld and some other mystics, as many things in his system closely agree with their writings. His entire doctrine may be regarded as the point of union where the naturalistic theosophy of Paracelsus, the Lutheran mysticism of Schwenkfeld and the decidedly mystical theosophy of Weigel, intersect and find their solvent unity.

The book (*Aurora*) which Böhme had achieved after the efforts of twelve years was, according to the original plan, designed to exhaust the whole sphere of theosophy; but it is scarcely half completed, and certainly not to the regret of posterity. Rude form encumbers the pearls, which lie at the bottom of the troubled sea. If there were not effused over the style of the whole a strange spirit of directness and heartfelt sentiment,—the earnestness of strong feeling that struggles (but in vain) for clearness,—the naïveté of individual passages would remind one only too much of a marionette play of little angels and devils. Böhme indeed was far from believing in the sensible and spatial existence of a heaven of angelic choirs and a hell of devils with horns and hoofs; but through default of philosophic notions, and through being unused to hold fast by non-sensible conceptions, his homely, energetically sensuous nature seized the vivid images which were furnished him by his studies, nature, scripture and the theosophists and alchemists, so as to fix with cyclopean power the speculative thoughts in his simple unlearned head. The immense effort involved in his thinking took as an aid gigantic similes or figures, which we would have to term childish, did not consciousness of the Divine immanence extend over them the halo of solemnity.—On continued reading of the works, the understanding accustoms itself to the strange mode of expression, and becomes capable of discovering the deep poetry, and the kernel of speculation towards which the dim crepuscular method of mysticism works. Böhme did not conceal from himself either the great obscurity of his phraseology in general, or the imperfection of the *Aurora* in particular. He cannot recommend to the reader sufficient caution in connection with the study of his writings: 'Thou must understand this properly, in the same way as it is meant, for when I speak in simile etc.' 'The great secrets are in the *Aurora* still very deeply hidden in mystery, but it was not possible for Reason to comprehend the first time.' [1]—'The book *Aurora* was my childlike beginning. Thus I wrote in the refulgence of the light without Reason, merely according to vision or beholding, in almost a magical manner.' [2] 'Therefore, if thou understandest not these writings, do not as Lucifer did. Take not up the spirit of pride with mockery, and ascribe it to the devil; but seek the lowly heart of God, and it will bring into thy soul a little grain of mustard seed from the plant of Paradise; and if thou persevere in patience, a great tree will grow from it.' [3] —When Böhme, after the lapse of some five years, again took pen in hand, he felt that his style had changed with his mode of view. In the twelfth Epistle he writes: 'Then I attained a better style of writing, and likewise a deeper and more thorough knowledge. I could bring everything better to outward expression, as indeed is shown by the book of the *Threefold Life*; and the lover of God, if his heart be opened, shall see [that it is so].'

Böhme affirms in many places that he composed the *Aurora* only for a memorial, so as to possess in it a fixed point for his further reflection, and a consolation in his hours of gloom, when he comprehended not how he came by his illumination. He asserts that he did not write the book with the view of putting it in circulation. These statements are to be understood in such a way that, without having the intention of burying the creations of his mind always in

[1] *Epistle* x. 36. [2] *Epistle* xviii. 13. [3] *Three Principles*, ix. 45.

darkness and never communicating them to the eye of another, he did not purpose bringing his writings either by printing or by self-promoted transcribing into publicity. While such bringing into publicity would have been a contradiction to his inwardly felt vocation, which was fond of representing itself as the lily which puts forth blossoms unto the northern countries; so the frequent addresses to the reader, not only in the introduction, but also in the body of the *Aurora* itself, show the contrary. And these addresses cannot even be reckoned among the spurious interpolations of a later modified text, as they are expressly given prominence to by the editors.

Karl von Ender, who read the *Aurora* with rapture, caused it to be transcribed at once, and to be circulated in many copies among his friends. He attached himself more closely to Böhme, and became his first patron and admirer. In the first Epistle (which is addressed to Karl von Ender) mention is made of Balthasar Walther, a theosophical physician of Glogau, a learned man well known to both parties. Like most of the physicians of his day he was a follower of the Theophrastic school. He had travelled much in the East, and on his return found unexpectedly in the head of a German shoemaker the information which the parchments of Egypt had not unfolded to him. For three months he resided with Böhme, and then went as Director of the Chemical Laboratory to Dresden. Walther declared Böhme's book to be the most perfect product of Magic. It is a pity that the side of Böhme's theosophy which transported the alchemist is the very same that we would gladly do without in it, and which has so often occasioned what is good and useful to be overlooked and the theosophist to be reviled as a half-crazy individual. Dr. Walther was a vigorous propagandist of Böhme's doctrine. His zeal once drew down upon him a well-merited reproof from his friend, when he had revealed mysteries to impure ears: 'They are not everyone's food. We must not cast the pearl into the way, to be trodden under foot. My writings are of no use to a full belly, but only minister to a hungry stomach. I have not written them either for the unlearned or for the wise, but for myself, and for those to whom God shall give them and with them understanding.'[1]

The adherents of Böhme in Görlitz itself were for the most part physicians of the Paracelsian school, like Balthasar Walther. The best friend among those at Görlitz was Dr. Tobias Kober. With him was Böhme in correspondence when he undertook the journey to Dresden. Kober had even undertaken the guardianship of his household, and after Böhme's decease cared for the family that was left behind. He called Böhme a *θεόπνευστον*. To him, as well as to Balthasar Walther, is to be attributed no small influence upon the theosophist's line of thought. It were even to be wished that he had not had these companions. Then perhaps we would be without many a nonsensical alchemistic phantasy and many an absurdity that runs into detail, this coming out always more and more strongly the longer Böhme cultivated their conversation. Even Frankenberg says that he made use of strange Latin terms, particularly in his writings; and that it was not voluntarily he had learnt them, but from intercourse with theosophists. We are told that he often went for a walk with Kober in order to botanize, and that by means of the external signature and form of a plant he recognized the internal power, influence and property, and designated them with the syllables of the name as given and spoken to him. On this point he would get someone to tell him the learned name of the plant, and liked best to hear it in the Hebrew tongue. When they could not tell him this name, he asked for it in Greek, and finally in Latin. Now, if the physician had given a false name, Böhme soon observed the fraud by comparing the property of the name with that of the plant, the signature with the colour, and said that such could not be the right name. Just as a panacea, an elixir of life, a philosopher's stone, was sought for, which, created from the centre of the Deity that is operative in nature, was to put man in possession of the forces of nature, so likewise it was supposed that an original and primitive language could be found, by the aid of which every language of the earth might become in-

[1] *Epistle* vii. 1-5.

telligible. 'The language of nature,' he says in the *Aurora*, xx. 90, 'is the root or mother of all languages which are in this world, and in it lies the entire perfect knowledge of all things. For when Adam first discoursed, he gave names to all the creatures in accordance with their qualities and inherent workings. And this is the language of the whole of nature, but it is not a language everyone knows. For this is a mystery that was communicated to me by the grace of God from the Spirit, which had delight in me.'

Such was Böhme's own view regarding the language of nature, and into what abortive attempts he worked it out, a few lines will show. Not in the sense and sound of the whole word did the mystery appear to him to lie, but in the disarticulation of the several syllables to an atomistic division and in the interpretation of the letter,—a micrology in the case of which, as in the case of the specialised alchemistic philosophy, understanding ends for any other ear than the sharp-pointed organ of the theosophist. Thus in the *Three Principles*, xxii. 85, he says: 'The word *Himmel* has another meaning in the language of nature. The syllable *Him* goes out of the heart, as out of the power of the Father, or out of the soul's essences, and strikes upwards into the *Ternarius sanctus*. Then it is formed with the two lips and carries the angelic name downwards, that is, the syllable *Mel* indicates the humility of the angels, that they elevate not their heart aspiringly into the Trinity through pride.'

Silesian soil was fruitfullest in the propagation of Böhme's doctrine. Abraham von Sommerfeld of Wartha, Frankenberg's uncle, sought the friendship of the shoemaker through a letter, in which he asked him for the expedition of his writings. He had read the *Aurora*, and forwarded the transcript which he had used to Jacob Böhme with the request that he would peruse it, so as to judge of its correctness. Böhme did this and sent him his work *Forty Questions on the Soul*, together with some directions and hints which were to serve for the understanding of his writings. Sommerfeld's nephew Frankenberg, the biographer of Böhme, became acquainted with Böhme's works through his uncle, but made the acquaintance of the theosophist himself in the winter of

1623, and in the summer of 1624 met him repeatedly. Abraham von Frankenberg was born in 1593 at Ludwigsdorf, and is lauded even by his opponents on account of his philanthropic disposition, which he gave active proof of during the long period of plague. He possessed an extensive erudition, was a great bibliophile, engaged considerably in the study of mathematics, natural science and medicine, but above all cultivated theology. He avoided the war of opinions carried on between the learned; his soul desired peace; *Jesus mea nobilitas* was his motto. His internal conversion to mysticism and contemplativeness took place in the year 1617. By continual watching and praying for the true religion, he was drawn into the Sabbath of rest, and he came to participate in mystical illuminations. He appeared as an author under the name of Amadeus von Friedleben and Friedericus de Monte. But his mode of writing and thinking leads to exaggeration of the doctrine of Böhme. Playing with the letters of a name and toying with magical terms and ambiguities gain ground in such a way that good judgment is lost still more than in the case of Böhme's obscurity. The greater clearness of expression only causes the attractiveness of mysticism to take the shape of a rigid formula. The spirit of profoundness perishes completely in the learned chatter and the scholastic aridity of thought.

Information concerning the highly-gifted shoemaker spread to Breslau and even beyond that city. In Lower Silesia Christian Bernhard, a young member of the theosophic school and collector of customs at Sagan, was the most zealous propagator of the writings and doctrine of Böhme. It was owing to him and Balthasar Walther that Böhme summoned up courage to take pen in hand afresh after the forcible inhibition of his calling by the magistrates. A considerable number of Epistles are addressed to him. Bernhard was the means of bringing about intercourse with the two noblemen, Rudolph von Gersdorff and Friedrich von Kregwitz; as well as with Caspar Lindner, a toll-gatherer in Beuthen.

On the side of adeptship and love of the miraculous the influence of friends upon Böhme was not the most favourable. One of the strangest examples illustrative of this is to be found in the twenty-second Epistle, in which is very neatly shown the possibility of tombstones shedding tears when beneath them repose sympathetic defuncts whose sidereal element penetrates and pervades the stone. Further, in the twenty-eighth Epistle a certain Valentin Thirnes receives a strange instruction. He is advised to read 'The Water-stone of the Wise,' a theosophico-alchemistic work, in which he would find how to prepare the philosophic tincture from suitable minerals for not more than two florins. Böhme's learned friends led him away to concern himself with astrology and alchemy more than was wholesome for himself and his reputation. To the strange inquiries that were put to him, there came to light still stranger replies. From friends come his Latin expressions, which have of Latin little more than the terminations, and conceal rather than define the concept. To friends is due the tendency to arrange his categories according to a varied contignation, by which only boundless confusion can arise in the mind of the reader, who tries to force himself to understand these infinitely finely divided and coalescing images of unintelligible signification. The happiness which is promised in the forty-seventh Epistle (in a footnote to Table I), namely, that if all this were understood, all conflict and questioning would cease in the reader, and Babel would stand in shame and reproach,—this happiness appears indeed rather to be desirable than, on the most honest endeavour, to be attainable.

When weary of these absurdities, it reconciles us again with the personality of Böhme to hear how, guided only by his individual reason, he could set bounds to the excesses of such extravagant enthusiasts. An anecdote, which Frankenberg relates, seems all the more worthy of credence as recorded by such a believer in wonders and lover of symbols, and yet puts this mystery-mongering in an unfavourable light: 'A stranger of small stature, sensible and intelligent, once came to Böhme in the belief that he was an alchemist *ex professo*, and required of him to sell his secrets for money. Böhme answered him, that he lived in God, and not in any singular or familiar spirit; and that if he wanted his secrets, let him return in penitence to God. When, upon this reply, the stranger began to make use of magical formulae, Böhme turned him out of doors, with the exhortation to meddle no more with such simony and devilry' (Frankenberg, 22).

Böhme's social position with reference to his friends was, relatively to his origin, a highly honourable one. Owing to his religiousness he was able to drop the distinctions of rank, which were then strictly and rigidly observed. In this connection the sentiment of his followers responded to him. In no way did he exhibit humiliation in his letters. He writes to high and low in the same God-conscient, direct, naïve and childlike style. With confidential intimacy, which rested upon a background of Christian love, he approached the newly-won scholar of wisdom. So also his adherents came together in friendly union, without regard as to whether they were of noble or burgher extraction. Böhme was invited to their table by noblemen, and stayed with them for weeks and months together. The respect with which his name is mentioned in the writings of these men shows that he was looked upon, not as a court-fool, but as a master of theosophy.

His adherents showed even so much regard for him as to assist him faithfully in straitened circumstances. By the somewhat lengthy residence on their estates he was freed from the immediate cares of life. From time to time they gave him direct assistance in money and articles of food, which frequently were not to be obtained for money in the distress and evils of the war. From literary work as such he had little profit. Only once (in the fifty-first Epistle) is there a statement that he was offered money for his manuscript. Moreover, he had entirely neglected his trade. During the years of dearth of the war, the gifts from friends became an important help to the poor author; and in order to dispense them not wholly in the form of alms, and avoid the irksomeness of such a relationship, it appears that Böhme occasionally defrayed the cost to the sender.

3. *The persecution of Böhme; his sojourn in Dresden, and his death.*

The Tolerationists, the Crypto-Calvinists and Theosophists, from whose ranks Böhme obtained his followers, formed but a small portion of the population; and that they flocked so quickly round their new light was due to the fact that the dominant party exercised not a little oppressive fanatical power upon intellectual freedom and civil life. Philosophic thinking was now neither popular nor present generally in Germany. The two schools, which were continually attacking each other, had grown on religious soil. The one was the spiritual progressive party of Mystics, Theosophists and Crypto-Calvinists, or all those who subjected to their independent examination the rule of faith which had been laid down once for all, and hence were regarded as heretics; the other was the stationary party of orthodox theologians, whether Catholics or Lutherans or theologians of the Reformed Church. However absurd the excesses and ridiculous extravagances of the Adepts might be, their principle commands the immediate respect of posterity on account of the doctrine of toleration and intellectual freedom which they maintained as a result of trust in a mystical, subjective revelation. It was otherwise with the orthodox guardians of the Church, whose principle—the power of a single ecclesiastical communion united by love—had long since passed over into a blind fanaticism through persistence in formulae of faith that were frozen and fixed once for all, without reason, without thought of progress. The worth of a good Christian was judged, not by inward disposition and moral conduct, but by oral readiness to defend the doctrines which had been set up. Theological and dialectical subtleties were taught in the universities and pulpits, and thus odious discord was sown in the hearts of the hearers. Hatred towards Sectarians was the first Christian duty, and servile subjection to the arrogant priesthood was the second. The body of clergy who sought to combine love and toleration with orthodoxy was but small, and these few were exposed to the hate of their colleagues. The Wurtemberg theologian Johann Valentin Andreae did not conceal from himself the great deficiencies of his orthodox clergy, 'who prefer explaining the Trinity to worshipping the Trinity, and prefer proving the presence of Christ to honouring him at all times and in all places; who choose rather to describe repentance of sins than feel it in themselves, choose rather to lower the merit of works than do good works, and more often turn over the pages of the sacred writings than occupy themselves with the practice of Christian love. They make religion a science, the knowledge of which, like the knowledge of logic and metaphysics, may be very useful with the view of acquiring a reputation for learning.'—On one occasion he exclaims in disgust: 'Farewell, Reformation, for on this earth we shall never see thee.'

Accordingly, it was not to be wondered at that an individual like Jacob Böhme became a thorn in the side of the leading expounders of orthodoxy. Dialectic subtlety was contrary to his nature. He desiderated a pure upright heart for religion. He opposed intolerance as being blasphemy against God, who has diffused spiritual gifts variously; and as being the work of Satan, who alone can forbid inquiry. This mode of thinking and call for intellectual freedom soon met with its opponent, with whom it had to try conclusions before the public.

It was in the year 1613 that Böhme had first had to suffer attacks from the orthodox clergy at Görlitz, who already had furnished proof of the fact that in the east of Germany also fanaticism had found admittance. The Primarius assumed pre-eminently the rôle of ecclesiastical opponent, full of his official consciousness of being unable from the orthodox standpoint to let it pass uncensured that a member of his congregation continued in a hitherto unheard of fashion to put a subtle interpretation on the literal word of Scripture and the history of creation until the matter had become wholly the property of the productive adapter; that Böhme, diverging from Luther's doctrines, nay even from the *Formula Consensus*, ventured to preach, and to explain the Lord's Supper, not by means of a positive miracle, as the stricter

Flacians required, but in a mystical way as a spiritual union with the heart of God; that he dared to attack as irrational the doctrine of Election, and to raise undauntedly the banner of free inquiry over religion, the Bible and human ordinance. But the motives of the pastor were not so innocent and pure when he thundered excommunication against the poor religious thinker. How could a cobbler, one of the lowest of his parishioners, venture to entertain a view of his own, and along with this to wish to appear as an author! He had not been to the universities, and undertook to solve problems with regard to which the most eminent men of learning were divided, and the bottomless abyss of which he himself, the Primarius, could only conceal by means of blind zeal and dead faith in the letter! Now, the expression of this solution in Böhme's treatise was obscure, and forcibly impressed the clergyman, to whom the breath of prophecy was unpleasant; for his arguments reached not so far as its depths. Therefore it must be the work of the devil. And this was too difficult for him to understand, as the author asserted that he was inspired by God. He, the Primarius, made a similar assertion; and since he had the right God, the other was from the devil. Personal reasons—envy and anger at the boldness of the layman—mainly goaded the priest on to extirpate such a heretic from the congregation.

Gregorius Richter, *Pastor Primarius* at Görlitz, was born in 1560 at Ostritz, a little town between Görlitz and Zittau. He was the son of the smith of the monastery there. When as a pupil in Breslau he lived at a smithy, the paternal trade attracted him so strongly, that for a certain period he exchanged his studies for the hammer and anvil. Subsequently, however, he turned again to the study of theology, and in 1584 got an appointment as teacher at the Görlitz Gymnasium. In 1587 he obtained from the Council the place of pastor at Rauscha, a village in the forest lands of Görlitz, and finally in 1590 became deacon at Görlitz. In 1606 he attained to the position of Primarius; yet his vehemence in preaching led even then to a reproof on the part of the Council. Again, in the year 1618, his violence had to be checked by the authorities. He also got involved in a quarrel with the rector Dornavius. And in the pulpit he had reviled as a bad Samaritan a physician in charge of those infected with the plague, on the ground that he kept his patients waiting. With the view of avoiding disturbances, Richter was directed by the Council to keep his room. The plague furnished the pretext, and the people made a pasquillic couplet :

'*Quaeritur inclusus cur sit Richterus in aedes?*
Me Samaritani calce petivit equus.'

These few traits are sufficient in order to put the behaviour of the Primarius to Böhme in the right light. The picture of an orthodox fanatic becomes complete by the following modes of procedure with regard to the quiet theosophist. Owing to Karl von Ender's zeal in circulating the *Aurora*, a copy fell in the way of the Primarius Richter. He began at once to pour out from the pulpit—the place where his activity was safest and might become most dangerous—violent abuse on the poor shoemaker, who knew not how he came by such hostility. It was long since he had seen his manuscript, and he did not know in whose hands it was. After a sermon preached by Richter (in July 1613) on false prophets, the excitement of the people was so great that the Council could no longer ignore a fact which had obtained publicity and was malevolently blackened by the priest, without having to fear violent scenes on the part of the wrought-up populace. For, as everywhere, so likewise at Görlitz, the common people exercised under the guidance of the priests a considerable and formidable dominion, before which innovators, as well as magistrates of cities, and even princes, were compelled to bow. The Council of Görlitz, which already had striven after a worthy impartiality in earlier religious disputes with the Schwenkfeldians and Crypto-Calvinists, and even now found in its midst enlightened individuals, had recourse to a prudential measure, so as not to be forced to bow to the raving of the fanatical priest and the rage of the rabble, and in consequence of civic overthrow see an innocent citizen sacrificed to a blind vindictiveness, so long as it could be checked in its worst outbreaks by a semblance of punishment. On the 26th of July the Council caused the persecuted man to be arrested by a town-officer. After a hearing he was indeed released, but had to promise to renounce his visionary philosophy, and above all his writing of books.

Had the Council had in view the complete suppression of the work (the *Aurora*), then the confiscation of Böhme's own manuscript would have been a wholly mistaken measure, as by the care of his friends very many transcripts of the wonderful book had been put in circulation. This punishment gave less pain to the author than the prohibition to write. Such an interdict amounted to killing him spiritually, because the expression of his internal world of thought had become to him a duty and an unquestionable personal need, which asserted its claims always more and more strongly. For a long time he restrained himself. Persecution had lowered his courage. He even supplicated God, that if his gift came not from His counsel, to take it from him, and let him know nothing at all in this way. He purposed writing nothing more, but rather keeping still as one who is obedient to God. But many an assault befell him, and 'what he suffered cannot well be told.'[1] 'His reason was weak and timorous, for the light of grace was withdrawn from him a good while, and burned in him faintly like a hidden fire, so that there was nothing but anxiety within him. Outwardly he found derision, and inwardly a fiery impulse.'[2] 'As a grain that is sown in the earth grows up under every storm and tempest, contrary to all reason,—for in winter everything appears as if dead, and reason says: All is gone!—so did the noble grain of mustard seed grow up again under every assault, under reproach and derision, like a lily, and returned with fruit an hundredfold.'[3]

During the period (five years) in which his spirit did not impel him to write, he had not remained without intercourse with mystics and theosophists. Friends continued to gather round him, and exhorted him to again give free scope to his Talent. Bernhard and Walther knew how to work upon him with such persuasive power, that he, the conscientious

[1] Epistle x. 5, 6. [2] Epistle xii. 13. [3] Epistle x. 7.

Böhme, full of the inward feeling of the heart, who could not bear to see his divine truth condemned to the sleep of death without being able to produce light for his neighbour, resolved through the highest stirring to again take up the pen, in spite of the edict of the authorities. 'Seeing I know in power and light that it is a mere gift from God, who giveth me further a will impelling thereunto, so that I must write; therefore I will obey God rather than man, lest my office be taken from me and given to another, which would cause me to repent eternally.'[1] The discouragement, which once pressed heavily upon him, had disappeared; so that now he would have regarded as an intolerable evil that for which not long ago he fervently prayed. The severe censure of the Council, the rage of the priest, the dark looks of the people (who in Böhme gazed at a heretic and sorcerer, and with offensive fabrications brought dishonour upon his reputation), were no longer so fresh in his memory; the storm itself in fact had somewhat abated. Silesia, Saxony, Meissen and the Marches were already full of his fame, when, with the exception of his followers in his native town, no one was acquainted with his book. The breath of the Most High came again to his aid, and awakened him to new life. His first work was *The Three Principles of the Divine Nature.* His second period of book-writing had dawned, in which he composed in quick succession thirty larger or smaller works.

At this point the mystic succumbed to a form of self-deception, which followed from the too great security given by the Divine influx. Resumption of authorship was plainly opposed to the edict of the magistrates; and his mode of conduct cannot stand before a strict tribunal. There were other means of escape in order to satisfy the inner craving. Böhme's friends could have facilitated for him a change of abode, so that he would have been freed from the fetter of the prohibition. Day had now overtaken the dawn. Although at the outset Böhme did his utmost to prevent publication of his activity and engage his friends to silence, this was not possible with his extended acquaintance and their over-officious zeal. Perhaps among the adepts were

[1] Epistle ii. 8.

to be found also betrayers, who viewed unwillingly the rise of the layman.

Here and there arose anew an evil report; and it was not long before the Primarius recommenced fulminating anathema against the unfortunate man. The people were already murmuring again; and the priest spared neither time nor trouble, by dissemination of the writings, to accuse Böhme of heresy. A scandalous affair, recorded indeed by an unreliable authority, may have contributed to embitter the relationship between clergyman and parishioner. The story comes from an officious friend of Böhme, one Cornelius Weisner, who pieced it together from uncertain statements so as to prefix an external tangible starting-point to the second conflict with Richter. Böhme himself makes no mention of the occurrence in the letters that are extant. Nevertheless, the narrative is not to be rejected on internal grounds. Rather it gives a sketch of the character of an orthodox clergyman, who, in spite of a humanistic training, displayed an egregious want of culture in his fanaticism, even though the writer may now and again overdo the picture. If it transmits only a popular tradition, it possesses on that account more credibility, as it is the only record of this kind which relates something favourable about the theosophist.[1]

[1] The substance of the narrative is as follows: Böhme's brother-in-law had borrowed a thaler from the Primarius Richter in order to buy wheat to bake white bread at Christmas; and instead of the interest for a fortnight brought him a large white loaf. The clergyman, incensed at this, threatens him with judgment from Heaven. The young man, a baker, falls into a melancholy; and at last confesses the reason to his brother-in-law Jacob Böhme. The latter goes to the Primarius, speaks mildly in favour of his relative, and offers him the interest. But the Primarius shouts: What has the ragabash [*i.e.* J. B.] to do at my house, to be disquieting, molesting and disturbing me! Jacob Böhme asks for grace, but the Primarius shows him the door, telling him he must clear out! Puffed up with pride and at his ease, Richter was sitting in his elbow-chair. Now, when Jacob Böhme was about to go out at the door, and said: God preserve your Reverence, Richter throws his slipper after him. But Böhme brings it back respectfully, and replaces it beneath his foot, though the Primarius says: Why shouldst thou wish me good-night, thou godless knave; what care I for thy blessing! Böhme replies: Sir, be not angry, I do you no harm, farewell, and withdrew. The Primarius now began on Sunday from the pulpit to accuse him of heresy and to condemn him, to curse his books, to threaten the city with a judgment from Heaven and enjoin the Council to take vengeance, lest a

The real reason, and the one that lies nearest at hand, of the rancour which broke out anew, was that Böhme's friends had had printed in 1623 the writings *On the Eternal Life* and *On True Repentance*, which afterwards were embodied in the series of tractates that bear the name of *Christosophia* or *Way to Christ*. This might appear to the Primarius as an open revolt against the interdict that was published in 1613, and as a presumptuous encroachment upon the rights of a learned man. He did not shrink from taxing Jacob Böhme with vices, and representing him as a despiser of the Church and sacraments; declaring that he got fuddled every day with brandy, as well as beer and other liquor, and was a rogue and vagabond; 'all which,' adds Böhme, 'is untrue, and he himself is a drunken man.'[1] In short, 'he raged violently against the printed book, as if his son had been murdered and all his goods burned, and poured out a heap of lies against me, along with wanton defamation.'[2] He wrote to Pastor Fries in Liegnitz, and required of him not merely to touch upon this in the pulpit, but also to put it in print, and that he should complain of Böhme to the Council at Görlitz, and so lodge the complaint as if it were made in the name of all the priests in the precincts of Liegnitz. Fries complied with the

heavy judgment befall it, as befell the company of Korah, Dathan and Abriam. After the sermon Böhme went up to the Primarius, and inquired what harm he had done to him; that he would fain make amends, if he could but call to mind his misdeed. Instead of an answer he got only furious looks. At last, with curses and revilings, Richter burst forth: Get thee hence, Satan, get thee gone with thy restlessness into the abyss of hell. Canst thou not leave me alone? Must thou insult and molest me here? Seest thou not that I am a clergyman, and proceed in the functions of my office?—Whereat Jacob Böhme was troubled, and answered: Yes, reverend sir, I see indeed that you are a clergyman, and have heard in the church how it is, and have seen that you are there in the functions of your office, and hold you justly and unquestionably to be a clergyman. Will you tell me what harm I have done to you?—Böhme then turned to the other clergyman, the chaplain, and besought him, saying: Reverend and dear sir, help me to solicit the Preacher to grant my supplication, and tell me in your presence what I have spoken or done against him, about which he was so zealous in the pulpit, and enjoined the magistrates to take vengeance.—Whereupon the Primarius assumed a still more wrathful attitude, and turning round to his servants bade them summon the town-beadle, in order to have Böhme thrown into prison. This, however, the chaplain prevented.

[1] Epistle lii. 1.

[2] Epistle liii. 5.

demand, and presented the complaint to the Görlitz Council. Richter himself vigorously stirred the fire, and he even stooped to go pretty often to the notables of the town and traduce him. He demanded that Böhme should be clapt in prison as soon as he came home, and then be expelled from the city. Ultimately he himself presented to the Council another communication, in which he had 'made it infernally hot for Böhme.' [1]

Now, although the Councillors had read this printed book, they could find absolutely nothing offensive or heretical in it. Some even praised it, and with the citizens it met with no little approval. The desire of the Primarius to impose upon him a judicial examination seemed therefore unjust. He was gainsaid; for it was held that 'this religion is nothing new, and is the very ground adopted by the ancient holy Fathers, where more such like works would be found.' [2] But the Council could now no longer escape from the importunate fanatic in an indulgent way. The common people were already in so irritable a mood that troublesome scenes were to be feared, as in the sequel they did not fail to come; moreover, the complaint possessed the formal legal title of Böhme having disregarded the prohibition of literary activity. The poor persecuted one was summoned before a sitting of the Council as soon as he returned from his journey into Silesia, where he had been staying with Hans von Schweinichen. Böhme went with the fixed resolve to tell the truth on principle, and to regard no creature, even though it should cost him his life. He thought that the hour of the Reformation had come. The municipal decree in the minute-book of the Council of Görlitz runs thus:

'Anno 1624, the 23rd of March. As regards the shoemaker of this city, named Jacob Böhme, it is decreed that, on account of manifold complaint respecting his alleged pernicious doctrine, he be summoned before the Council and enjoined to seek fortune elsewhere.' Three days after, on the 26th of March, Böhme appeared before the meeting, and was asked whether he had written and had had printed

[1] Epistle liii. 8. [2] Epistle liii. 9.

the work on *The Eternal Life.* In the minute-book the record of the proceedings is as follows:

'Jacob Böhme, the shoemaker and confused enthusiast or visionary, says that he composed the book of *The Eternal Life*, though he did not have it printed, but that one of the nobility, Hans Sigismund von Schweinichen, had it printed. Was warned by the Council to seek fortune elsewhere, or in default of fair means this must be reported to the Illustrious Prince Elector. Thereupon he declared that he would take his departure as soon as possible.'

Böhme drew up a vindication in writing (the Apology or Defence against Gregorius Richter) and presented it to the Council. In it he relates simply and plainly the story of the circumstances which may probably have given the Primarius ground for complaint. He derives his wisdom, he says, from the Saviour alone, who is enamoured of and betrothed to him in the inward life of the soul. He states that his first book through divine providence and without his wish came into the hands of the Primarius, and that the latter quoted it and railed at it with external understanding. Finally he confesses, he says, that he promised in accordance with the first judgment to write no more, but the Primarius himself is partly to blame for his wide reputation, seeing that he lent his book out into other places, cities and villages, and circulated it without his knowledge, till it reached even the Duke of Liegnitz. That at his court and at Dresden it is eagerly read. That many learned men and noblemen have come to him in person, and as he was threatened with a judgment from God if he did not develop his gift, he began again to write, although he had no share in publishing his printed book. The reproaches of drunkenness and godlessness are, he states, unfounded. Let the Primarius, he goes on to say, put down his complaints item by item, and let the Council listen quietly to him [Böhme] but once, and they will easily recognize his innocence. He declares he is no heretic nor despiser of the Church, no fanatic nor vagabond. He despises not the sacraments, he says, but worships Jesus Christ, from whom he has his religion.

The Council did not accept this apology or written defence,

because the Primarius stepped in with his authority. He was afraid, as Böhme observes, that he would have to answer concerning his lies. The Council once more warned the unfortunate one to take himself off, or, as other persons were fond of having him with them, to take up his abode with them, that at least they might be at peace. To which he replied as follows: 'As they will not hear my answer, that I may discover my innocence, and as I cannot be afforded protection or support in consequence of the imputations and unjust invectives of the Primarius, I must commit it to God, and see if He will lead me somewhere to pious people, and finally appoint me a place, that I may at last be lost sight of by the Primarius.'

When he went home from the Council, there were standing at the door of the Council-house some caustic mockers, adherents of, perhaps even sent by, the Primarius, and they began to ridicule him. 'One of them,' so Böhme relates, 'a low loose fellow, anatomized me from head to foot, in reference to my clothes and my endowments. He violently assailed the Spirit of God, and mocked at it, and finally said: The Holy Spirit would at length become as common as pieces of hide at the skinners'.'

On the 27th of March Richter had published a lampoon against Böhme, which exhibits in a clear light the terrible priestly fanaticism of that period. All the powers of heaven and earth did he conjure, in order to punish the transgressor. In this connection he gave not much attention to elegance of expression:

> *Liber sutorius nil nisi picem redolet sutoriam,*
> *Atrum et colorem, quem vocant sutorium,*
> *Pfuy! Pfuy! teter sit foetor a nobis procul.*

Further, in the *Propempticum*:

> *Nostram incestarunt urbem tua stercora sutor;*

and again:

> *Ergo abeas, nunquam redeas, pereas male, Sutor,*
> *Calceus in manibus sit tibi, non calamus.*

In return, Böhme wrote on the 10th of April an apology or defence in detail, wherein Richter's invectives are taken up point by point, repudiated, and by imputations relating to the Primarius paid back. It is written in a sharp and bitter tone, and shows that in controversy even Böhme could be wholly the child of his time. 'O Primarius! Satan hath blinded you, and led you into wrath.—It is to be regarded as a sign, that the way of repentance, which leads to Christ, stinks to you like filth.'

Böhme would have done most prudently to be silent. The Council saw more clearly in commanding him to leave the city. It was a command dictated by caution, that the weaker party, who moreover had been guilty of an infringement, must yield to the stronger, so as to avoid brawls which it were impossible to see to the end of, and dangerous riots. Jacob Böhme was himself sensible of the impropriety of his Defence, as he excuses himself at the end for having composed it: 'Dear Reader, I regard the pasquil as deserving of no reply, because nothing but untruth and reviling are found in it. I wished, however, to make a reply for the sake of those who do not understand and have not read my book, nor know my person.' The Council purposely allowed it to pass unnoticed that he made no haste to carry out the command. The edict of banishment had been drawn up on the 26th of March, and it was the middle of May that the condemned man first thought of leaving the city. The storm had for a time cleared off.[1] Even the Primarius, before so many voices which were raised in support of the assailed theosophist, could not but shrink from still accusing him of heresy. The priest had on his side only the opinion of the rabble. In the street, and even in his own house, Böhme had to suffer insults, abuse and ridicule. He writes (Epistle lix. 2) that although some said: He is pious and a prophet, yet a common saying was: He hath a devil. His bodily condition, he states, is still tolerable, for which he thanks God; but he is entirely covered with pharisaical aspersions, so that the common people hardly recognize him to be a man. Under such circumstances residence in his native place could not appear to him desirable. His

[1] Epistle lviii. 12: 'The enemy's intention is evil, but he thus publishes my talent; it is in great request at present, though the ignorant crowd rails against it.'

steadfastness was put to a severe test, and the sensitive, nervous,[1] sanguine man was again near losing his courage, like the first time in 1613, when the breath of the Most High had left him in the lurch. It was his way to view all his states in a religious light, as directly subject to the influence of the Deity. Thus he often breaks out into bitter and almost woeful complaints regarding perverse Christendom. Now and again would awake in him a defiant joy, when in the midst of the darkness of attacks a ray of recognition illumined him with a kindly gleam, and the clamour of the imperious priest became silent for a while before the testimony of his friends. In the fifty-eighth Epistle he laments thus: 'Alas! there is now only a professing and titular Christendom; the heart is worse than when they were heathens! O dark night! Where is Christianity? Has she become a perfidious whore? Where is her love? Has it turned to copper, steel and iron? Whereby is Christendom to be recognized now? What distinction does she possess over Turks and heathens? Where is her Christian life?'

His fame had likewise attracted the attention of the court at Dresden. The event itself, that a cobbler was an author and had moreover obtained a considerable following, could not but excite to the highest degree the curiosity of the ecclesiastical dignitaries, in whose diocese he lived, to become acquainted with the simple and wonderful man. There was

[1] How easily excitable and accessible to disturbances his nervous nature was, is shown by his account when the Görlitz bridge had collapsed before his eyes: 'We cannot at present enter the city on account of the bridge that has given way, with an entire pier in the middle of the bridge, from top to bottom; which happened in a flash, as if a gun were fired off. This I myself saw, and discerned the great power of God almost in a supernatural way; which gives rise to considerable reflection, whereof I would discourse with you orally. For such a thing as I beheld threw me into sore consternation. For I was stationed not above three yards from the break, at a [side] window [of the bridge], in order to look into the water, but I ran away in terror. I saw it only with one glance, and before I looked round, all was to the bottom in a moment. P.S. I should think about ten persons fell with the structure; some were much hurt, but none killed. There is no knowing whether any stranger may have fallen, for there were many people on the bridge. The case is not yet rightly understood; information will come to hand when the timber is raised' (Epistle 66).

added to this, that Richter had sounded a violent alarm, as if the theosophist was a detestable heretic. The consistories were at that time very jealous of the subject's orthodoxy. Thus one reason more was presented for submitting to an interrogatory the shoemaker who, in Richter's view, might already be regarded as the head of a sect, and threatened the constitution of the Church by his mystical doctrines. Lastly, the Saxon court, like most courts of that period, entertained the well-known predilection for gold-making and alchemical arts. The Elector kept up a laboratory, the director of which was first Balthasar Walther, and afterwards Benedict Hinkelmann, a practising physician and the alchemist to the court, just as the Emperor Rudolph had maintained in his service the great Kepler. Now Böhme is to be reckoned among these alchemists. His letters bear indubitable evidence of the fact that he held gold-making and the discovery of a material Philosopher's Stone to be possible. Hinkelmann doubtless had been in close connection with Walther, that zealous follower of Böhme; and hence perhaps it was believed at the court that advantage and profit could be derived from the gold-maker. Clergy, nobles and the learned accordingly summoned the wonderful man, not in order to drag him before a consistorial enquiry, but to sound him, to determine whether nothing but wind and words, whether an orthodox but calumniated individual, whether a heretic and false prophet, or something else, perchance a gold-maker, could be sought for in him. They seem to have inclined principally towards the latter opinion. Hinkelmann, the alchemist to the court, offered his dwelling to him as a guest. They certainly had no inkling of the significance which posterity would find in Böhme. The highest that they were prepared for in him was a genius who had gone astray through a fanatical enthusiasm. Böhme viewed the summons in a rosy light. Hitherto he had been invited only to friendly colloquies by adherents, and such persons as sought his acquaintance on the ground of a previous esteem. Now, elevated by his success, he surveyed the immense distance between him and that supreme consistory, at the head of which stood Hoë von Hoënegg. The court presented itself to him only as a brilliant abode, whence fresh recognition beckoned to him.

He had received the summons prior to the fifteenth of March. Through the medium of his adherents his fame had spread to Dresden even before he had been cited by the Primarius before the Council, nay even before Richter tried to blacken his character to the court. Böhme had promised to obey the summons after the Leipzig Fair. On the ninth of May he set out upon his journey, which led him by way of Zittau. Some friends had invited him to come to this place, where he met with a hospitable reception. A conference was held, in which Johann Molinus, Doctors Johann Hartig and Matthias Rhenisch, and Herr von Fürstenau took part. Further, they animadverted upon the conduct of the Primarius, and declared they could find no trace of a good spirit in him. Finally, Böhme received from them some money for travelling expenses, and was asked to continue to keep up their acquaintance. Melchior Berndt, his host, accompanied him to Dresden. A few days afterwards the two arrived at the place of residence of the Electoral court, and were received by Benedict Hinkelmann, who was a Christian gentleman (Epistle 62), with all Christian love and friendship. Through him, as physician to the Elector, acquaintanceships among the courtiers and Church dignitaries were opened to Böhme. The long misunderstood theosophist, who also aroused interest by his personality, found more and more widely extended sympathy. Almost all with whom he became acquainted read and loved the printed book, acknowledged it to be a gift of God, and used it daily.

The Saxon clergy, the members of which were not all so orthodox as Hoë von Hoënegg and Richter, now had the printed book of the supposed heretic in their possession. Fortunately, in the two tractates *On True Repentance* and *On the Supersensual Life* there was nothing of Schwenkfeldt's doctrines, nothing of Theophrastian chemistry and physical theory, nothing of a decided and blasphemous Weigelian mysticism, and lastly nothing philosophical. In them Böhme had described only what he himself had experienced. It was a description of the surrender of the individual self, the doctrine of entrance into God and sinking the whole will; of deep penitence, and the Christian's struggle if he would attain to inwardness with the Deity; of the thorny path of him who is tempted by the ego to fall away from the heart of God; of the blessedness of union with the body of Christ. This presented nothing heretical. It was the Lutheran doctrine of justification by faith, as Tauler and the 'German Theology' already possessed it, from which sources Luther derived the essential fact of his Reformation. It is no wonder, then, that the clergy did not understand how the author of such orthodox writings could be persecuted to extremes by a clergyman; it is no wonder, then, that Böhme himself heard Hoë von Hoënegg teaching from the pulpit the doctrine of regeneration and the inner man exactly as was written in his own little book. The Superintendent of Dresden, Aegidius Strauch, openly and publicly commended his work, and granted the author the privilege of a conference at his lodging.

In the case of an individual unused to the world the transition from so severe a persecution to so eulogistic a recognition was too rapid for him to be able to curb his delight. He rejoiced loudly and scoffed at his vanquished opponent, which before was not his way at all, and can only be explained by surprise affecting his temperament, which had been wrested out of customary circles. He threatens Richter with punishment by the Electoral court, of which indeed there was far from being any question. 'They might be able to put him to rights on the score of his lies and shameful slanders' (Epistle 62). 'If the Primarius has any complaint to make against me, he might now present it to the Prince Elector's Council. I would stand confronting him, and set forth his lies to his face, which lies he has poured out in a venomous way regarding me, both before the congregation and in the pasquil. He brings shame and reproach upon the city of Görlitz by such defamation. His mouth might be stopped; to keep his mouth from reviling would be good for him. If the Primarius aims at checking and repressing me, he should have time to convene a council and take in hand a reformation' (Epistle 63).

The climax of his good fortune seemed to him at hand when there was announced to him, after a tarrying of more than six weeks, a solemn conference with the supreme consistory, perhaps even in the presence of the Elector, who with many councillors had been away during this period. Without this solemn conference, the whole journey of Böhme to Dresden, which was only undertaken for this purpose, since his position with reference to the Church was to be decided, would have been entirely useless.

After the conference Böhme was discharged 'in all favour to his home.' Subsequently Weisner heard Professor Gerhard declare in the presence of Meisner, that 'he would not take the whole world, and help to condemn the man.' To which Meisner replied: 'My brother, neither would I. Who knows what lies behind this? How can we judge what we have not understood nor are able to understand, whether it be right, black or white? May God convert the man if he be in error, and keep us to His divine truth, and enable us to know it always the longer the better; likewise give us mind and heart to express it, and power to propagate it.' Weisner, on another occasion, heard that the late Dr. Meisner at Wittenberg, when Jacob Böhme was spoken of, being asked what judgment he would give of him, answered, 'He desired not to contribute to condemning, suppressing or banishing the man; that he was an individual of wonderfully high mental endowments, whom at present it were impossible either to condemn or approve.'

The examiners had recognized that Böhme was an unassuming man, that his book contained no heresies, and, probably also, that he had not the remotest idea how to make gold. The greatest part of his answers was certainly so obscure, that the meaning of what he said was not understood. This man, who was so little formed for intercourse with the world, was, in oral discourse, even more stiff and awkward than in written exposition. The cumbrousness, slowness and unreadiness of his conceptions was the reason that acute logicians easily gained the victory over him in a theological colloquy. With the astronomers he had so far come to an understanding, that he recognized and approved the discoveries made by Copernicus, Galileo and Kepler; but, just as in his writings, he declared that his proper sphere embraced the *depth* of this science, that is to say, metaphysics, philosophy of nature and theosophy,—not the empirical science of nature, in which his attainments were not brilliant, but only consisted in popular barbarism. The court and the clergy found themselves deceived in their expectations. They did not exactly care to condemn his unintelligible discourse; accordingly they let him go his way, after the Elector's curiosity was satisfied.

By this decision, and by the favour of the Elector, Böhme had obtained a splendid vindication: his victory over the Primarius was complete. The ecclesiastical tyrant had been placed in an exceedingly doubtful light with regard to his supreme board. But if for the unassuming modest thinker this vindication sufficed to consider the event as the culminating point in his career, recognition of his worth had remained nevertheless an empty phrase. There was now no more any reference made to those promises on the part of the court, which had filled him with such great delight that he himself wrote his wife word that there was hope of being able to find in Dresden a new home and a refuge from the persecutions of the Primarius and his rabble. The poor needy theosophist was put off with audiences and colloquies, without having obtained even a formal protection from the enemy in his city, whose behaviour however had been publicly disapproved. With impunity and freedom from censure the Primarius Richter continued to practise indignities towards his person and his family. Jubilation over the victory was soon spoiled for the unfortunate man. Six weeks in vain he had had to wait in the capital; and when at last, full of disillusions, he returned to his home, there fresh sufferings and fresh persecution received him.

During his absence the Primarius had unceasingly stirred up the rabble. Böhme's family were exposed to its continual abuse and insults. Before his house tumultuous gatherings took place, in connection with which his windows were broken.[1] From Dresden Böhme had often to speak words of comfort to his wife, and direct her thoughts to his early return. In the meantime he commended her to the protection of his friend Dr. Tobias Kober and his own son Jacob, who had just returned home from his travels. The latter found no peace at home. His brother had to suffer harsh treatment from his master Hans Bürger, who was a faithful follower of the Primarius. In these circumstances complaint sounds forth ever more clearly and loudly from Böhme's letters.[2] The long waiting, and the desire of his family for the head of the household, put his patience to the test. He had already resolved to return to Görlitz, even if he should have to travel back to Dresden again. Yet the joy of reunion with his family was but brief. He soon accepted an invitation from Hans and David von Schweinichen and Abraham von Frankenberg to come to Silesia and visit them on their estates. As regards this stay in Silesia, Frankenberg's account is more worthy of credence than in the case of other events, which he did not experience as an eye-and-ear-witness. And therefore a certain narrative is not to be passed over, though it was written down for the glorification of the master.

Jacob Böhme was once on a visit with David von Schweinichen to a nobleman living in the neighbourhood, and from there he was to return to Seifersdorf, Schweinichen's seat. A lad was to conduct him thither, but was bribed by a physician to throw him into a miry slough. He carried out the revengeful plot, and ran off to fetch assistance from Seifersdorf on Jacob Böhme (for whom probably only a fright was intended) unluckily falling on a stone and being wounded somewhat severely in the head. The victim was

[1] 'If the high priest choose to break open my house, let him do it, that it may be known in all countries what a stirrer up of riots he is; it will redound to the great honour of him and his. If others should do it, or give occasion to it, the Council would not suffer them in the city.'—'My wife need not have any window shutters made. If they will break them, they may; and then the fruits of the high priest will be seen' (Epistle 64).

[2] He complains thus of the people of Görlitz: 'Their steadfastness is very well seen: what they approve now, at another time they disavow. Oh, if the Jesuits should come, and the churches were reclaimed from Luther again, what good Papists they would make' (Epistle 64).

conveyed to his hosts, where he received at once the necessary care and attention. When he had recovered, the family often assembled in order to hold converse with him. On one of these occasions a brother-in-law of Schweinichen's fell out with the theosophist, and heaped such shameful taunts upon him, that at last Böhme became exasperated, openly reproved his frivolous life and warned him of judgment from Heaven. Afterwards, the nobleman is said to have fallen from his horse and broken his neck when he was about to ride home, being enraged at the tribute of approbation which was paid to the learned cobbler.

After a stay of some months Böhme was seized with a burning fever, so that he had to depart hurriedly, and, on the malady growing worse, had to be conveyed to Görlitz. A grave abdominal complaint developed; [1] his early end was to be feared. Dr. Kober, his physician, consulted with Dr. Christopher Kutter of Sprottau. No remedies took effect. Melchior Berndt, a friend of the theosophist, came from Zittau. The illness had lasted a fortnight. Then the patient desired the Lord's Supper.

The Primarius Richter had died on the 24th of August 1624. Nicholas Thomas had delivered a brilliant funeral oration for the sturdy orthodoxist. 'It was known,' he said, 'to each and every one how the Primarius by his teaching and mode of life comported himself in his function and calling; that before all else he preached and taught God's word purely and in accordance with the prophetic and apostolic writings, and at the same time with due zeal steadily and undauntedly refuted and reproved the prevailing gross *errores* and *delicta*, according to the command of God, as is incumbent upon and properly belongs to every sincere teacher; notwithstanding he was well aware that he made for himself thus not a few enemies.' Later generations, however, from a right sympathy for the victim of fanatical priestly persecution and from a favourable senti-

[1] Kober has thus recorded the symptoms of the disease: *alvi fluxus, rugitus ventris, dolores lancinantes lateris sinistri, excrescentia ventris et pedum, angustia pectoris, hians os, siccitas, consumptio summa thoracis et faciei, urina ruffa circulo nigro, quae semper talis erat.*

ment towards the mild representative of toleration and honest inquiry in the sphere of religious thought, have covered his adversary with ignominy. So long as self-examination, self-reflection and respect for the convictions of others are held to be a sacred duty of the teaching profession, the human mind being unable to grasp the complete truth, so long will the name of Richter stand as the symbol of a fanaticism deserving of condemnation.—His successor in office was his funeral orator, and worthy he was of such succession. Under his direction the clerical board made the last hours of the hounded-to-death theosophist more difficult, and set a stigma upon his mortal remains.

The Primarius Thomas gave permission to *Mag.* Elias Dietrich to administer the Lord's Supper to the requestant, only when the confession of faith of an orthodox Lutheran should be obtained from him. Dietrich's report (as delivered to the ecclesiastical authorities) of the examination imposed runs as follows: List of some questions that were put to Jacob Behmen, formerly shoemaker at Görlitz, in his sickness, previous to his absolution and partaking of the Lord's Supper, together with his answers to these questions.—I asked whether he believed

I. That God is one in essence or substance, and threefold in person, God the Father, Son and Holy Spirit? Answer: Yes.

II. That God at the beginning created man in true holiness and righteousness, in his own image; but man, of his own will, by the devil's guile, turned himself away from God, and in consequence fell into sin, into temporal and eternal death; and on its account he must have remained therein eternally and perished, if God had not taken pity on him and shown interest in him? A. Yes.

III. That in the middle person of Christ there are two distinct natures, Divine and human; and that by his Divine nature he has existed from eternity, equal in essence, honour and glory to the Father and Holy Spirit. That in the fulness of time he assumed humanity from *Maria Virgine, operatione Spiritus Sancti*, in oneness of person, unmixed and undivided;

and brought not his flesh from heaven, much less laid it away after his resurrection and ascension, but is and remains God and man in eternity? A. Yes.

IV. That there is no other mediator nor any other way to salvation but Christ, who must be laid hold of by us through our own real faith, and be applied by us along with his merit and all benefits; and that this faith is a gift of God? A. Yes.

V. That a Christian ought to lead a holy and blameless life, according to God's command, so far as is possible, *in hac corrupta natura*; yet with God he can gain nothing by this, according to the saying of Christ, when ye shall have done all those things etc., but is justified and saved by pure unmerited grace, *propter meritum Christi fide apprehensum*? A. Yes.

VI. That the preached word and the sacraments were *medii salutis*, which are to be made use of and not despised, if they can be had; but that God is not tied to them, and can in case of need bring about salvation without them (this I illustrated to him *simili & exemplo*)? A. Yes.

VII. I asked whether he held the doctrine which is presented in our churches to be correct and conformable to Scripture? A. Yes.

VIII. Whether henceforth—for God might prolong his life and restore his health—he would keep to our church and doctrine, and abandon whatever was contrary to it? And when he expressed himself affirmatively on this point, I referred him to the Scriptures, and reminded him that he was to draw near to God, that is, be content with His revealed word. With occult revelations and visions it were quite an uncertain thing. For a man could imagine something which never took place *in rei veritate*; and the devil too could cast a mist before a person's eyes. But God's word was certain, and whoever trusted and believed it could not be deluded. To which he returned answer, that he had the New Testament and read it diligently. But I exhorted him to combine the Old and the New. For the Old

Testament had reference to the New, and the New to the Old; and the New Testament was the explanation and fulfilment of the Old. *Item*, he was to abstain from the writing of books, in accordance with reasons advanced. Then he gave me an account of *occasionem scribendi*, which however I do not pretend to pronounce upon, and consider unnecessary to relate here.

IX. Whether before this he had partaken of the Lord's Supper? A. Yes, often, and about three quarters of a year ago with his wife and two sons in public church-assembly. (According to the statement of his wife, he was absolved then as well as a certain number of times previously by Herr Andree).

X. Whether his repentance amounted to a real earnestness, and whether he desired with his whole heart the Lord's Supper? A. Yes, he was in earnest, and desired the Lord's Supper from the bottom of his heart. Thereupon he was exhorted by me to consider well what he was doing; that he could indeed deceive me (who could not see into his heart and judge *de occultis*), but not God in heaven, who trieth the heart and reins. Now, if his repentance were a real earnestness, then God would pardon and forgive him all his sins, and by Christ's command, in virtue of my office, I would announce to him the gracious forgiveness of sins, and thus my absolution would be of use to him and have its effect. In the contrary case he would get no comfort or enjoyment from it. Upon this he repeated his last answer.

His praemissis, I prepared for the act in question. And before absolution and administration of the Lord's Supper, I interrogated him once more to superabundance, and with a view to better caution and defence on my part *contra calumniatorum morsus et Satanae mendacia*:

1. Whether he confessed himself to be a sinner? A. Yes.

2. Whether he sorrowed with his whole heart for the sins he had committed? A. Yes. *Manibus complicatis, oculis elevatis.*

3. Whether he believed that for his sake and for his benefit Christ died and shed his blood on the tree of the cross? A. Yes, for he himself says: Come unto me all ye etc.

4. Whether he believed that God, for Christ's sake, would pardon and forgive him all his sins, and be gracious and merciful? A. Yes, firmly.

5. Whether with God's help he would amend his life, and so far as it were possible for him, be on his guard henceforth against sin? A. Yes.

6. Whether he was ready to pardon and forgive from the bottom of his heart everyone by whom he had been injured? A. Yes, with his whole heart he forgave them, and desired of others in turn a like forgiveness. Was insistent in his prayer that this should be done publicly in his name, but passed away before it was able to be carried out.

I next heard his confession, absolved him, *praemissis praemittendis* administered to him the Lord's Supper, and performed fully whatever pertains to my office in the case of sick persons. But seeing that he was weak, I accommodated myself to the occasion, and dealt with him in a gentle and kindly way, according to the admonition of Paul and the example of Christ. And indeed it is not my custom to treat people harshly and sharply. For, from experience in my ministry as well as in common life, I have observed that more is accomplished with gentleness and kindliness than with violence and rudeness.

Haec non ficta, sed facta sunt (sensu et rebus iisdem immo fere verbis) Anno Christi 1624 *d.* 15. *Nov. hora* 8. *matu.*

To whom God wills not of His grace the denial,
To him of my service I make not refusal.

Semper in dubiis benigniora praeferenda sunt. Et recte, ne praecipitanter et cum scandalo judicem id, quod nobis nox tenebrosa, aliis autem clara dies est.

Given in Herr *Mag.* Elias' own hand.

On the 16th of November Böhme had declared to Hans Rothe and Michael Kurz that in three days he should go into the other world. But his end overtook him sooner. On the 17th of November, a Sunday, he asked his son at two in the morning whether he heard the sweet music. When the son answered no, he said: 'Let the door be set open, so as to hear the singing better.' Then he asked what the hour was. When told it was two o'clock, he replied: 'My time is not yet. O thou strong God of Sabaoth, deliver me according to thy will! O thou crucified Lord Jesus Christ, be merciful to me, and take me into thy kingdom!' At six in the morning, before the gates of the city were opened or his friends had come to him, he suddenly bade farewell to his wife and children, murmured some unintelligible words, and exclaimed: 'Now I go hence into Paradise.' Whereupon he turned round and departed, as the record says, with joyful mien, peacefully and happily. He was in the fiftieth year of his age.

ON THE ELECTION OF GRACE
ETC.

DE ELECTIONE GRATIÆ

OR

OF THE WILL OF GOD IN REGARD TO MEN

THAT IS

A SHORT EXPOSITION AND INTRODUCTION CONCERNING
THE HIGHEST GROUND, SHOWING HOW MAN MAY
ATTAIN TO DIVINE KNOWLEDGE

FURTHER, HOW THE PASSAGES OF SCRIPTURE ARE TO BE
UNDERSTOOD THAT TREAT OF FALLEN CORRUPT ADAM
AND OF THE NEW BIRTH FROM CHRIST

Written in accordance with Divine illumination
by
JACOB BÖHME
in the year 1623

AUTHOR'S PREFACE TO THE READER

1. WHEN Reason hears any one speak of God, as to what He is in his essence and will, it imagines that God is to be regarded as being something remote and strange, dwelling beyond the place of this world high above the stars, and governing only by his Spirit with an omnipresent power in the place of this world; but that his Majesty in threefoldness, where God is specially manifest, dwells in heaven, outside of the place of this world.

2. And hence Reason falls into a creaturely delusion, supposing that God has, before the times of the creation of the creatures and of this world, held a consultation in himself, in his triad through wisdom, as to what he should make, and wherefore every being should exist; and has thus drawn for himself a purpose in himself, what way he would dispose every particular thing.

3. And therefrom has arisen the contentious opinion of a decree in regard to men, as if God had by his purpose chosen one part of mankind to the kingdom of heaven, to enter into his holy bliss, and chosen the other part to eternal damnation: in the latter he would manifest his wrath, whereas in the others, the Elect, he would manifest his grace. And it is held that he has thus by his purpose made a distinction in order to exhibit his power in love and wrath. And therefore everything has to take place by necessity; and the part of mankind belonging to wrath becomes so hardened and reprobate in consequence of God's

purpose that there is no longer any possibility of their attaining to the grace of God; in the others, on the contrary, there is no possibility of damnation.

4. And though in certain passages the Scriptures speak almost in such a manner, to which creaturely Reason (that understands not what God is) assents; yet, on the other hand, they say also the direct opposite, namely, that God neither wills nor, as the result of his purpose, has made anything that is evil. Now as regards these two opposites, how they are to be understood according to their true ground, we will (in order to unite them and establish the real meaning) furnish to the Christian impartial reader, to the seekers and lovers of the ground and the truth, a short statement for further reflection; and with a good intent and affection will set forth our gift which we have received (as this has been laid hold of in the grace of the highest Good) for the reader to consider of. Not with a view to attack or to despise any one thus for his formed opinion; but in order to a Christian and brotherly union of our gifts, which we have together from the Divine grace.

5. As the branches and twigs of a tree are not like each other in form, and yet live in one stem; and one gives to and introduces into the other power and virtue, and all rejoice, blossom and bear fruit in a single stem; and there is no envy on account of strength or inequality, but every branch labours to bring forth its fruit and harvest: so also it may be with our dissimilar gifts if we introduce our desire into the right true mother, as into our stem, and each branch of the tree continually give to the other its virtue in good will, and we bring not ourselves into a selfness and a lust of self-love, i.e. into pride (being minded to fly out above our mother in whom we live,

and above all her children, and wishing to be a special individual tree), nor take into ourselves the devil's poison of self-will and false magnetic impressure, whence strife, contrary will and divisions arise, whereby one twig of the human tree separates itself from the other, grudges it its power and virtue, and proclaims it to be apostate and false, and yet itself is exhibited and seen in a false lustre as an apostate twig in relation to its brethren. And therefrom have arisen the multiplicity of contentions among men.

6. To all these [our fellow-branches] we would indicate what the origin of contention and controversy is, and whence opinions and divisions naturally take their rise ; further, what the true ground of the one religion is, out of which so many schisms have arisen ; and we will indicate from whence opposition has originated from the time of the beginning of the world : to promote understanding of the divine Will according to love and wrath, showing how all this is fundamentally to be understood.

7. And we exhort the loving Reader to sink himself in divine humility into God and his fellow-branches or brethren. In this way he may lay hold of our deep thought and knowledge which we have received, and be turned from all errors to the true rest (wherein all things do rest in the Word and power of God). And we commit him to the effectual working love in the being of Christ, and commend our well-disposed will and desire into his will. Amen.

CHAPTER I

Of the one will of God, and of the introduction of what he has revealed as his being. What the one God is.

1. God says in Moses in a manifested voice to the people of Israel (by which voice he brought himself out of his hiddenness into a manifest sound in an express creaturely manner, and made himself heard, so that the creature might apprehend him) : I the Lord thy God am one God only ; thou shalt honour no other gods beside me (Ex. xx. 2, 3 ; Deut. vi. 4). And again, Moses says : The Lord our God is an angry, jealous God, and a consuming fire (Deut. iv. 24). And then again : God is a merciful God. His Spirit is a flame of love (Deut. iv. 31).

2. These passages seem to involve a contradiction, inasmuch as God calls himself an angry God and a consuming fire, and then again, a flame of love,—he who can be nothing but good, else he were not God, viz. the one good.

3. For it cannot be said of God that he is this or that, evil or good, or that he has distinctions in himself. For he is in himself natureless, passionless, and creatureless. He has no tendency to anything, for there is nothing before him to which he could tend, neither evil nor good. He is in himself the unground, without any will towards nature and creature, as it were an eternal nothing. There is no pain or quality (*Qual*) in him, nor anything that could incline either to him or from him. He is the one sole existence, and

there is nothing before him or after him by or in which he might draw or grasp a will for himself; neither has he anything that generates or produces him. He is the nothing and the all, and is a single will in which the world and the whole creation lies. In him all is alike eternal, without beginning, equal in weight, measure and number. He is neither light nor darkness, neither love nor wrath, but the eternal One. Therefore Moses says: The Lord is one God only (Deut. vi. 4).

4. This unfathomable, incomprehensible, unnatural and uncreaturely will, which is one only and has nothing before it nor after it; which in itself is but a one, which is as nothing and yet is everything,—this will is called and is the one God, which seizes and finds himself in himself, and begets God from God.

5. That is to say, the first unoriginated single will, which is neither evil nor good, generates within itself the one eternal good as an apprehensible will, which is the Son of the unfathomable will, and yet co-eternal with the unoriginated will. This second will is the first will's eternal feeling and finding, for the nothing finds itself in itself as a something. And the unfathomable will, *i.e.* the indiscoverable One, by its eternal discovery goes forth, and brings itself into an eternal intuition of itself.

6. Thus the unfathomable will is called eternal Father. And the will that is found, grasped and brought forth by the unground is called his begotten or only-begotten Son; for it is the Ens of the unground, whereby the unground apprehends itself in a ground. And the outgoing of the unfathomable will through the apprehended Son or Ens is called Spirit, for he leads the apprehended Ens out of itself into a movement or life of the will, as a life of the Father and of the Son. And what has gone forth is joy, viz.

the discovery of the eternal nothing, in which Father, Son and Spirit behold and find themselves; and this is called God's wisdom or intuition.

7. This threefold being in its birth and in its self-contemplation in wisdom has been from eternity, and possesses in itself no other ground or place than just itself. It is a single life and a single will without desire. It has in itself neither thickness nor thinness, neither height nor depth, nor space nor time; but is through all and in all, and yet is to all as an unseizable nothing.

8. As the lustre of the sun works in the whole world, in all things and through all things, and yet all this can take away nothing from the sun, but must suffer him and work along with the power of the sun: in such a way is God to be considered, as to what he is apart from nature and creature in himself, in a self-comprehensible Chaos, independent of ground, time and place. In this Chaos the eternal nothing comprehends itself in an eye or eternal power of seeing, for the beholding, feeling and finding of itself. In such case it cannot be said that God has two wills, one to evil, and the other to good.

9. For in the unnatural, uncreaturely Deity, there is nothing more than a single will, which is called also the one God; and he wills in himself nothing more than just to seize and find himself, go out from himself, and with the outgoing bring himself into an intuition; by which is understood the triad of the Deity together with the mirror of his wisdom or the eye of his seeing. Therein are understood all powers, colours, wonders and beings, in the eternal (one) wisdom, in equal weight and measure without properties, as a single ground of the Being of all beings. And a longing that is found in himself or a desire for somewhat, a longing

for manifestation or discovery of properties, which divine longing or wisdom is in itself, in the primal Ground, wholly without properties. For if there were properties, there would have to be something to produce or cause the properties. But there is no cause of the divine powers and of the divine longing or wisdom save the one will, that is to say, the one God who brings himself into a threefoldness as into an apprehensibility of himself. This apprehensibility is the centre, as the eternal apprehended One, and is called the heart or seat of the eternal will of God, in which the unground possesses itself in a ground. And it is the one place of God, but with no partition or separation; moreover immeasurable, without any form or parallel, for there is nothing before it to which it might be compared.

10. This heart or centre of the unground is the eternal mind of the will, and yet has nothing before it that it can will, save only the one will that apprehends itself in this centre. The first will to the centre likewise has nothing that it can will, save only this one place of its self-discovery. The first will is therefore the Father of its heart or the place of its discovery, and a possessor of what is found, viz. its only-begotten will or Son.

11. The unfathomable will, which is the Father and a beginning of all being, generates itself within itself into a place of apprehensibility, or possesses the place; and the place is the ground and beginning of all beings, and possesses in its turn the unfathomable will, which is the Father of the beginning and so of the ground.

12. Thus the Father and his Son (as the place of a selfhood) is one God only, with one only will. This one will in the apprehended place of the ground goes

out from itself, from the apprehension, and with the outgoing it is called a spirit. Thus the one will of the unground through the first, eternal, unoriginated grasp divides into three kinds of working, and yet remains but one will. The first will, which is called Father, produces in itself the Son as the place of the Deity. And the place of the Deity, which is the Father's Son, produces in itself, in the discovery, the power of wisdom,—all which powers take their rise in the Son. And yet here all powers are but one power, and that power is the perceptible, discoverable Deity in itself, in one only will and being, with no distinction.

13. These found, generated and produced powers, as the centre of the beginnings of all beings, does the first will in the perceptibility of itself breathe forth from itself, from the one power which is its seat or Son, in manner as the sun's rays shoot forth from the magical fire of the sun, and reveal the sun's power. Accordingly this outgoing is a ray of the power of God, as a moving life of the Deity, in which the unfathomable will has brought itself into a ground, as into an assurgent power. Such a power does the will to power breathe forth out of the power, and the outgoing is called the Spirit of God, and makes the third kind of working, as a life or movement in the power.

14. The fourth kind of working takes place in the outbreathed power as in the divine intuition or wisdom, where the Spirit of God (which arises from the power) with the outbreathed powers as with one power sports with himself, and in the power introduces himself into forms in the divine longing, as if he wished to bring an image of this generation of the triad into a particular will and life as a representation of the one trinity. And this imprinted image is the joy of the divine intuition, though we are not to understand a

comprehensible, creaturely image possessing circumscription; but the divine Imagination as the primal ground of Magic, from which the creation has had its beginning and origin.

15. And in this imprint or magical representation in wisdom is understood the angelic and soulic true image of God, whereof Moses says (Gen. i. 27): God created man in his own image, that is, in the image of this divine imprint according to the spirit; and in the image of God created he him as to the creature of created corporeal form. So likewise is it to be understood with regard to the angels, in respect of the divine existence out of the divine wisdom. But the creaturely ground, wherein lie the properties, shall be indicated hereafter.

16. In the foregoing account we understand in a summary way what God apart from nature and creature is, when He declares in Moses: I the Lord thy God am one God only. His name in the sensual tongue (this Divine process of birth in the powers of the one wisdom bringing itself into a framing of the image of itself) is called JEHOVA, as an embodied longing of the Nothing in a something, or the Eternal One. This in a manner might be delineated thus △, and yet there is no measurable or divisible form or thing; but it is for the mind to reflect upon.

17. For this inward figuration is neither great nor small, and has nowhere either a beginning or an end (save where God's longing is carried into a being of his intuition, as in the creation), but it is infinite and its form uncircumscribed,—just as the modelizing in man's mind remains immeasurable in a constant form, where innumerable thoughts may fashion and define themselves in the one mind; which, however, in the earthly creature take their rise for the most part from

the phantasy of the astral mind, and not from the powers of the inward ground of the Divine wisdom.

18. Here we remind the reader that God in himself (so far as he is called God apart from nature and creature) has no more than one will, which is, to give and bring forth himself. God Jehovah generates nothing but God; that is, there is generated one Father, Son and Holy Spirit, in the one Divine power and wisdom.

19. As the sun has but a single will, which is, to give itself, and with its desire to press forth in all things, and yield up to every life power with itself; so likewise is God apart from nature and creature the one good, that neither wills nor can give anything but God or the good.

20. Out of nature God is the greatest gentleness and humility, wherein is found no trace either of a will to good or a will to evil inclination; for there is neither evil nor good before him. He is himself the one eternal good, and a beginning of all good being and will. Nor is it possible for anything evil to penetrate into him, in so far as he is this one good; for to everything that is posterior to him he is a nothing. He is a power operative within itself, essential and spiritual, the supremest purest humility and beneficence, namely, a feeling, a tasting of love and goodness in the Sense of the sweet bringing-forth, a ravishing and delightful hearing.

21. For all senses inqualify [in God] in equal harmonious accord, and there is nothing but a lovely assurgency of the Holy Spirit in the one wisdom. In this connection it cannot be said that he is an angry God or that he is a merciful God, because here there is no cause of anger, nor any cause to love anything; for he is the one Love himself, who in pure love

gives birth to himself in and ushers himself into threefoldness.

22. The first will, which is called Father, loves his Son, viz. his heart of his self-revelation, because the Son is his discovery and power. As the soul loves the body, so the apprehended will of the Father is his power and spiritual body, as the centre of the Deity or Divine something, in which the first will is a something.

23. The Son is the first will's (*i.e.* the Father's) humility, and in his turn desires powerfully the Father's will, for without the Father he would be a nothing. And he is rightly called the Father's longing or desire for the manifestation of powers, viz. of the Father's taste, smell, hearing, feeling and seeing. And yet here distinctions must not be made or understood, for all these senses are in equipoise in the one Deity. Let it only be considered that these senses, which have their origin in the ground of nature, arise by the Father speaking forth these powers from himself into divisibility.

24. And the holy Spirit is therefore called holy and a flame of love, because he is the emanating power from the Father and the Son, viz. the moving life in the first will of the Father, and in the second will of the Son, in his power; and because he is a shaper, worker and leader in the emanated joy of the Father and the Son in wisdom.

25. Therefore, ye dear brethren, ye poor men confused by Babel, who has confused you through Satan's envy, observe this: When you are told about three persons in the Deity, and about the divine will, know that the Lord our God is one God only, who neither wills nor can will anything evil. For if he willed something evil, and then willed something good in himself,

there would be a separation in him; and thus there would have to be something that were the cause of opposition.

26. Seeing there is nothing before God, nothing can move him to anything. For if something did move him, then that something would be prior to and greater than himself, and it would be the case that God were divided in himself; and hence too that moving something would have to be of another beginning, as having moved itself.

27. But, in regard to the declaration of the One, we tell you that God's essence (so far as this is called the one God) is to be understood apart from ground, place and time, dwelling in itself, and not to be considered in any region specially with a particular abode. But if thou wilt know where God dwells, abstract nature and creature, and then God is all. Abstract the expressed formed word, and then thou beholdest the ever-speaking Word which the Father speaks in the Son, and thou seest the hidden wisdom of God.

28. But thou sayest: I cannot abstract from myself nature and creature; for if that were done, I should be a nothing. Therefore I must represent to myself the Deity by means of images; because I see there is evil and good in me, as well as in the whole creation.

29. Hearken, my friend: God saith in Moses, Thou shalt make thee no likeness of the one God, neither in the heavens nor upon the earth, nor in the water nor in anything; to signify that He is no image, nor needs a place for an abode, and that He should be sought nowhere but in His formed expressed Word, that is, in the form of God, in man himself. For it is written: The Word is nigh thee, even in thy mouth, and in thy heart (Rom. x. 8). And this is the nearest way to God, namely, that the form of God sink down in itself

from all imprinted images, abandon all images, disputation and contention in itself, despair of its own will, desire and opinion, and merely sink into the eternal One, into the pure single love of God, and trust in that; which love after the fall of man God introduced again, in Christ, into humanity.

30. This I have set forth at some length, that the reader may learn to understand the primal Ground, what God is and wills; and that he seek not for an evil and good will in the one, unnatural, uncreaturely God; and that he leave the images of the creature if he would consider God, His will and His ever-speaking Word. Further, if he would consider from whence spring evil and good, with regard to which God calls himself an angry jealous God, then let him turn to the eternal Nature, *i.e.* to the expressed compacted formed word, and also to the temporal Nature that has a beginning, wherein lies the creation of this world.

31. We now proceed to inform the reader further concerning God's word (which He speaks forth from His powers), and will indicate to him the process of separation, that is, the origin of properties, from which a good and evil will take their rise, and to what end this must inevitably be. And we will show him how all things depend on such inevitable separation, and how badness originates in the creature.

CHAPTER II

OF THE ORIGIN OF GOD'S EVER-SPEAKING WORD; AND OF THE MANIFESTATION OF THE DIVINE POWER, THAT IS, OF NATURE AND QUALITY.

1. CREATURELY Reason is found in the formed, comprehended, expressed word, and therefore it is a figurate being, and it thinks always that God too is a figurate being, who can kindle himself into wrath and bring himself into properties for evil and good. In like manner, with regard to this high article of the divine will, Reason has imagined that God from eternity has made a resolution and choice, decreeing what he would do with his creature; and so has passed into a condition of avengement, in order that he might manifest his love and mercy to his elect; and that therefore his wrath must be a cause of his mercy becoming known. All this really at bottom may be stated thus, that God's wrath must reveal his Majesty, as fire reveals the light.

2. But concerning the will of God, as also concerning the separation of the formed word in the creature, Reason has no right idea. For had God ever held a consultation in himself, so to reveal himself, then his revelation were not from eternity, beyond the sphere of mind and place. Thus this consultation must have had a beginning, and there must have been a reason in the Deity for which God in his triad had deliberated; and thus also there would have to be thoughts in God, as one who fashioned for himself a form representing how he would deal with a thing.

3. But now he himself is the sole and single, and the ground of all things, and the eye of all beings, and the cause of all essence. From his proprium arises nature and creature. Why then should he want to deliberate with himself, if there is no enemy before him nor behind him, and he himself is alone all,—the will, the capability and the power ?

4. Therefore, if we wish to speak only of God's unchangeable essence, as to what he wills, or has willed and ever wills, we ought not to speak of his deliberation, for there is no deliberation in him. He is the eye of all seeing and the ground of all beings. He wills and does in himself always one and the same thing, that is, he brings forth himself so as to give birth to Father, Son, Holy Spirit, and the wisdom of his manifestation. Other than this, the one unfathomable God wills in himself nothing ; neither has he in himself any deliberation about several. For if he willed in himself several things, he could not in such a willing be powerful enough to effectuate them. Thus he can will in himself nothing more than just himself; for what he has willed from eternity, he himself is. He is therefore one only, and nothing more. But a single thing cannot fall at variance with itself, whereby a deliberation might arise to decide the dispute.

5. So is it also with the things that proceed from the eternal, unoriginated ground. Each in its selfhood is an individual will, which has nothing before it that can break it, unless it bring itself into an alien form that resembles not the primal ground from which it arose ; and then there is a separation from the whole. As is to be understood in the case of the fallen devil and the soul of man, that the creature has broken itself off from the whole will and brought itself

into a selfhood of a different form, which is opposed to the one divine bringing forth. But in order to understand this, we must look at the principal cause, to see how such a position could have come about.

6. For, if the powers of the one Divine proprium had not passed into divisibility, this could not have been; and then neither angel nor other creature would have arisen, and there would have been no nature nor quality, and the invisible God would have been manifested to himself only in the calm working wisdom in himself, and all beings would have been a single being. And yet we cannot speak of a being, but rather of a longing that is active within itself; which indeed is just so in the one God, and no more.

7. But when we contemplate the divine revelation in the whole world of creation, in all things, and consider the sacred writings, then we see, find and understand the true ground. For it is said (John i. 1-3): In the beginning was the Word, and the Word was with God, and the Word was God. The same was in the beginning with God. All things were made by him, and without him was not anything made that was made.

8. In this brief statement we have the whole ground of the divine and natural revelation in the Being of all beings. For, 'In the beginning' means the eternal beginning in the will of the unground for a ground, that is, for the divine apprehension, since the will apprehends itself in a centre for a foundation, as for the Being of God, and brings itself into power, and goes out from the power in spirit, and in the spirit configures itself into a perceptibility of powers. Thus these powers, which are all contained in one power, are the primal being of the word. For the one will apprehends itself in the one power, wherein lies all

hiddenness, and breathes itself forth through the power into an intuition, and this wisdom or intuition is the beginning of the eternal mind as the conspection of itself. This amounts to saying, The Word was in the beginning with God, and was God himself.

9. The will is the beginning and is called God the Father, and he apprehends himself in power, and is called the Son. And the being of the power is the scientia and cause of the speaking, as the essence or separation of the one power, and is the partition of the mind, which the Spirit by its out-going from the power renders divisible.

10. Now there could be no utterance or sound (for the powers all lie in a single power in great stillness) if the one longing in the power did not comprise itself in a desire, as in a scientia or drawing-in. That is, the free longing comprises itself in a scientia of itself for a forming of the powers, that the powers may enter into a compaction in order to a manifest sound. And therefrom arises the sensual tongue of the five senses as an inward beholding, feeling, hearing, smelling and tasting, which however must not be understood in a creaturely way, but only in the manner of the primal feeling and finding in a sensual way.

11. And in this connection it is said: The Word (*i.e.* the formed power) was in the beginning with God. For here two things are to be understood, namely, the unformed power, *i.e.* the *In*; and the formed power which is the *With*, for it has come into something and so to motion. The *In* is still, but the *With* is formal or compacted; and from this compaction and motion arise nature and creature, together with all being.

12. We must now open wide the eyes of our understanding, so that we may be able to distinguish

between God and Nature, and not merely say: God wills, God has created. It is not enough to juggle with the Holy Spirit and call him a devil, as imprisoned Reason does, which says: God wills evil. For every evil will is a devil, for it is a self-comprehended will for selfness, an apostate from the whole of being, a vain imagination.

13. Therefore I highly exhort the reader to lay hold of our meaning aright, and to avoid the phantasy of forming conclusions without the true inward ground. We will here exhibit to him the true ground.

14. The powers for the word are God, and the scientia [desire] or the magnetic attraction is the beginning of nature. Now the powers could not be manifested without this desire of attraction; God's majesty would not be manifest in actual power, joy and glory without the attraction of the desire; nor would there be light in the divine Power unless the desire attracted and overshadowed itself. Here we have the ground of darkness, which is carried even to the kindling of fire; here God calls himself an angry God and a consuming fire; and here the great separation, as also death, dying and the great manifest creaturely life take their rise.

15. A similitude of this is seen in a burning candle, where the fire absorbs and consumes the candle. There the being or substance dies, that is, in the dying of the darkness it is transformed in the fire into a spirit and into another quality (which is understood in the light), for in the candle no true feeling life is understood. But with the kindling of fire the being of the candle passes into a consuming process, into a painful feeling motion and life; and as the result of this painful feeling life the Nothing or the One becomes light and shining in a large room.

EXPLANATION OF THE SEVEN PROPERTIES OF THE ETERNAL NATURE. Rev. i.

Principle	Properties		Hellish / Heavenly properties		The third Principle, or this world with its creatures, evil and good, according to hellish and heavenly properties.
First Principle. Wrath.	I. Sour, Desire, Will.	Hellish properties.	1. Hard, Cold, Covetousness.	World with properties of the first Principle.	1. Coldness, Hardness, Bone, Salt.
	II. Bitter, Attraction, or the Sting of sensibility.		2. Sting, Envy.		2. Poison, Life, Growth, Senses.
	III. Anxiety or Mind.		3. Enmity.		3. Sulphur, Perception, Pain.
	IV. Fire or Spirit.		4. Pride, Anger or Dark-fire.		4. Spirit, Reason, Desire.
Second Principle. Love.		Heavenly properties.	Love-fire or Light-fire.	Earthly kingdom with properties of both Principles.	
	V. Light or Love, from which flows the water of eternal life.		5. Gentleness.		5. Venus-play, Life's light.
	VI. Sound or Understanding.		6. Divine Joy.		6. Vocality, Outcry, Distinction.
	VII. Body or Being.		7. Heaven.		7. Body, Wood, Stones, Earth, Metals, Herbs.

Remark.—Nos. I. II. III. are also called the Dark-world, of which we have a similitude in the stem of a candle. No. IV. is called the Fire-world, whereof we have a similitude in the fire of a candle. Nos. V. VI. VII. are called the Light-world, of which we have a similitude in the light of a candle.

16. So in like manner we are to conceive with regard to God. He brings his will into a scientia [desire] for nature, that his power may be manifested in light and majesty, and that a kingdom of joy may be produced. For, if in the eternal One no nature were to arise, all would be still. But nature is carried into pain, sensation and perception, in order that the eternal stillness may attain to motion, and that the powers for the production of the word may be manifested. We are not on this account to understand that the Eternal comes into a state of pain (no more than light comes into such a state from fire); but we are to consider that the fiery property in pain puts in motion the still longing.

17. Nature is the instrument of the still Eternity, by which it forms, makes and separates, and therein embodies itself in a kingdom of joy; for the eternal will manifests its word by means of nature. The word takes to itself nature in the scientia; but the eternal One, viz. God Jehovah, assumes no nature, but dwells through nature, like the sun in the elements, or as the Nothing in the light of the fire, for the brightness of the fire causes the Nothing to shine. And yet one ought not to say a nothing, because the Nothing is God and all things; but we speak thus, if haply we might impart our thought and knowledge to the reader.

18. Nature with its origin in the scientia, namely, in the desire that draws, is understood as follows. I will set before the reader a similitude taken from fire and light, whereby with the assistance of the divine Power he may be brought into the true sense and meaning.

19. Look upon a lighted candle, and thou seest a similitude of the divine and also of the natural being. In the candle all lies together in one substance, in

equipoise without distinction, viz. the fat, fire, light, air, water and earth ; further, the sulphur, mercury, salt and oil from which the fire, light, air and water have their origin. In the candle we can make no distinction and say, this is fire, this is light, this is air, this is earthy. We see no reason for sulphur, salt or oil. We say, there is a fatty substance, and that is true ; yet all these qualities are contained therein, but in no perceived distinction, for they are all in equipoise in the temperament.

20. So likewise we are to understand with regard to the eternal One, or the hidden unrevealed God apart from the eternal scientia, that is, apart from his word as his manifestation of power. All powers and qualities lie in the imprincipiate Deity Jehovah in the temperament. But the eternal will (which is the Father of all beings and of every origin) comprehends itself in wisdom in a mind for its own seat and for power, and breathes forth this comprehension, and its will in the outbreathing of its power in the temperament, in the outgoing of itself, forms itself into a desire for separation and for manifestation of powers, that there may shine forth in the One an infinite plurality of powers as an eternal gleam or lustre, and that the eternal One may be divisible, perceptible, sentient and essential.

21. In this scientia or intrahent desire the eternal Nature begins, and in Nature being begins, that is to say, a spiritual being, viz. *Mysterium magnum* or the revealed God, or, as it might be expressed, the Divine manifestation. For Scripture speaks of God and his distinctions, as for example, God is good, God is angry and jealous, God can will nothing evil, God hardens their hearts lest they believe and be saved. *Item,* Shall there be evil in a city, and the Lord hath not

done it? For this cause have I raised thee up, for to show in thee the power of my wrath. *Item*, the whole doctrine of election as in relation to good and evil, and all whatsoever the Scriptures speak of. Further, the great distinction of evil and good in the created world, there being evil and good creatures; as also is to be seen in metals, earths, stones, herbs, trees and elements, all which have their origin and beginning from thence.

22. In nature one is always set in opposition to another, so that the one is the enemy of the other, and yet not to the end that hostility should show itself; but that in conflict the one should excite and reveal the other, so that *Mysterium magnum* should enter into divisibility, and that there should be in the eternal One an elevation and joyfulness, and that the Nothing in and through the something should have wherewith to operate and play. And this is the Spirit of God, who has through wisdom introduced himself from eternity into such a spiritual mysterium for the contemplation of himself. This mysterium he likewise brought into a beginning for creation and for time, and compacted it into a being and motion of four elements, and has thus made visible with and in time what is invisible and spiritual.

23. We will show you a true figure of this in the world, *i.e.* in sun, stars and elements, as well as in the mystery from which the four elements take their rise. We see that the sun shines in the deep of the world, and its rays kindle the ens of the earth from which everything grows. We understand also that the sun kindles the ens in the great mystery or *spiritus mundi* (*i.e.* in sulphur, mercury and salt), whereby the magical fire is revealed from which air, water and earthiness have their origin. That is, the single ele-

ment in the great mystery of the outer world thereafter divides into four elements. These indeed exist before in the mystery, but they lie in the scientia [temperament], united together in the magnetic impression, hidden in the great mystery, and have their subsistence in one being.

24. Now as the power and rays of the sun disclose the mystery of the outer world, so that creatures and plants proceed from it; so, on the other hand, the mystery of the outer world is a cause by which the sun's rays are disclosed and enkindled. If the great mystery in sulphur, salt and mercury, of a spiritual nature and character, existed not in the *spiritus mundi,* viz. in the scientia of the properties of the stars, which is a *quinta essentia* above the four elements, then the sun's rays could not be manifested. But because the sun is nobler, and a degree deeper in nature, than the mystery of the outer world, that is, than the *spiritus mundi* in sulphur, salt and mercury in the *quinta essentia* of the stars, it penetrates into the outer mystery and kindles it, and thus too kindles itself, so that its rays become fiery, for they would not be fiery without the scientia in the mystery of this world.

25. And as the sun introduces its desire eagerly into the mystery, that is, into the first three forms, viz. salt, sulphur and mercury, in order to kindle and to manifest itself in them; so in like manner the mystery brings its desire out of the *quinta essentia* of the stars, through the first three, eagerly towards the sun as its Nature-god, which is a soul of the great mystery in the outer elemental world, a similitude of the hidden inner God.

26. We see also that the stars are so greedy and hungry for the power of the sun, that they introduce their desire in a magnetic manner in the *spiritus*

mundi into the first three forms, and draw the sun's power into themselves. The sun, on the other hand, penetrates powerfully into the stars to receive their desire, so that they get their lustre from the power of the sun. The stars, again, introduce their enkindled power as a fruit into the four elements ; and thus they qualify one into another, and one is the manifestation power and life, as also the destruction of another, that one property mount not above all the others.

27. The most High has spoken them forth thus into a time out of his ever-speaking Word, out of the great Mystery (which is wholly spiritual) for a likeness of his own being, and has exhibited the Eternal in a time by means of a figure, in which all creaturely life has its origin and dominion ; except the angels and eternal spirits, as well as the right inner soul of the true man,—these have their origin from the eternal unbeginning scientia or Nature, as shall be set forth later.

28. God is the eternal Sun as the eternal one Good ; but out of the eternal scientia or Nature he would not be manifest with his Sun-power or Majesty ; for out of Nature there were nothing in which God in his power could become manifest. He is the beginning of Nature ; and yet he does not bring himself out of the eternal One into an eternal beginning of nature because he wills to be something evil ; but in order that his power may come into Majesty, as into divisibility and sensibility, and that there may be in him a moving and playing, where the powers sport one with another, and thus manifest, find and feel themselves in their wrestling sport of love, so that thereby the great immeasurable love-fire in the bond and in the birth of the Holy Trinity may be actually operative.

29. We will give you another similitude of this in

fire and light. Fire in its painfulness denotes nature in the scientia [the first ternary], and light denotes the divine love-fire. For light is also a fire, but a giving fire; for it gives itself to all things, and in its giving there is life and being, *i.e.* air and a spiritual water; and in this oleous water the love-fire of the light has its life, for it is the food of the light. Otherwise, if the light were to be cooped up, and the spiritual water could not separate itself from the fiery nature and resolve itself within itself with the nothing or the unground, the light would be extinguished. But when it resolves itself with the unground (in which lies the eternal foundation or ground), that is, with the temperament, where all the powers lie in one power, then the light-fire or love-fire draws this spiritual water (which in the resolving becomes an oil or tincture, as a power of fire and lustre of light) again into itself for its food.

30. And here we have the great arcanum of feeding spiritually. Dear sons, if this were known to you, you would possess the ground of all mystery and of the being of all beings; and concerning this Christ said, He would give us the water of eternal life, which should spring up in us into a fountain of everlasting life (John iv. 14),—not the external water generated from the external light-fire, but the inner water generated from the Divine light-fire, of which the external is a figure.

31. Know then and understand this similitude thus: The eternal one Good, as the Word of the holy mental tongue, which the most holy Jehovah speaks out of the temperament of his own being into the scientia [attraction] for nature; this Word he speaks forth into a distinction or into an opposition only in order that his holy powers may become separable and enter

into the splendour of Majesty, for they must be manifested by means of the fiery nature. For the eternal will, which is called Father, brings his heart or Son, viz. his power, out through fire into a great triumph of joy.

32. In fire is death : the eternal Nothing dies in the fire, and from the dying comes the holy life. Not that there is a dying, but the life of love arises in this way from the painfulness. The Nothing or the Unity thus takes an eternal life into itself, so that it becomes sentient, but proceeds again out of the fire as a nothing. As indeed we see that light shines forth from fire, and yet as a nothing, that is, merely a lovely, giving, working virtue.

33. Understand, then, (in the separation of the scientia, where fire and light separate) by fire the eternal Nature, according to which God says, that he is an angry jealous God, and a consuming fire. This, however, is not the holy God, but his jealousy, as a consuming of what the desire immasses in itself in the divisibility.

34. As where a separable form in the scientia [attraction] elevates itself into and comprehends itself in an individual will in order to fly out above the temperament, and breaks itself off from the whole will, and introduces itself into the source of phantasy. As Lord Lucifer and the soul of Adam did, and even to-day is done in the human essence and in the soul's property, by which a thistle-child of false disposition (devilish nature) is born. These the spirit of God knows, and concerning them Christ said, They were not his sheep (John x. 26). And in another passage, that he alone is God's child, whose soul has sprung, not from flesh and blood, nor from the will of man, but from God, that is, from the right Divine desire,

from the temperament, from the root of the love-fire (John i. 13). Into this corrupt Adamic nature God has again introduced his love-fire in Christ, and implanted it again in the constitution of the light; which hereafter shall be further treated of.

35. Now as in the kindling of fire we understand two natures, namely, one in fire and the other in light, and thus two principles; so likewise it is to be understood with regard to God. He is only called God according to the light, that is, according to the powers of the light, in which indeed the kindling is manifested, and moreover in infinite divisibility, but all in the fire of love; where all the propria of the powers yield their will to the One, *i.e.* to the Divine temperament, where in all the properties only a single spirit and will rules, and the properties all give themselves up to a great love in and to each other, where each property desires to taste the other in great fiery love, and all is but one lovely power inqualifying together; and yet through the distinction of the kindling they are brought into manifold colours, powers and virtues, for the manifestation of the infinite divine wisdom.

36. We have an example of this in the flowering earth, in herbs and plants, where from the temperament, from the good element, pleasant fruits grow. And on the other hand, from the fiery nature along with the impression of the curse of the earth (the Lord having cursed it because of man's and the devil's fall, and reserved it for a refining upon His cupel), nothing but evil prickly thistle-like fruits grow. These, nevertheless, have in them something that is good in consequence of their origin, where in the *quinta essentia* the temperament is still found, and at the end shall be separated.

37. And here we must rightly understand that in the Divine power, in so far as God is called God, in the word of the Divine propria, there can be no will to evil, nor any knowledge thereof; but knowledge of good and evil exists only where the unfathomable will separates into the fiery scientia [enkindling], in which lies the natural and creaturely ground.

38. For no creature can be born and subsist solely from the divine love-desire, but it must have in itself the fiery triangle in accordance with painfulness ; that is, it must have an individual will, which goes forth as an exspirated power and as a ray from the whole will, out of the temperament of the primal unfathomable will, the Word of power separating itself in fire, and passing out of the fire again into the light.

39. Here [at this point of separation] the angels and the soul of man have their origin, namely, from the fiery enkindling of the beginning of the eternal Nature ; and here this ray of the fiery kindling must unite itself again to the constitution of the light, that is, to the whole. And then it eats of the holy tincture of the fire and the light, *i.e.* of the spiritual water by which the fire becomes a kingdom of joy.

40. For the spiritual water is a daily mortification of the fiery enkindling, whereby the fiery kindling along with the fire of love becomes a temperament; and then there is but a single will therein, which is, to love all that has its subsistence in this root. As is to be understood of the angels of God and blessed souls, who have all of them their origin from the enkindling of fire. In this enkindling the light of God shines, so that they have a continual hunger after Divine power and love, and introduce the holy love into their fire

for food, whereby the fiery triangle is transformed into pure holiness and love, into great joy. For nothing exists or subsists eternally unless it have its origin from the eternal unoriginated will, from the fiery enkindling of the Word of God, as shall be set forth later.

CHAPTER III

OF THE INTRODUCTION OF THE FIERY ENKINDLING INTO FORM FOR NATURE AND FOR BEING. HOW THE SCIENTIA OR DESIRE PASSES INTO THE CONDITION OF FIRE; WHAT THAT IS, AND HOW MULTIPLICATION ARISES.

The gate of the great Mystery of all mysteries.

1. WHEN the dear Moses describes the creation of the world, he says: In the beginning God created the heaven and the earth. And God said, Let there be: and there came to be (Gen. i. 1, 3). And John i. 3 runs thus: God made all things by his Word.

2. In this lies the foundation and deep meaning. For from eternity there has been nothing but God in his threefoldness with his wisdom, and therein the scientia, as the speaking, self-breathing-forth, circumscribing, forming and bringing-into-properties. The circumscribing is the fiat; and the scientia or desire is the beginning that springs from the temperament for differentiation. The whole ground is contained in the passage where it is said, God created by the Word. The Word remains in God, and with the scientia or desire proceeds out of itself into a division. This is to be understood thus: The scientia is eternally in the Word, for it rises in the will. In the Word it is God; and in the division, in the circumscribing, it is the beginning of nature.

The first species naturae.

3. The first form of nature is *sour*, as it were the enclosing of itself. Its forms, which arise in its enclosing, are as follows: First, darkness, for the confining or enclosing overshadows the free will in the attraction. Secondly, it is the cause of hardness, for what is drawn-in is hard and rough; and yet in the Eternal only spirit is to be understood. Thirdly, it is a cause of sharpness. Fourthly, it is a cause of coldness or the cold fiery property. Fifthly, it is a cause of all substance or materiality. In *Mysterium magnum* it is the mother of all salts, and a root of nature; and in the Mystery it is designated by the term *Sal*, that is, a spiritual sharpness,—the origin of the wrath of God, and likewise the origin of the kingdom of joy.

Of the second species naturae.

4. The second form in the scientia is the *sting of sensibility*, and is attraction itself, whence feeling and perception take their rise. For the more the sourness impresses itself, the greater becomes this sting, like a rager, raver and destroyer. Its division into forms is as follows: Bitter, pang, pain, movement, a beginning of the contrary will in the temperament, a cause of the spirit-life, a cause of flowing and streaming forth, a father or root of the mercurial life both in animated and vegetative beings, a cause of the forth-flying senses, a cause of the exulting joy in the light, and a cause of the hostile opposition in the austere impression of the hardness, whence strife and contrary will take their rise.

Of the third species naturae.

5. The third form in the scientia is *anxiety*, which arises in the opposition between the sourness and the stinging bitterness, as a root of feeling, the beginning of essence and mind, a root of fire and all painfulness, a hunger and thirst after freedom or the unground, a manifestation of the eternal unfathomable will in the attraction, where the will is brought into spiritual forms; further, a cause of dying, as it were the birth of death, though not death, but the beginning of the nature-life arises, and is the very root where God and nature are separated,—not by way of a dividing off, but by reason of the temperament in the Deity, in that here the manifest sensible life arises, from which the creation has had its origin.

6. These three forms, viz. sour, bitter (sting) and anxiety, are the first three in the scientia [attraction] of the one will, which is called the Father of all beings; and they take their rise from the triad of the Deity.

7. We are not to understand that they are God, but the revelation of God in his Word of power. Sour is the beginning of strength and might, and is a ground from which all springs, arising out of the Father's property in the Word.

8. The bitter sting or life's beginning has its origin from the Son's property, from the Word; for it is a cause of all divisibility, as also of speech, understanding and the five senses.

9. Anxiety arises from the property of the holy Spirit in the Word; for it is the cause of both fires, viz. of the light-fire or love-fire and the painful fire of consumingness. It is the true origin of the creaturely life, as well as of the dying to joy and sorrow, the root

of every life springing from the scientia [attraction] of the one eternal will.

10. These first three forms in the nature-life are named, according to the compaction in the creation, salt, sulphur and mercury, and in them the spirit-life has introduced itself into a visible comprehensible matter. This matter is in all things, in what is living in the flesh and in what grows from the earth, both spiritually and corporeally, without any exception; for all the beings of this world are rooted in it, as is plainly to be seen.

11. Thus the invisible or spiritual world has by these first three forms brought itself into a visible graspable being, that is, as regards spirits in a spiritual way, and as regards bodies in a corporeal way. The whole earth moreover, with all material things, arises therefrom, as well as all the stars and elements. But we must look further, and go through all the seven forms, if we are to give explanations of sun, stars and elements.

Of the fourth species naturae.

12. The fourth form in the scientia as arising out of the one will is the *kindling of fire,* where light and darkness separate, each into a principle. For here is the origin of light, as also of the right life in the sensibility of the first three forms, and likewise the origin of the true separation between anxiety and joy. This is effected as follows :

13. The first will in threefoldness, which is called God (as beyond nature and creature), seizes itself in itself so as to become its own seat in the process of birth of the triad with the attraction, and brings itself into power. And in the power it is brought into the generating Word, as into an essential sound for the

manifestation of power, and furthermore into a desire for the feeling and finding of power, that is, into the first three forms of nature, as set forth above.

14. But when it is brought into anxiety, as into the origin of the spiritual life, it seizes itself again in itself through the longing of Freedom to be delivered from the anxiety. That is, it embraces in itself the unground, viz. the temperament of the divine longing and wisdom, which is lovely, gentle and still. And in such comprehension there takes place in the anxiety the great terror, for the painful anxiety is terrified at the great gentleness, and sinks down in itself as a trembling, whence the poison-life in nature has its origin and beginning; for in the terror there is death. And in the terror the sourness compacts itself into being, viz. into a mercurial spirit-water, from which, in the impression at the beginning of the creation of the earth, stones, metals and the mercurial sulphureous water were produced.

15. This terror makes in the first three forms, according to the dark impression in itself, the hostile terrible life of the wrath or anger of God, of devouring and consuming. For it consists in the kindling of fire, in the essence of the painfulness or consumingness of fire, and is according to the dark impression called hell or hollowness, as an individual self-comprehending painful life which is manifest or perceptible in itself only, and is with reference to the whole unground rightly termed a hidden hollowness, which is not revealed in the light, and yet is a cause of the kindling of light. This is to be understood in the way night dwells in day, and one is not the other.

16. Understand then the enkindling of fire correctly thus : It is brought about by a conjunction of the first three forms, in their impression in the wrath ; and,

on the other side, by the lovely freedom of the Ens in the temperament, for love and wrath enter into each other. As when water is poured into fire, there is a shock; so likewise when love enters into wrath, there is a terror and shock. In the love the terror is a beginning of the lightening or brightness, whereby the one Love becomes perceptible, majestic and shining, and is the beginning of the kingdom of joy, in manner as light becomes shining in fire. In the love too is the commencement of the separation of powers, so that the powers press forth in the terror, whence the smell and taste of difference arises. And in the first three forms the painful nature of fire is to be understood.

17. For (1) *sour* impresses and devours, and (2) *bitter* is the sting of pain, and (3) *anxiety* is death and likewise the new fire-life, for it is the mother of sulphur. And the ens of love gives to the anxiety or mother of sulphur a refreshment for new life, from which arises the lustre of fire; for we see that light is gentle and fire painful. We understand, then, that the ground of the light springs from the temperament, from the divine union, from the ungroundedness of the one love which is called God; and that fire springs from the ruling will in the Word, from the desire through impression and introduction into the first three forms.

18. Now in the light is understood the kingdom of God, viz. the kingdom of love; and in the fire God's strength and omnipotence, viz. the spiritual creature-life. And in the darkness is understood death, hell and God's wrath, and also the anxious poison-life, as is to be understood in earth, stones, metals and creatures of the external created world.

19. And I exhort the reader not to understand in an earthly manner the high supernatural meaning (when I speak of God and the generation of the Great

Mystery), for I thus only indicate the origin from which the earthly has arisen. And I must often speak so, in order that the reader may understand and reflect, and plunge into the inward ground; for I must frequently give earthly names to what is heavenly, because the earthly has been spoken forth therefrom.

20. In the enkindling of fire lies the entire ground of all mystery. The terror of the enkindling is called in nature *sal nitri*, as a root of all the salts of the powers; a divisibility of nature, where the scientia [kindling] divides to infinity, and yet always continues in the terror, as a terror of separation in being. In the enkindling of fire (understood according to the inner magical fire) the Spirit of God becomes moving, in manner as air arises from fire. For here arises the one element, which in the outer world has unfolded into four elements. Understand this as follows:

21. In the flash of fire and light is the separation. The spirit passes upwards, that is, into the fiery enkindling of the powers, for it proceeds out of the fire-terror as a new life, and yet is not a new life, but it has in this way assumed nature. And the ens of love remains in the midst as a centre of the spirit, and produces from itself a spiritual oil in which the light lives; for it is the ens of the fiery love. From this fiery ens of love there ascends with the spirit the *tincture*, as the spiritual water or the power of fire and light, whose name is called Virgin Sophia.

22. Dear philosophers, if you knew this Maiden, it were well for you. This water is the true humility, which is straightway transmuted in accordance with the temperament, and absorbed again by the light, for it is the soul of the light according to love; and fire or the fire-soul is man, as the Father's property. In this [spiritual water] are the two tinctures, male

and female,—the two loves, which in the temperament are divine, and which in Adam were separated when the imagination went out from the temperament, but in Christ were reunited.

23. Dear philosophers, understand the meaning thus indicated; for here is the pearl of the whole world. We have hinted enough for the understanding of our condisciples: we must not give the pearl unto beasts.

24. The third separation arising out of fire comes from the mortification of the fire, from the essential nature of the first three forms, from the spirit of sulphur, mercury and salt. It goes downwards like an inert insentient life, and is the water-spirit, from which the material water of the outer world has its origin, and in which the first three forms have by their working produced metals, stones and earth from the properties of the salniter. In the precious metals and stones must likewise be understood the higher being arising from the impression of the Love-ens. This salnitrous ground is opened up by the sun, so that it possesses a growing life; which is sufficiently understood by those that are Ours, for it is covered with the curse. We of right content ourselves with what rejoices us eternally, and would not furnish a delight to the beast, and yet afterwards point out what is profitable to us.

25. The fourth separation goes into darkness, where all beings exist and move as in the light-world and in the outer elemental world. But all goes into phantasy according to the property of the quality. Whereof no further mention is made here, because of the false light which is understood therein, and also on account of man's rashness. But it is herewith intimated to the Pharisee, that he has no true understanding of hell and phantasy, as to what their quality and purpose

are, and to what end they exist; seeing there is nothing out of God, and yet they are out of God, but only in another source or quality; as well as a different life, and also a different nature-light, as is known to the Magician.

Of the fifth species naturae.

26. The fifth form in the scientia is the true *love-fire,* which separates itself in the light from the painful fire, and therein the divine Love in being is understood. For the powers separate in the fire-terror, and become desirous in themselves. In this form also is understood every characteristic of the first three forms, yet no longer in pain, but in joy; and in their hunger or desire, so to speak. That is, in the desire they draw themselves into being: they draw the tincture of fire and light, viz. Virgin Sophia, into themselves, and it is their food, as the great sweetness, or pleasing delight and agreeable savour. This becomes embodied in the desire of the first three forms in being, which is called the corpus of the tincture, and is the divine essentiality, Christ's heavenly corporeality.

27. Dear Sons, if it were but understood by you where Christ says (John iii. 13), that he had come down from heaven, and at the same time was in heaven. This tincture is the power of speech in the Word, and the entity is the Word's comprehension, where the Word becomes essential. The entity is the heavenly water, of which Christ said, he would give it us to drink, and it would spring up in us into a fountain of eternal life. The tincture transforms this water into spiritual blood, for the tincture is its soul. It is Father and Son, from which the holy Spirit proceeds as power.

28. O ye dear Sons, if you understand this, suffer not your spirit to elevate itself therein in joy, but make it bend in the greatest humility before God, and show it its still existing unworthiness, lest it pass therewith into self-love and self-will, as Adam and Lucifer did, who introduced the pearl into phantasy, and broke themselves off from the whole. Consider well in what a hard lodging the soul is imprisoned. Humility and willing nothing but God's mercy, is, for those who have known Virgin Sophia, the best and most useful thing to practise. It is a high matter which God reveals unto you. Take heed what ye do. Make not an aspiring Lucifer of it, or you will eternally repent it.

29. This fifth form has all the powers of the divine Wisdom in it, and is the centre in which God the Father manifests himself in his Son through the speaking word. It is the root-stock of the plant of eternal life, a food of the fiery soul, as also of the angels, and that which cannot be expressed. For it is the eternal perpetual revelation of the triune Deity, where all the propria of the holy Wisdom do qualify inwardly in a sensual way as a taste, smell and unitedly inqualifying life of the love-fire. And it is called the power of the Glory of God, which has been effused in the creation into all created things, and is in everything according to the property of the thing, hidden in the centre, as a tincture in the living body. By means of this power all things grow, blossom and yield their fruit; and this power is contained in the *quinta essentia*, and is a cure of disease.

30. If the four elements can be brought into the temperament, then the glorious pearl in its working is revealed. But the curse of God's anger keeps it imprisoned in itself, because of man's unworthiness. This is well understood by the physicians.

Of the sixth species naturae.

31. The sixth form in the scientia, in the divine power, is speech, namely, the mouth of God, the *sound of the powers,* where the holy Spirit in the love-comprehension brings itself manifestly out of the comprehended power; as we are to understand in the image of God in man, by reference to man's speech. So likewise there is a sensual effectual speaking in the divine power in the temperament. And by this effectual speaking is rightly understood the five senses, namely, a spiritual seeing, hearing, smelling, tasting and feeling, where the manifestation of the powers work together unitedly. This operancy the Spirit speaks forth into a distinct sound, as is to be understood in man, as well as in the expressed word in the created creatures,—both in animated and also in insensible vegetative beings.

32. For the spiritual world or the spiritual sound has been incorporated in the creation, and therefrom the sound of all beings has its origin. This sound in material things is called a mercurial power, as arising out of the fiery hardness; and here the other powers co-operate and lend assistance, so that a tune or song is produced, as is to be seen in animated beings, whereas in insensible things there is a sonorousness; as we see in a concert of music, how all the melody which the understanding can bring forth is united together in a single composition.

33. Further, we are to understand in the sixth form the true meaning of the thoughts or percipient senses. For when the spirit has brought itself out of the [separated] qualities, it is in the temperament again, and has all the qualities in it. Of whatever the body

is a substantial power, of that the spirit is a soaring power, wherein mind is understood, from which the thoughts take their rise. For the thoughts have their origin from the infinite number of propria springing from the fire-terror, and therefore they have in themselves both centres, viz. God's love and anger. As long as they remain in the temperament, they are right; but when they pass out of it and plunge into individual proof of themselves, in order to find themselves in properties and know themselves, then lying is born, so that they speak from their own will, despise the other properties and hold them to be false, and forthwith bring themselves into self-ful desire, wherein we are to recognize the heavy fall of Adam and Lucifer.

34. For Adam was placed in the temperament with the properties, but his will introduced itself into division or into false longing by the influence and persuasion of the devil. Through this persuasion desire elevated itself in the temperament, and brought itself into multiplicity of properties, each property passing into a selfhood.

35. For the soul [of Adam] wished to taste how it would be if the temperament should disunite and fall asunder, that is, how heat and cold, wet and dry, hard and soft, sour, sweet, bitter and acid, and all the other properties, would taste in distinction. This did God forbid him, warning him not to eat of such growth, that is, of the revelation of the knowledge of good and evil. And by this taste the fiery hunger first arose, so that the forms of life lost the manna, viz. the bread of God which springs from the love-nature, and could no longer taste how it was in the temperament in one united will. Whence immediately the forms of life impressed themselves into a great hunger, whereby the coarseness of the flesh arose, and bestial lust

became manifest in Adam through the multiplicity of the attraction of the properties of the powers. And forthwith also the separated qualities in the *spiritus mundi* penetrated into him, as heat and cold, likewise bitter-stinging pain moved him, all which could have had no existence in the temperament. And thereby too disease at once arose in his flesh, for the qualities had entered into conflict and contrary will.

36. Now as soon as one quality elevates itself above another, or becomes enkindled by something, so that it soars aloft in its qualification, then this constitutes for the others a hostile contrary will, from which arises pain and sickness. For strife is straightway introduced into the first three forms, whereby the *turba* is brought forth, and the chamber of death awakens, so that the poison-source gets the dominion. And this in fact is the heavy fall of Adam.

Of the seventh species naturae.

37. The seventh form in the scientia, in the divine power, is the comprehended being of all the powers, where the Sound or the speaking Word embodies itself in being, as an entity in which the Sound [spirit] embodies itself for manifest utterance. The fifth comprehension in love is wholly spiritual, viz. the purest essentiality. But this seventh form is a comprehension of all the qualities, and is properly called the *whole of nature*, or the formed expressed word. It is the inner divine uncreated heaven, but stands connected with the divine active birth of the temperament; and it is called Paradise, as a growing life of the comprehended working divine powers, in manner as the scientia [attraction] draws out of the earth by the sun's desire a growth of wood, herbs and grass;

for the scientia [desire] of the earth also has its origin from thence.

38. For when God introduced the spiritual world according to all the properties into an external being, the internal remained in the external,—the external in the form of a creaturely existence, but the internal as a generative nature. And therefore we see the world only half; for we have lost Paradise or the internal world, which in Adam's innocency budded forth through the outer earth.

39. Further, we are to understand that the seven days and their names have their origin from these seven forms, all seven arising from a single one, which was the beginning of the motion of the *Mysterium magnum*. The seventh is the day of rest, in which the working life of the six properties reposes: it is the temperament in being, in which the working life of the divine powers rests. Therefore God commanded man to rest in it, for it is the true image of God, wherein God has perpetually fashioned himself from eternity into an eternal being. And if we would but see, it is Christ, that is, the right man as created in Adam, who fell, and in the works of the six days brought himself with desire into unrest, and awakened and set up the dark world, which God with his supreme love-tincture, in the name Jesus, tinctured again in man, and introduced into the eternal sabbath of rest.

40. Such then are the seven properties of the eternal and temporal nature, being according to eternity spiritual and appearing in a clear crystalline transparent being. And according to the external created world they have arisen in conflict with each other in evil and good, to the end that the inner spiritual powers might be brought by the nature which is at strife into creaturely forms and births, that the divine

Wisdom might be manifested in wonders of formation in manifold lives. For no creature can be born in the temperament, for the temperament is the one God. But in the out-going of the scientia [desire] of the one will, since the will separates itself into particular existence, a creature as an image of the formed word can arise.

CHAPTER IV

OF THE ORIGINAL CONDITION OF THE CREATED WORLD

1. KINDLY reader, I exhort thee, be a man, and not an irrational animal, and let not the prating of the sophists lead thee astray with their calvish understanding: who know not what they prate, and do but wrangle and jangle, yet understand not what excesses they commit, and have no foundation in sense.

2. And be not offended at this pen or the hand that holds it. The Most High has cut this pen so, and breathed his breath into it. Therefore we know, see and understand this [that we write] very well, and write not out of the delusion of another source or by virtue of astral fancies, as we are accused of. A door is opened to us in the holy of holies, to see and to be cognisant of what the Lord will know in man at this time: that controversy may have an end, and that men may no longer wrangle about God. He reveals himself accordingly in this way, and it should be no marvel to us; but we ourselves should be the marvel, which he has brought forth in the fullness of time, if we know ourselves and recognize what we are, and withdraw from contention into the temperament of the one will, and love one another.

3. The whole creation, both of the eternal and also of the temporal creatures and beings, lies in the Word of divine power.

4. The eternal creatures spring from the scientia of

the speaking, viz. from the one will of the unground, which with the Word of the speaking has disposed itself into particular beings.

5. The temporal creatures have their origin in the expressed word, viz. in an image of the Eternal, as the expressed word in its substantiation has brought itself into an external mirror for the beholding of itself.

6. The partition of the scientia as proceeding out of the unground into a ground, with the introduction of the speaking Word into a re-utterance of the Being of all beings, to and in evil and good, is understood as follows: There arise in the Being of all beings three Principles, that is, three kinds of life or three distinctions of divine revelation, whereof always one is the cause of another.

7. The true Deity in itself in threefoldness, in the scientia [attraction] of the unground in the one will, where God begets God as the one will which brings itself into triplicity, is not a principle. For as God has nothing before him, neither has he any beginning; but he himself is his beginning, the nothing and likewise its something.

8. But in the Word of the one divine power, where the one desire [scientia] in the generation of the triad breathes itself forth from itself, the beginning of the first Principle takes its rise. And yet not in the ground of the speaking or triad, but in the embodiment of the distinguishableness, where the distinguishableness embodies itself in nature so as to attain to sensibility and mobility. There the sensibility divides into two entities, viz. into fierceness according to the impression in the darkness, and a cold painful fire, in which heat arises. This is the first Principle in the fire-root, which is the centre of nature.

9. The second Principle is found in the separation of fire, as the divine desire in the fire separates into light, and there passes into nature and being: so as to reveal the divine kingdom of joy, in which the Word of power is in an actual process of birth, where the mens works in the ens. Here is the separation between the two principles, whence God according to the first is called an angry jealous God and a consuming fire, and according to the second a lovable compassionate God, who neither wills evil nor can will it.

10. And by the third Principle we are to understand the seven properties of nature, as where these in the seventh are brought into a being and so to an inclusion. This being, in itself holy, pure and good, is called the eternal uncreated heaven, the place or the kingdom of God; it is also called Paradise, the pure Element, the divine Ens.

11. This one being of the divine operancy, which has existed from eternity, God has immassed and moved with the scientia [attraction] of his unfathomable will, and comprised in the word of his speaking; and has spoken it forth out of the first Principle of the painful dark fire-world, and also out of the holy light-flaming love-world, as a representation of the inner spiritual world.

12. And this is the external visible world with the stars and elements, which existed not before in a tangible being of distinctions. It was the *Mysterium magnum,* where all things stood in wisdom, in a spiritual form, in a wrestling sport of love; not in the form of creaturely spirits, but in such a model that wisdom has thus in the power sported with itself. This model the one will has comprised in the word, and suffered the attraction to work freely, so that every

individual power in the separation might be brought into a form according to its quality.

13. This it is that the divine creative word, or the desire of the Eternal Nature, which is called the fiat of power, has immassed into a compaction of qualities. As Moses says : In the beginning, *i.e.* in this immassing of the *Mysterium magnum,* God created the heavens and the earth, and said, Let there arise all manner of creatures, each of them according to its property.

14. At the word *fiat* the great Mystery became compacted into a being, that is, emerging out of the inward spiritual being into a palpable tangible being, and in the compaction lay the attraction belonging to life. And that in two propria, viz. a mental and an ental one. That is (1) a truly living proprium springing from the ground of eternity, and which is rooted in the wisdom of the Word, and (2) a proprium budding forth from the being's own desire as generated in itself, and which forms the growth wherein the vegetative life stands.

15. Through this mysterium the *quinta essentia,* viz. the ens of the Word, originally became manifest and essential, and to it all the three Principles were suspended. And here the ens has separated,—what is spiritual passing into spiritual beings, and what is inert into inert senseless beings, as are earth, stones, metals and the material water.

16. The first three forms have embodied themselves in a spiritual being, viz. in the heavens, fire and air ; for Moses says : In the beginning God created the heavens and the earth. The word heavens comprehends the spiritual element, that is, the spiritual upper-world with the operation of the four elements, as the one element has unfolded itself through the properties of the first three forms of nature. This

spiritual being has thrust out from itself the coarse compacted senseless being, viz. the matter of the earth and whatever is contained therein according to and as derived from the characteristics of the seven forms of nature, where every form with its multiplication has brought itself into being. As is seen in the vegetative spirit, which, springing from the salnitrous seething of the two fires, carries the desire of every property aloft out of itself into desire of the upper spirit-life, from which then the earth also receives power. And in connection with this upper and lower power the power of the earth passes into the condition of vegetation, which vegetation the sun kindles with its light-fire so that fruit grows from it; in manner as the inner magical sun of the light of God kindles the inner nature wherein Paradise grows and buds, that is to say, in the temperament of the one element, which is hidden to the earthly nature.

17. The inner, holy, spiritual world is the speaking Word of God, which brings itself into a being and working according to love and wrath, where in the impression of darkness evil is understood; and yet in God it is not evil, but only in its own comprehension of selfhood, as in a creature; although there also it is good, in so far as the creature lives in the temperament.

18. And in the comprehension of the light is understood the kingdom, viz. the revealed God with his active power, which in the fiery nature embodies itself in a manifest word for divine revelation in the holy Spirit. This operating word, which sprang from all the powers, from good and evil, viz. from the fire of light and love, and also from the painful dark nature-fire, and which in eternity consisted in an active being in two Principles, viz. in light and darkness,—this word has been spoken forth into a time and brought

into a being with a beginning and end, and fashioned into the created world as its self-revelation.

19. That is to say, this external world with its hosts and all that lives and moves therein is shut up into a time of a clockwork, which runs on from its beginning continually to the end, as into that First out of which it proceeded. And this has been made manifest in order that the eternal Word in its active power might become image-like and creaturely, and that as it has formed and fashioned itself from eternity in wisdom, so it might likewise be fashioned in a particular life, to the glory and joy of the holy Spirit, in the Word of life in himself.

20. And God has, therefore, in the eternal scientia [desire] of the eternal unfathomable will created angels from the two fires, from the fire of nature and from the fire of love; although the fire of love cannot constitute a creature, but dwells in the creature and fills it as the sun fills the world, that the holy Spirit may thus have a sport of joy in himself.

21. And you must understand us correctly in regard to the angels, for here we have the reason why the question of Election comes to be discussed, wherein Reason goes astray.

22. The sacred Scriptures call the angels flames of fire and light (Ps. civ. 4), and also ministering spirits (Heb. i. 7), which is so. And though they have their high princely dominions, yet they are all of them only a prepared instrument of the one Spirit of God in his joy, which he manifests by means of them, for he reveals himself through them.

23. Their substance and being, in so far as they are something individual and are called creatures, is a compaction of the Eternal Nature, which stands without beginning in a Divine working to its self-manifestation

in the eternal bringing forth. Viewed as to the creature, the angels are of all the seven forms of the Eternal Nature in great differentiation of powers. As the first three forms in nature dispose and shape themselves into infinite distinctions, so in like manner is the creaturely being of the angels to be understood in many properties, every one in its own property.

24. But there are especially seven high dominions in three hierarchies, according to the fountain of the seven properties of nature. Every form of the Eternal Nature has immassed itself into a Throne, as for a dominion, wherein distinctions are understood as well as the will of obedience to the holder of the Throne.

25. This dominion they have under their administration, as creatures of divine endowments, God having given them for a possession the sphere (of which they are an image) wherein they dwell, which is the holy spiritual power of the world of the temperament. Their inmost foundation, which springs from the divine proprium of eternity, is constituted by the one will of the unground as passing into a ground. They have their origin, therefore, in accordance with the beginning of nature from the scientia [attraction] of the free will, from and in which free will God begets his Word. This free will has in the birth of nature, as in the first Principle of the kindling of fire, introduced itself into divisibility ; and out of this divisibility in the origin of fire the angels have been carried in the free will (as a particular existence of the unfathomable free will), to turn themselves with the free will to the first or second Principle, and to manifest themselves.

26. As God himself in this free will is free and is all, and in this same free will brings himself in nature, in fire, light and darkness, into pain and torment (*Qual*), as well as into love and joy ; so likewise the particular

element has power, as deriving from the whole free will, to bring itself into a creaturely property in the three hierarchies or principles, as it pleases. That is, the scientia [essence] may comprehend and manifest itself in the three hierarchies, wherein it possesses power, just as the divine scientia has brought itself into a being and working, namely, one part in the fiery principle according to cold, the second part in the fiery principle according to heat, the third part in the fiery principle according to light, and the fourth part into phantasy, as into a play of the selfhood of Nature, where Nature in the inequality sports with itself in the [separated] properties.

27. The three hierarchies are to be understood in three principles, as in three kinds of natural light. The first hierarchy is founded upon the nature of the eternal Father's property, according to the fire of strength, as upon the tincture of fire, upon the essence of Nature. The second hierarchy is founded upon the tincture of the fire of light, according to the Son's property in the Eternal Nature, and is the holiest. The third hierarchy is founded upon the selfhood of Nature, where it sports in the properties as opposed to one another, just as the four elements sport in the astral power. This hierarchy is manifest according to the centre of darkness, and has also a natural light in itself, namely, the cold and hot fire-flash in which transmutation is understood, where the creature is able to transmute itself into this or that form, and which in Nature is called false magic. To this hierarchy Prince Lucifer turned himself, and departed out of the temperament with the scientia. His kingdom is called hell or a hollowness, because it dwells in itself, in the darkness, and possesses a false light which exists not in the temperament, but has a desire or

phantasy of building up and pulling down. For here a form is fashioned, and in accordance with the wrestling forms of Nature is very soon broken down again and transformed into something else. This kingdom is in dominion in the locus of this world; not indeed according to the stars and the four elements, but nevertheless hidden in them and penetrating also into the creatures; and in it the devils and the spirits of phantasy dwell in the four elements.

28. If sun and water were to disappear, then this kingdom would be manifest. It takes form in certain plants, likewise in metals which are not fixed and resist not fire; further, in herbs, trees and creatures in which the false magic of sorcery is understood, and in them Christ calls the devil a prince of this world.

29. When he was expelled from the Light, he fell into the realm of phantasy, into the centre of Nature, out of the temperament into the darkness, where he may initiate for himself a false light from the hot and cold fire through the attraction (scientia) of the might of eternity. For that is Lucifer's fall, that of his own will he revealed the realm of phantasy in his creaturely being, so that he brought the eternal will out of the temperament into division, namely, into the dissimilarity of imagination or phantasy. This imagination took him immediately and carried him into an unquenchable cold and hot fire-source, into the contrariety of forms.

30. The fierceness of the Eternal Nature, which is called God's wrath, manifested itself in them [the fallen angels], and led their will into phantasy. And therein they still live, and can now do no otherwise than what the property of phantasy implies, namely, practise foolery, transform themselves, and break

down the existing being ; likewise elevate themselves in the cold and hot fire-power, frame in themselves a will to fly out above the hierarchies of God's holy angels, and exhibit themselves in their fierceness in the pompous might of fire according to the first Principle. Their will is mere pride, a greed of plurality of properties, a stinging envy from the bitter pang, a rage springing from fire, a despair arising out of anxiety.

31. In sum, as the first three forms (*i.e.* the spirit of Nature in the spiritual sulphur, salt and mercury) are, so is the fallen angels' inward disposition, from which the thoughts come. Understand it thus : As the first three forms are in their primitive condition out of the light of God, so also is the devil in his heart and will. For his elevation was according to the first Principle, that he might be a lord over and in all being, even over all the angelic hosts. And therefore he turned away from the humility of love and wished to rule in the might of fire, which spewed him out from itself, and established itself as a judge and took away from him the divine power.

32. And with reference to this elevation we are to consider and highly recognize (seeing the angels were created in the first divine motion, before the time of the third Principle) that the realm of phantasy in the fierceness of Nature has powerfully moved and impressed itself, and in such impression earth and stones have had their origin. Not that the amassment has been produced by the devils, but they have roused and excited the matrix of nature, viz. the wrath of God, so that it has shut up existence into a compaction and brought it into a mass, because they would carry on jugglery in the *matrix naturae.* This pursuit they are now deprived of, so that they must lie captive

in the spiritual ground, in that womb of phantasy; and they are the poorest creatures, for they have lost God and His being. He that would be too rich became poor. In humility he might have had all and worked with God, but in selfhood he is foolish, that it may be known what folly or wisdom is. God has therefore shut him up in his own will through his own elevation, namely, in folly as in an eternal prison.

33. And here Reason says: It was God's will that his wisdom should be distinguished from folly, and that it might be understood what wisdom or folly is. Otherwise it would not be known what wisdom is. Therefore God suffered Lucifer to fall and hardened him, so that he necessarily had to do this; else it would not have been done. So far does Reason go, and understands no further.

34. Answer: When the unground with the one will introduced itself into a fiery separation, the attraction in the fire became free in the separation. There every attraction in the partition has separated into its own will, and the multiplicity of wills were all brought into the temperament, and had depending on them the three hierarchies (light, fire and darkness). There every host, with the comprehension of its creaturely being in the first three forms, could introduce itself into any hierarchy, according to its will. And that such is true is evident by this, that the devils originally were angels, and stood in the temperament in the free will. Then they could turn themselves whither they pleased, and there they were destined to be established.

35. But thou sayest: No; God did with them what he pleased. Answer: The scientia [attraction] is God's eternal unfathomable will, which has intro-

duced itself into nature and creature. But in the attraction of the creature there arose the will to introduce itself into phantasy, as into the centre for the fire-life. Thereupon followed confirmation and separation, and also expulsion from the temperament into the source to which the attraction had turned itself with the free will.

36. This hierarchy of darkness and phantasy assumed such a will, and confirmed it in itself. Thus from an angel was produced a devil, viz. a prince in the wrath of God, and there and in it he is good. For as God's wrath is, so is its inborn royal prince. He is and remains eternally a prince with his legions, but only in the kingdom of phantasy. For as the kingdom of those powers is in itself, so likewise is its inborn prince. The essence of the fierce wrathful kingdom is the mother of his selfhood, and is his God. He has to do what his God wishes, and therefore he is an enemy of the good; for love is his poison and the killing of him. And even though he sat in the holy power in the Light, yet he would draw to himself only a poisonful quality, for such is his life and nature. Just as if a toad were put into a sugar-canister, it would draw only venom therefrom, and would poison the sugar.

37. Reason now says: If God had re-infused his love into the devil, he would have become an angel again; and therefore it depends upon God's purpose. Answer: Hearken, Reason! Consider a thistle or nettle, upon which the sun shines the whole day, and penetrates with his power into it, and willingly gives his rays of love to its prickly stinging ens. The thistle rejoices in the ens of the sun, but grows thus always only into a thistle, and becomes the more prickly and proud. So is it also with the devil. Though God

should have infused his love into him, yet the scientia [attraction] of the unfathomable will would have introduced itself into the thistly nature: namely the eternal will, which apart from ground and place is in itself a will, and which nothing can break.

38. We are not to understand that the will of the unground has done this, for it is neither evil nor good, but merely a will, that is, a scientia without understanding for anything or in anything. For it is one thing only, and is neither desire nor longing; but it is a moving or willing,

39. Just as the outer world in the *spiritus mundi* has a will, or as the air is a gentle moving, and neither evil nor good. But we understand that the first three forms with the ground of sense penetrate thereinto, and take the will into their possession; and though they arise from this same will, yet they take it into their possession.

40. So likewise we are to understand with regard to the scientia, viz. the one eternal will springing from the unground. This will has its origin from the eternal One, and has given itself to the creature of phantasy, to the wrath of the eternal Nature, and so to what is bad. This will is not the cause of phantasy. The first three forms, wherein the creature is understood, *i.e.* Nature in the eternal bond, from and in which the understanding as well as phantasy takes its rise,—this Nature is the cause of the fall. For the unfathomable will is not the creature, as it is not a mode of imagination; but in the eternal Nature there arises imagination, as well as the creaturely will for something or plurality.

41. The unfathomable will is of God, for it is in the One. And yet it is not God; for God is only understood when the will of the unground shuts itself into

a centre of threefoldness in the divine bringing forth, and leads itself out into the joy of wisdom.

42. From the will in which the Deity encloses itself in threefoldness, the ground of Nature has also eternally been generated. Here is no purpose, but only a process of being born. The eternal birth is the purpose, namely, that God wills to beget God and to manifest himself through Nature.

43. Nature, however, shuts itself up in its own will, as in a painful and hostile life; and this hostile life is the cause of the fall. For it has given itself up to the phantasy of Nature or the play of production, and made itself a leader or lord of this phantastic Nature; and phantasy has taken this life into itself, and given itself wholly to it. Phantasy and life have thus become one thing. This existence has in it the will of the unground (*i.e.* the divine attraction in which God begets himself in God), but in such a shut up attraction God does not bring forth himself. He begets himself indeed in it, but he is not manifested in the attraction in so far as it embraces or comprehends Nature. God is immovable and inoperative in it. He generates not in it a Father, Son, Holy Spirit and Wisdom, but a phantasy according to the property of the dark world. God is indeed a God in this shut up attraction, but dwelling wholly in himself, not in the creature. He dwells in the unground out of the motion, and out of the will and out of the life of the creature.

44. Now if the creature does something, God does it not in the will of the unground, which is likewise in the creature, but the life and the will of the life of the creature does it, as may be recognized in the devil. It repenteth him that he has become a devil, seeing that he was an angel. Yet he repents not this in his

life's will according to the creature, but he repents it according to the will of the unground, in which God is so near him. There he is ashamed before the holiness of God, in that he was a holy angel, and is now a devil. The scientia [attraction] of the unground is ashamed that such an image exists in it, in its manifestation, and that it (the scientia) is outwardly a phantasy. But the will cannot destroy the phantasy; for the will is one only, and without any feeling of the phantasy. The will is a scientia in which the phantasy forms itself. This phantasy receives nothing into it but its own likeness, the likeness is the power of its life. If, however, something else should enter into it, the phantasy would have to perish. And there would also pass away with it that out of which it was produced, viz. nature. And if nature were to pass away, the Word of the divine power would not be speaking or manifest, and God would remain hidden.

45. Understand, then, that it all amounts to an inevitable thing that good and evil exist. In God all is good, but in the creature there is difference. The life of the creature was in its beginning wholly free, for it was manifested in the temperament. The angels were created for heaven, and though the dark world with the kingdom of phantasy was therein, yet in heaven it was not manifest. But the free-will in the fallen angels made it manifest in themselves. For the free-will inclined itself to phantasy, and phantasy accordingly has laid hold of the free-will and given itself up to its life.

46. Thus this dark realm of phantasy and the creaturely existence of the fallen angels is now wholly one thing, one will and one being. But because this apostate will wished to dwell and rule, not only in phantasy, but also in the holy power in which it

originally dwelt, the holy power in the light of God thrust it out from itself, and concealed itself from it. That is, the inner heaven excludes from itself the apostate will, so that it sees not God. It has died to the kingdom of heaven or the good will, and is now in God as the night in the day, which in the brightness of the sun is not manifest. It is there, but dwells only in itself, as said in John i. 5: The light shines in the darkness, and the darkness apprehended it not. And so it is with the devil and God. The devil is in God, but in the divine Night, in the centre of Nature, shut up with the darkness in the essence of his own life. And he has a magical light of fire from the ens of cold and heat, which is a terrible light to our eyes. But to him it is good.

47. The Scripture says: The great prince Michael fought with the dragon, and the dragon prevailed not (Rev. xii. 7, 8). And in another place: I beheld Satan as lightning fall from heaven (Luke x. 18). This prince Michael is a throne-angel, and has in the power of Christ, *i.e.* in the Word of the holy power, fought with the dragon; and in this Word Adam was created.

48. By this Word of power is to be understood all the three Principles. For when Lucifer fell and betook himself to the kingdom of phantasy, he lost the kingdom in the holy power and was thrust out. This was accomplished by the function of the angels, who thrust him out as an apostate by means of the divine power. And in this same power (viz. in the Word consisting of all the three Principles) man was created.

49. But when the kingdom of wrath overpowered man and expelled him from the temperament, there manifested itself in him the supreme name of the

Deity, that is, the most sweet power of Jesus, which overcame the kingdom of phantasy and wrath, and tinctured it with the highest love. There the devil's kingdom and dominion was broken to pieces as regards the power of man, and from thence springs the name Christ.

CHAPTER V

Of the original state of man

1. Moses says: God formed man of the dust of the ground (Gen. ii. 7), namely, the body, which is a *limus* of the earth. And the earth is an ens consisting of all the three Principles, viz. an ex-spired, formed, coagulated power derived from the Word of all the three Principles, from the *Mysterium magnum,* from the seven forms of Nature, which in the enkindled desire or in the fiat have impressed themselves, and brought themselves into a being, each property in itself so as to make a compaction, which God in the fiat or in the essential desire has comprehended in a mass, and in which all the powers of the spiritual world according to God's love and wrath, as well as according to phantasy, lie in a fixed condition; not after the manner of the Mens, but after the manner of the Ens.

2. In the Mens is understood the living essentiality, which is spiritual, that is, a wholly spiritual being, or a spiritual being of the tincture, as the highest power of fire and light brings itself into a being.

3. And in the Ens is understood the life of the seven properties of Nature, as the sensitive growing life, that is, the expressed word, which in the process of growth again expresses, forms and coagulates itself.

4. The Mens is contained in the Ens, like the soul in the body. The mental word speaks forth the ental word. Heaven encompasses the Mens, and phantasy the Ens. In the Mens is understood the divine holy

power in the comprehension of the Word, where the Word of power comprehends itself in a spiritual being, as the Word of power is essential.

5. The Mens is the spiritual water, and the power therein that forms itself in the spiritual water is the highest tincture, which stands in the temperament. And the ground of this tincture is the divine wisdom, and the ground of wisdom is the triad of the unfathomable Deity, and the ground of the triad is the one unsearchable will, and the ground of the will is the Nothing.

6. The mind therefore should first learn to discover what is comprised in the earth, before it says: Man is earth; and it should not look upon the earth as a cow does, who supposes the earth to be the mother of grass, nor does she require any more than grass and herbs.

7. But man desires to eat the best that springs from the earth, and therefore he should learn to know that he is the best that springs from the earth. For every being desires to eat of its mother from which it came. Man requires not for his vitality to eat of the coarseness of the earthly being, but of the fineness, viz. the Quintessence which he had as food in Paradise.

8. But when he went out from the temperament into the desire of distinction or difference, God established the curse between the Element of the temperament and the four elements, so that man, since he had gone by desire into inequality of the properties (which had compacted themselves in him into an animal, hard, material and sensible being of enmity, *i.e.* into the quadri-elemental coarseness of heat and cold and into the poison-source of the dark world, or into mortality), had necessarily also to eat of those properties in himself. For to inequality belongs not the tempera-

ment of the one holy Element, but to it pertain the four elements. The curse is therefore the dividing bound, so that what is impure may not enter into what is pure. For the curse is nothing else than a flight of the good, whereby the one Element has comprehended itself within itself, and concealed itself from the being of badness.

9. For in Adam's innocency the holy Element budded forth in the temperament through the four elements, and produced through the four elements heavenly fruit, which was pleasant to the sight and good for food, as Moses says. And in such budding forth is Paradise to be understood. For this fruit stood in the temperament, and Adam also stood in the temperament; accordingly man could and was to eat of the fruit of Paradise.

10. But when Adam introduced himself by desire into multiplicity of properties, viz. into the phantasy of inequality, and would know everything and acquire wisdom, and wished to try how heat and cold and all the other properties would taste in wrestling combat; then these properties in conflict took him prisoner, arose in him, and compacted themselves by desire into the being of phantasy. Thus the image of God in the temperament was destroyed, and the light in the being of the holy Element, wherein he knew God, was extinguished in Adam. Hence he died to the temperament, and awoke to the four elements and unequal attraction, which now plague and finally kill him.

11. But that we may satisfy the seeking mind which inquires after its native land, and is on the road of its pilgrimage, we proceed to present man to it as follows: (1) what he properly is, (2) from what he was created, (3) what his soul and body are, (4) his fall, and (5) his redemption or restoration; and thus we shall

be able to show fundamentally to the seeking mind the ground of the divine will in its relation to man. After that we will test the same by the Holy Scripture, and exhibit this Scripture with its supposed contrary, if perchance the eyes of any might thus be opened. All which we shall do faithfully according to our gift.

12. Moses says quite rightly: God created man in his own image, in the image of God created he him. And further: God made man out of the *limus* of the earth. When Moses says that God created man in his own image, he means not that God is an image and has created man after the model of it; but he understands the attraction in the Power, as from eternity all things have been imprinted in the powers in the spirit of wisdom; not as creatures, but as a shadow or form in a mirror, in which God from eternity has seen in his wisdom what might be. And with this figuration the Spirit of God has sported in wisdom. In this comprehended form (where the spirit of the attraction in wisdom, in the nature of the powers, has been configured from eternity into a divine play) God created the creaturely man, as for man's image proper, which however was not a man, but was God's image, wherein the spirit of God has imprinted itself from all the principles in a shadow of uniformity to the Being of all beings. As a man before a mirror beholds himself, for in the mirror is his image, but without life; so in like manner we are to consider the image of God presented in man, as also the whole creation, how God has seen all things from eternity in the mirror of his wisdom.

13. When God had comprehended in a being all the powers of all the three Principles contained in the attraction, and had drawn them into a mass which is called earth, as into a fixed condition of the generating

spiritual powers, then he separated the elements in the constitution of the one Element into four elements, to make a moving life. Further, he formed the spiritual powers of Nature into stars. For of whatever being the earth is corporeally, of that being the stars are spiritually ; and yet not as living spirits, but a spiritual being or a *quinta essentia*, that is, the subtle power from which the earth, viz. the coarseness, has been separated, and which God in the scientia of his Speaking has formed into distinction of powers.

14. And they are called stars, because what we have here is a moving, eager, strong being, in which the properties of Nature are understood. All that Nature is in itself spiritually in the temperament, that the stars are in their difference or distinction. If the stars all dissolved, and entered again into the One out of which they have proceeded, then Nature would be as it was from eternity ; for it would be again in the temperament, as indeed this shall come to pass at the end ; yet so that all beings shall be proved by fire and separated into their proper Principle. By this division and comprehension of the powers of the stars and four elements, we understand time and the creaturely beginning of this world.

15. Now when God had created the earth and the starry firmament, and had arranged in the middle the planetary wheel of the seven properties of Nature with their regent the sun, then the *spiritus mundi* was disclosed from all the properties of the powers, from the stars and elements, for in the speaking Word every power is emanant according to the right of the Eternal Nature. This eternal Word had here shut itself up in a time, as in a figure of the spiritual *Mysterium magnum*, like a great clockwork, where the spiritual Word is understood in a work.

16. The whole work is the formed word of God or the natural word; for the living Word of God, which is God himself, is understood within. This speaks itself forth through Nature for a *spiritus mundi,* that is, for a soul of the creation. And in the speaking forth separation appears in the fiery astral kindling in the *spiritus mundi,* the fiery kindling developing into a spiritual separation. And in this severance are understood the spirits in the elements, and these according to the separation of the four elements, in every element according to its quality.

17. For in every element there are its indwelling spirits, according to the quality of that element, and these are a shadow or image of the Eternal, yet with a real life derived from the desire of the nature of the expressed formed word,—not belonging to the true divine Life, but to the natural life. And they rule in fire, air, water and earth, in orders, as the stars have their inherent orders; and so it is to be understood at each pole.

18. The *spiritus mundi* is the life of the outer world. The firmament is round about, and has in itself the first three forms in a hard fiery enkindling. They are in fact a part of this very sphere, but in great partition and separation. Such separations of power proceed outwards and are a hunger, according to the being that they possess, after the earth and its material things. And the earth is a hunger after the *spiritus mundi,* for the earth is separated from it.

19. Thus the higher desires the lower, and the lower desires the higher. The hunger of the higher is strongly set on the earth, and the hunger of the earth is set upon the higher. Therefore everything that is material falls towards the earth, and indeed even water is attracted towards the earth. On the

other hand, the fiery *spiritus* in the higher again draws up the water into itself for its refreshment. This *spiritus* produces the water, gives it forth, and draws it again into itself after it has been tempered with the earth. And these two are in relation to each other as body and soul, or as man and wife who beget children together.

20. From this birth [of the higher with the lower], or from the matrix of nature, God, by the fiat, *i.e.* by the essential desire of the powers, on the fifth day caused all creatures to proceed according to every movement of the properties, the body deriving from the fixed earth and the spirit from the *spiritus mundi*. This was effected by the conjunction of the higher and lower; that is, the inner divine Word spoke itself through the outer expressed word in every attraction, passing out of the fiery proprium of the powers into a creaturely life. This includes the creatures upon earth, in water and in the air; every creature under guidance of its own attraction, of good and evil, according to the characteristics of all the three Principles; every creature an image and likeness of the inward ground, and springing from the kingdom of phantasy as well as from the original good life. For we see that there are good and evil creatures, as venomous beasts and worms according to the centre of nature of the darkness, and arisen from the power of the fierce wrathful property, which desire only to dwell in the dark and conceal themselves from the sun. In contrast to them we find many creatures which the *spiritus mundi* has fashioned from the realm of phantasy, as are apes and such beasts and birds as play monkey-tricks and disturb and torment other creatures; so that each is the enemy of the other, and hey all contend against one another, in manner as the

three Principles sport together in their powers. God has this sport before him, and by the *spiritus mundi* has brought it into a living creaturely being. We find likewise good friendly creatures in imitation of the angelic world, as the *spiritus mundi* has formatively introduced itself into the good forth-spoken powers, and this gives the tame beasts and birds; although many evil properties mingle with the tame animals, who thus have been laid hold of among mixed properties. By the food and dwelling of any animal we see from whence it came; for every creature desires to dwell in its mother, and longs after her.

21. The *spiritus mundi*, from which by their spirit all external creatures have arisen, is shut up in a time, limit and measure, as long as such existence shall continue, and is like a clockwork composed of the stars and elements wherein dwells the supreme God, who uses this clockwork as his instrument and has enclosed his making in it. This clockwork goes spontaneously of itself, and produces according to its minutes. Everything is contained in it, whatever has been done in the world and whatever shall yet be done. It is God's purpose with reference to the creature as well as in the creature, and in it he rules over all things by means of this government of nature.

22. In God himself, in so far as he is and is called God, there is no purpose with a view to evil or with a view to anything; for he is the one only Good, and has in himself no other comprehension than just himself. And in his word, which he has spoken forth from himself out of the great mystery of the Eternal Nature, he has grasped his purpose and comprised it in the free clockwork, in the *spiritus mundi*. This clockwork produces and breaks up everything acording to its instant course, and brings fruitfulness and unfruitfulness.

23. But God in his being pours his love-power into it, that is, he pours himself into it, as the sun does into the scientia [power] of the elements and fruits; that is, the holy divine scientia [power] gives virtue to the natural power. God loves all his works, and he can do nothing else but love, for he is the one Love itself. But his wrath lies in the eternal and temporal nature. In the eternal nature it is found in the centre of darkness, in the cold and hot fire-source; and in the temporal nature or in the *spiritus mundi* it is found in the fiery attraction belonging to the separation of all the properties.

24. Now if a city, country or creature awaken in itself this wrath in the fiery attraction, in the *spiritus mundi*, so that it introduces abomination into the fierce wrath, then the abomination is like wood in fire, where the fierceness becomes operative and spreads, and brings the life in the scientia [attraction] of the creature into the highest pain.

25. And thus speaks the wrathful, fiery Word in the awakened *turba* by the prophetic spirit in *Turba magna*: I will call for adversity upon a city and country, and will find my delight in this, that the wrath devours the abomination and consumes the wicked people. For it is just a joy and strong power of the fierce wrath in Nature, when such fuel (as blasphemy and other sins and infamy) is introduced into it. These it devours and consumes, for they are its food. And this is specially the case when the human scientia [will] breaks itself off from God's love, and plays the whore with the fierceness of Nature. In this relation the fierce wrath fattens itself much, till the clockwork is introduced into a fiery attraction, where all beings live under proof or trial. Here then the fierce wrath becomes inflamed, according as the *turba*

is enkindled in the wheel of the clockwork, so that a quality or property is manifested therein. Thus goes the plague, and thus it is poured out on such city, country or creature; often by poison and pestilence, frequently by unfruitfulness, and often by embittering the hearts of those in authority, whence war arises.

On Man.

26. From this great clockwork, as from the higher and lower, where all things are united together, man was created in the image of God. For Moses says that the Lord said: Let us make man in our image; and let them have dominion over the fish of the sea, and over the fowl of the air, and over the cattle, and over all the earth, and over every creeping thing that creepeth upon the earth (Gen. i. 26). Now if man was to rule over all these, he must have proceeded from the very same ground, and moreover from the best power of that ground. For nothing has dominion any deeper than its mother, whence it comes; unless it be transmuted into something that is better, and then it has dominion in that better thing, but no further than the ground of that thing extends.

27. Moses goes on to say: God created man from the dust of the ground, and breathed into him the breath of life, and man became a living soul (Gen. ii. 7). We are not to understand that God stood there in a personal creaturely manner like a man, and took a lump of earth and made a body from it. No; but the word of God or the speaking (fiat) was active in all the properties, in the *spiritus mundi* and in the earthly ens, and spoke into all the essences a life. That is, the fiat, which is the desire of the word in the attraction, existed in the eternally beheld model of

man that stood in wisdom, and drew the ens of all the properties of the earth and whatever may be therein, into a mass. This was a quintessence of the four elements, and in it lay the tincture of all the powers springing from all the three Principles, together with the proprium of the whole creation of all creatures, *i.e.* the being of all beings, from which all creatures have arisen.

28. Understand it aright: The earthly creatures belonging to time have by their body come from the four elements, but the body of man has come from the temperament, where all the four elements are united together in one being, and whence earth, stones, metals and all earthly creatures have their primal origin. The body of man has certainly come from the *limus* [original material] of the earth, yet not from the coarseness of the compacted being of separation in the properties, where every property has compacted itself into a particular being of earth, stones or metals; but it has come from the Quintessence, where the four elements are in the temperament, and where neither heat nor cold was manifest, but all things stood in equilibrium.

29. For if man was destined to rule in all the creatures, it was necessary for him to have in himself the higher power, as the supreme being of the creation, whereby the creatures were a degree lower or more external; that what is powerful might rule in what is impotent, as God does in Nature, which indeed is lesser than he. But we are not to think that in man the animal qualities had to be creaturely or manifest; on the contrary, the being of all the creatures lay in the human being in equipoise. Man is an image of the whole creation in respect of all three Principles: not only in regard to the being of the outer nature of

the stars and elements, *i.e.* the created world, but also in accordance with the being of the internal spiritual world, with the divine substantiality. For the holy Word in its being has embodied itself in the expressed word, that is, heaven has embodied itself in the being of the outer world. The budding in the being of the internal world, that is, Paradise or the holy Element, existed in the moving, surging [external] dominion.

30. In sum, the human body is a *limus* [extract] of the being of all beings, else it could not be called a likeness or image of God. The invisible God, who has from eternity brought himself into being, and likewise with this world into time, has by the human image that consists of all beings modelled himself into a creaturely image, as into a figure of the invisible being. Moreover, He gave man not merely the creaturely animal life (as springing from the attraction in the creature), which was to remain undivided in the temperament; but He breathed into him the living breath as the true rational life in the word of the divine power, that is, He breathed into him the true soul of all the three Principles in the temperament.

31. That is to say, (1) He breathed into him from within the magical fire-world or the centre of nature, being the true creaturely fire-soul according to which God calls himself a strong jealous God and a consuming fire.

32. And (2) along with the fire-world He breathed into him the light-world, or the kingdom of the power of God. Just as fire and light exist together unseparated, so likewise it is to be understood here.

33. And (3) along with these two He breathed into him from without the *spiritus mundi* and the air-soul. Thus the entire speaking Word breathed itself into the whole [human] nature according to time and

eternity. For man was an image of God in which the invisible God was made manifest, a true temple of the Spirit, as it is said in John i. 4: The life of man was in the Word, and was inbreathed into the created image. The Spirit of God breathed into it the life of nature in the temperament, *i.e.* the spirit of divine manifestation, in which the divine scientia passes into a natural life. And this divine and natural life is man, by his soul as the angels of God or the spiritual world, as it is written in Matt. xiii. 43 and xxii. 30: In the resurrection they are as the angels of God. Then we shall enter again into the first created divine image, and not into another creaturely existence.

34. Thus we are to know man rightly, viz. (1) what he was in innocence, and (2) what he afterwards became. He was in Paradise, that is, in the temperament. He was placed in a certain region where the holy world budded forth through the earth and bore paradisaic fruit, which in essence was also in the temperament. This fruit was pleasant to the sight, and good for food in a heavenly way; not to be taken into a worm-bag or miserable carcase as is done now in the awakened animal property, but to be eaten in the mouth in a magical way. But in the mouth were the centres of separation, each Principle separating into its own centre, in manner as this can be in eternity. As the *spiritus mundi* generates water from the first three forms, and gives it forth from itself in the salniter [ground] of the separation; and also draws it up again into itself from the earth, and yet becomes not full of it: so likewise is it to be understood regarding man.

35. Adam was naked, yet clothed with the greatest glory, as with Paradise, a most beautiful clear crystalline image. He was not a man nor a woman, but both of these, viz. a masculine virgin with the two

tinctures in temperamental equipoise, namely, the heavenly *matrix* in the generating love-fire, and, secondly, the *limbus* [quasi *lumbus*] from the nature of the essential fire. In these two the first and second Principle of the Divine Nature is understood. The tincture of Venus (*i.e.* the bringing forth and giving which belong to the Son's property) is to be regarded as the woman or the parturient mother, and the fiery property springing from the proprium of the Father is to be regarded as the man. These two properties have afterwards been separated into man and woman.

36. For if Adam could have stood firm, then the birth and propagation of men would have been magical, one proceeding out of another, as the sun penetrates glass and yet breaks it not. But because God knew Adam would not stand, He ordained for him the Saviour and Regenerator before the foundation of the world. He created him, however, originally in the right true image, and placed him in Paradise, where he was to be eternally. And there God let the trial come upon him, that he might fall into the paradisaic attraction,[1] and that the holy Word might not enter into the bestial attraction to be the subject of a process of regeneration, but into that which there would disappear, viz. the true image of God.

[1] '*Scienz* (scientia) in the writings of Böhme does not mean science, but he derives this term from *ziehen* (to draw), and thus has in mind an attracting or intracting power, the craving or longing of a being after its complete realization. Accordingly scientia denotes in particular the ruling activity of the first form of nature, especially in connection with the doctrine of creation.' —Hamberger.

CHAPTER VI

Of man's fall, and of his wife

1. Here we would exhort the lover of truth to take our meaning aright, for we shall point this out to him in such a way that he will be satisfied, if he do but understand us. That is, we shall show him where the divine will to good and evil originally arises, regarding which the Scripture says: He hardens their heart, lest they should believe and be saved (John xii. 40); and again, on the other hand: God willeth not the death of the sinner (Ezek. xxxiii. 11). And we shall proceed thus lest he [the lover of truth] should take his stand upon the delusion that God has formed a purpose to damn eternally one aggregate of persons, and to save the other aggregate in His purpose by grace; so that he may learn to understand rightly and fundamentally in what way the Scriptures (which speak so) mean this.

2. Consider the image of God in Adam antecedent to his Eve. This image stood in the temperament in Paradise, for Moses says: God saw every thing that he had made, and, behold, it was very good. Afterwards he said: It is not good that the man should be alone. Further, he cursed the earth for man's sake.

3. Dear man, tell me: Why did not God at once in the beginning make man and woman, as he did in the case of the other creatures? What was the reason he did not create them at the same time from one mass or lump? *Answer*: The reason was this, that the life of the two tinctures constitutes but one

only man in the image of God, and in eternity cannot exist in a twofold life as masculine and feminine: after the manner of the Father's and Son's property, which together are but one God and not divided.

4. Accordingly God created his image and likeness in a single image. For perfect love is not found in one tincture, but it is found in the two, one entering into the other. There the great fiery desire of love arises, for the fire gives light, and the light gives to the fire power, lustre and substance for its life, and these two make but one spirit, viz. air, and the spirit gives substantial being, viz. water. So long as these four (fire, light, air and water) are separated from each other, no eternal thing is there; but when they bring forth one another in the temperament, and flee not from each other, then we have something that is eternal.

5. And this holds also of Adam. When the tincture of light and water was separated from him into a woman, he could not exist eternally in the image which he thereby became; for his rose-garden of Paradise within him, wherein he loved himself, was taken away from him.

6. Reason now says: Why did God do this? Why did he divide Adam, and bring him into two images? It must have been his purpose, else he would not have done it. Moreover, he saw before the foundation of the world that he would will it and do it. Here Reason lies dead, and can advance no further without divine knowledge in the Holy Spirit; and therefrom comes all disputation and controversy.

7. God's purpose and ordaining, and God's foreseeing and knowing, are not one and the same thing. All things have been seen from eternity in the emanant spirit proceeding from the attraction of the fire and

light in the wisdom of God,—all whatsoever might arise if God's essence should move itself for the production of nature.

8. That is, in the property of the fiery attraction according to the darkness it has been clearly seen what would be a devil; and also in the attraction of the light-fire it has been seen what would be an angel, if the fiery attraction were to separate itself from the light. God, however, has created no devil; and had there ever been such a divine purpose, a devil would have been created in that purpose. The one will of God gave itself only to the angelic figure; but the fiery scientia [kindling] according to the property of the dark world pressed forth and embodied itself in a purpose, and would likewise be creaturely.

9. When the light and the shining fire became creaturely, then also the dark cold painful fire pressed forth with the formation of phantasy and united itself to the fiery kindling; and it (the phantasy) embraced the fiery kindling in itself as a delight, and pressed forth out of the temperament. And thus was born in opposition to the temperament the new will, which was expelled out of God.

10. It must be understood that the beginning of separation does not take place in God in such a sense that God has comprehended himself in a will for a devil; but the fiery scientia [kindling] originates in the Eternal Nature, in the speaking forth of the word according to fire and light. This was accomplished through the first three forms, so that a princely throne has separated itself in the fiery enkindling into the kingdom or dominion of phantasy.

11. The kingdom of phantasy according to the darkness has existed from eternity, and was an occasion of the devil's fall; although the fiery enkindling

of Lucifer lay in his own will, and he took up his abode in this realm without compulsion.

12. But man was deceived by the devil, so that he fell. For when, before the foundation of the world in the first motion or impression of Nature, Prince Lucifer fell and was thrust out from his royal position, Adam was created in his place. And because Lucifer had not stood firm, God created Adam as to the body in a material substance, *i.e.* in a watery property, that He might help him.

13. And then the holy name Jesus immediately embodied itself in man for a Regenerator. For Christ in Adam was to possess the royal seat of Lucifer, because Lucifer had turned away from God. And from thence comes great envy, so that the devil is hostile to man. Therefrom arises also the temptation of Christ in the wilderness, since Christ was to take away from the devil his seat and destroy his power in the creation, and be his judge that should cast him out eternally.

14. The soul of man and the devils, as well as the holy angels, all come from one ground, only that man has in himself the element also of the outer world, which indeed the devil likewise possesses, but in another principle, namely, in phantasy or false magic. And therefore the devil was able to deceive Adam; for he influenced Adam's fiery attraction by his speaking in the soul, and commended to him the inequality of the properties, and introduced his false desire into Adam. Hence Adam's free-will in the fiery attraction became infected (like a poison that enters into the body and begins to operate), by which a first will to individual desire arose. Whereupon it was all over with the temperament; for the propria of the creation (which in Adam all lay in the temperament)

awoke, every one in its selfness, and drew the free-will into themselves and wished to become manifest.

15. The *spiritus mundi* of the outer world, as the element of the external world in Adam, also drew the temperament out of Adam into itself, and wished to rule in Adam. Further, the realm of phantasy reached after Adam, and wished to become manifest in the image of God; as did also the fierceness of Nature, viz. the wrath of God in the envy of the devil: all drew Adam.

16. Here he was tried, to see whether he would stand. For the attraction (as springing from the separation of the magical fire in the Word of power, from the Father's proprium out of the will of the unground) was free. It stood in three Principles in the temperament, and it could turn whither it pleased. Not that it would have been free in the creature, for to the creature the commandment was given, not to turn away from God into the lust of evil and good. But the ground of the creature, that is, the fiery attraction as the root of the soul, lay in the unfathomable will of the beginning of all beings, and was a particle of the eternal will; and this eternal will in the fiery word of the separation of nature had divided into various scientia [or souls]. Thus the soul was a portion of the divisibility. And this divisibility in the Word of power in nature (in the first three forms and their extension) was figurized in angelic creatures and high eternal spirits, in which also the fiery inbreathed soul is understood.

17. But the entire holy speaking word of God according to love, *i.e.* according to the triad of the unfathomable Deity, gave a commandment to the fiery scientia [desire] of the soul, and said: Eat not of the tree of the knowledge of good and evil; else, if

thou dost, that very day thou shalt die unto the image of God (Gen. ii. 17). That is, the fiery soul would lose the light, and thus the divine power in the holy ens from the second Principle in the working of the holy Spirit would be extinguished.

18. For the Spirit of God reveals itself not in any animal property, and much less in the kingdom of phantasy. God therefore told him he was not to go out of the temperament into the desire of the properties, nor was he to prove these in their differences or their taste. Otherwise, mortality would appear and manifest itself in him, namely, the dark world's property from the centre of the first three forms, and would swallow up the kingdom of God in him; as indeed came to pass.

19. Reason says: Why did not God prevent this with his holy power? Is he not almighty, so that he could break the fiery attraction (whence the will to lust arose)?

20. Hearken Reason: The fiery attraction has come from the will of the unground, and this will is called a Father of all beings. And in this will God is born (the Son from the Father), and this will brings itself in powers to the word, as to an act of expression.

21. Know then that a particle of the highest omnipotence, of the Being of all beings, is to be understood in the soul, that is, in the scientia which has been from eternity. This scientia by the motion of the word of all powers formed itself into an image in the first three forms. Thus this scientia [essence] is a selfhood springing from the will of the unground, for there is nothing prior to it that can break it. The creature is indeed posterior to it; but the scientia to the creature exists from eternity, and has by the creature, *i.e.* in the first three forms, brought itself into a lust contrary to the temperament [harmony] in nature.

To the scientia of the soul the commandment was given, to keep the creature in the temperament, that is, it had to maintain the properties of nature in the sphere of equality; for the scientia was the power that could do so, being a spark of omnipotence. Moreover, the scientia had in itself the kingdom of the holy power in the light of God. What more should God give it, in order to hold it in check? He had given himself to it, as indeed also to King Lucifer.

22. But the scientia broke itself off from God's power and light, and would be a thing of its own; it wished to be a particular working God according to the properties of nature, and to work in evil and good, and to manifest such working in the kingdom of the holy power. This constituted a contrary rebellious will in the divine power and proprium, and on this account King Lucifer and also Adam were expelled from the kingdom of the holy power. Lucifer was cast out into the kingdom of phantasy, into the darkness, and Adam into the inequality of the created world, into the animal proprium, into the *spiritus mundi*, so that immediately the properties of all creatures in evil and good awoke in him. And on this account God has appointed the final judgment in the *spiritus mundi*, to separate the evil and the good, and to gather in all things, every one into its own Principle.

23. There all things (whatever the great clockwork in the *spiritus mundi* has generated, as well as in regard to the inner spiritual world) shall be put to the test of fire; that is, everything shall be proved by the fire of the Eternal Nature, according to which God calls himself a consuming fire. For how could God judge the creature, if it should do only what it would inevitably have to do if it had no free will?

24. The last judgment is nothing else than an in-

gathering by the Father of all beings and of all that he has brought forth through his Word. Into whatever any thing in free will has separated itself, into that will it enter; for in that eternal receptacle, and according to the property of that Principle, it is good.

25. God has brought forth nothing contrary to him, in him everything is good; yet every thing, however, in its own mother. But so long as it runs in an alien mother, it is in the contra-will. Consider a similitude: Heat and cold, also fire and water, come from one origin and separate one from another, and each of them moves in its own will as for a special quality. Now, if they should re-enter one into another, then there is enmity, and one kills the other; and this makes the particular will belonging to each quality. While they are together in the temperament, they have great peace; but as soon as they separate, each of them will be an individual thing and desires to rule over the other. Hence the struggle in the *spiritus mundi* between the four elements, as well as between heat and cold; each desires to prevail, and now one is victorious, now the other. Thus, at one time it rains, at another time it is cold, and at another hot; now the air sweeps along this way, now another way; all according to the power of the seven properties of Nature and their egress in the first three forms, from which all that moves is derived.

26. Reason says: God regulates this, that it happens so. Answer: Yes, that is true; but Reason is blind and sees not with what God rules, nor how this takes place. It understands not the divided word in the properties, wherein this government consists.

27. For in the *spiritus mundi* a great deal of evil activity appears, and this seems to be contrary to God: Item, that one creature injures and kills

another; and further, that war, pestilence, thunder and hail occur. All this lies in the *spiritus mundi*, and arises from the first three, viz. salt, sulphur and mercury, wherein the properties form themselves in their contrary will.

28. For God can give nothing but good, as he alone is the only Good, and never changes into any evil; nor is he able to change, else he would no longer be God. But in the word of his manifestation, where forms take their rise, and where nature and creature originate, working in evil and good arises.

29. This word has comprised itself in a clockwork of time, and therein lies the making of evil and good according to the separation of powers in the word, according as the powers of divine revelation have separated in the beginning into distinct principles, namely, into pain and joy, into darkness and light, into a love-fire of light and a painful fire of nature, as already set forth. Here now the whole ground of the divine will is understood in distinctions.

30. No creature is entitled to say that a will is given to it from without; on the contrary, the will to evil and good arises within the creature; but by outward influences of evil and good the creature is infected. As an outward poisonous air infects and poisons the body, so in like manner do outward things corrupt the individual will of the creature, so that the individual will comprehends itself in evil and good.

31. God has therefore given man doctrine and laws, that he should take occasion by the commandment to reject evil influences, and not say: If I do something wicked, I necessarily have to do it, for I am of evil tendency. But he is to know that the scientia [will] of the soul which could embody itself in evil was able also to embody itself in good, and that God is not

a cause of man's or the devil's fall; neither has He drawn man into it, in so far as He is called God.

32. But the differentiation of the manifested Word of power, as the powers have disposed themselves into properties, this it is that has drawn him. Man stood in the temperament; but outer influences from the devil and the dark world, as well as in the created world in the *spiritus mundi*, breathed into him, *i.e.* into the image of God, and awakened distinction in the image of God, in its harmonious constitution, so that the eternal scientia [will] of the soul entered into a desire for the manifestation of properties.

33. Understand this as follows: The soul of Adam was captivated with the creation of the formed word in its separation, and was cognisant in itself of the very same power of differentiation, and elevated itself into a longing for separation. And forthwith separation in the creature became manifest in respect of soul and body; but the devil was the greatest cause of it.

34. For when he, as a fiery spirit, had gone out from the temperament, from the image of God, he introduced his desire into the soul of man, in order to bring the soul into a longing or lust; for he marked well what Adam was, namely, a throne-prince in his (the devil's) former seat in the kingdom of God. But he knew not the name of Jesus, and that this name in the course of time would reveal itself in man; for his knowledge in God's love, where the name Jesus is the supreme sweetness of the Deity, had died at his falling away; that is, it had become changed into what is bad, and therefore he now knew only what is bad.

35. And thus is understood the ground and beginning of the fall of the devil and of man. Not that it

can be said that God has willed it, so far as he is called God; but the divisibility or distinction which proceeds from nature into the creature has willed it, and this divisibility is not called God.

36. God brings his one will into forms and representations of his Word for divisibility or distinction, that is, for the revelation of God; and here the divisibility moves in free-will. For the divisibility is nature and also the world of creation, and in the divisibility God wills evil and good. Namely, in that which has separated itself into what is good, as the holy angels, he willeth good; and in that which has separated itself into what is evil, as the devils, he willeth evil. As the Scripture says: Such as the people is, such a God do they have; with the holy thou art holy, and with the perverse thou art perverse (Ps. xviii. 25, 26).

37. Reason now says: If God in his emanated formed word is himself all, namely, evil and good, life and death, on what then rests human disputation and contention, that men dispute about God's will, seeing that God in his formed word is everything, and also wills everything, be it evil or good,—every thing in its property from which it originally arose?

38. Consider! Disputation and contention rest on the fact that Reason in its presumption and vain opinion, without Divine light, is a fool before God, and knows not what God is. It always imagines something strange and remote when it wishes to speak of God, and makes in the eternal unchangeable God, in his eternal Triad, a will and purpose that have a beginning. Reason understands not that all beginnings and purposes take their rise in the formed word through nature, where the Word comprehends and forms itself in nature, and that beginnings are all contained in the formation of the word, in the creation,

as in the great mystery of divisibility, in which the creatures have their origin, so that all evil comes from nature and the creature, and the hardening in nature and the creature originates in the scientia [attraction] of the creaturely selfhood; and that if the creature turn towards the wrath of Nature, it is laid hold of and hardened therein, so that the divine Speaking compacts it in the wrath and confines it in itself; and that all (as when it is written, He hardeneth their heart lest they believe and be saved) is done in the formed word of the eternal and temporal Nature.

39. God also speaks from this ground when He says in the psalm of David: Thou shalt see and have pleasure therein, when the wicked are requited (Ps. xci. 8). Further, Thou shalt rejoice when the wicked are overthrown; that is, when the wicked man, who has been an opposition and a continual source of poison to the holy man, is swallowed up in the wrath (Ps. lxiv. 8). When this poison is taken away from the holy soul, it rejoices that it is redeemed out of adversity. And therefore the Word also is in pain in nature, in order that joy may be manifested. But the divisibility that springs from the Word moves without constraint in freewill, every property passing into its own special existence. For in the holy Word all is good, but at the introduction of the individual will it becomes bad.

40. Now this takes place in nature and the creature, and not in God at all. Otherwise, if God in his Word did all things inevitably, even the devil's will would have to be in the Word of God. But the devil's will, as well as Adam's sinful will, arose in the self-attraction of the creature, and not in God. On the contrary, in the centre of nature the self-attraction embodied itself in a will of pride, desiring to be equal to and even more than the speaking Word in the trinity of

the Deity. Humility was despised and abandoned, and in its place the power of fire was assumed.

41. And that is the fall, that Adam and Lucifer put phantasy in the place of God; whereupon the Holy Spirit withdrew from their nature. They are now a spirit in their own self-will, and are imprisoned in phantasy, as indeed we recognize in Adam. When the scientia [will] of the soul, through the devil's hold or influence, elevated itself, the Holy Spirit retired into its principle, and Adam became weak and feeble in the image of God, *i.e.* in the temperament, and could not magically in the equality produce from himself beings like himself. His power, which he had in the temperament, was broken, for the animal properties of the creation were become active in him.

42. Moses then says: God caused a deep sleep to fall upon Adam, and he slept (Gen. ii. 21). Now he fell into sleep in the temperament, that is, he fell asleep to the divine world. Out of this sleep Christ must awaken him, else he can no more see God in the creation; for the falling asleep was nothing but losing God's light of love, or the love-fire. This became extinguished in the ens of the heavenly world, and hence Adam already was half dead.

43. The time that Adam remained in the right image of God is set before thee in the figures of Moses and Christ, as also the time of the sleep. Art thou seeing, then put Moses into Christ's figure, and Christ into Adam's figure, when Adam was yet in innocence.

44. Moses was forty days in the mount when Israel was tried. Israel was forty years in the wilderness, and Christ remained forty days in Adam's trial during the temptation in the wilderness. After his resurrection Christ walked forty days in the true perfect trial, in which Adam was to walk in his innocence for his

confirmation in the magical mode of production. But because this could not be (which indeed was well known in God), Adam fell into a sleep; and hence Christ afterwards had to rest in Adam's sleep forty hours, and awaken Adam in Him in the kingdom of God again. Consider this and reflect upon it, then wilt thou learn to understand the whole ground in the process of Christ. Put Christ in Adam's place, then findest thou the whole ground of the Old and New Testament. Place Adam in the formed word of the creation, and let him be the figure of the outer and inner Eternal Nature of all the three Principles; and place Christ in the ever-speaking Word, according to the true divine property wherein no evil can arise, but only the love-birth of the divine revelation according to the kingdom of glory appears; and introduce Christ into Adam, that Christ may regenerate Adam in himself, and tincture him with love, so that he may awake out of that deep sleep: then thou hast the whole process of Adam and Christ.

45. For Adam is the expressed formed creaturely word, and Christ is the holy ever-speaking Word. Thou wilt thus introduce time into eternity, and wilt see more than thou canst learn in all the books of men.

46. When Eve was made out of Adam during his sleep, this was done in the fiat, in the *spiritus mundi*. There they were made into creatures of the outer world, that is, fashioned into the external natural life, into mortality, with bestial members, and also a carcass or worm-bag to hold earthly food. For after the woman came out of Adam, the image of God in the temperament was destroyed, and Paradise could not continue to exist in him. For the kingdom of God consists not in eating and drinking, says the Scripture,

but in peace and joy in the Holy Ghost (Rom. xiv. 17). This could not be in Adam and Eve, for they had the mark of the animal nature. Although the animal nature was not yet wholly awakened, it was awakened already in desire.

47. The tree of the knowledge of good and evil was the trial or test, to find whither the desire of the human soul would will to turn itself; to see if it would remain in the creature, in the temperament, or if it would enter into the *spiritus mundi*, into the separated qualities.

48. Reason says: Why did God suffer that tree to grow? Answer: The trial attached to this world is better than making proof of the centre of fire according to the right and law of eternity, as Lucifer was tried. Moreover, God knew well man's fall in the *spiritus mundi*; for whatever the will of the soul desired, that the earth was compelled to give, because the soul's desire entered into the proprium of the earth. The earth had therefore to present to the desire whatever it wished to have; for the will of the soul is of a divine property in accordance with the divine Omnipotence. And in this lies the ground of all hiddenness; and the fall remains always, founded in man's own will and the devil's deceit.

49. The true real fall of man is as follows: When Eve was made out of Adam, the devil put himself into the serpent, and laid himself on the tree of temptation, and persuaded Eve to eat thereof, and then her eyes would be opened and she would be as God. He whispered her that she would know what was in all the properties, and what sort of being and taste was in them; how all the powers tasted in their properties, and what all the animals were in their characteristic qualities. Which indeed was all true; but her naked form, and

how heat and cold would penetrate into her, this the devil did not speak of. Neither did he come in his own form, but in the form of the most subtle beast. Thus it was the devil's aim to make Eve (as the matrix in the tincture of Venus) monstrous, that she should become enamoured of the serpent's subtlety; and from thence arose the desire to know evil and good as they existed in the serpent's subtlety, where the scientia [attraction] of Nature had brought itself into phantasy, into such a subtlety. Not as Reason says, that God armed the serpent's tongue, so that it had to do this. It may indeed be said that the devil armed it from the kingdom of phantasy, so that it has done this; but such cannot be said of God.

50. The serpent was a being in the first three forms, in the natural attraction, where fire and light separate, and the understanding lies as yet in the fiery sharpness; for the spirit of the understanding has not yet separated from the centre of the first three forms, but is mixed up with the painfulness, that is, with the root of the poison-quality. In the serpent therefore is found the highest cause of poison and false crafty will; and, secondly, there is found in it the highest preservation against poison, if the poison be divided from it, as may be conceived of Lucifer and his followers.

51. Satan was of the highest fiery enkindling according to the kingdom of Nature, and was one of the fairest in heaven. The fiery enkindling of Nature was a cause of his shining glory. He had taken to himself the worst and also the best; that is, the eternal scientia had assumed the fiery nature according to the highest motion (whence strength and power originates), and then in this fiery nature the scientia [desire] of the unground had formed itself in its own will

after the manner of subtlety, and had broken itself off from humility, and wished to rule in the light of God in its own lustre in all powers. And indeed it did in its beginning, whereby it poisoned the ens in the attraction of Nature with that property, and from this poisoned ens the serpent had its origin at creation. On account of this poisoning God cursed the earth, after man had poisoned it still more with the devil's poison and subtlety through his introduced false desire, whereby he poisoned the scientia in the being from which he had been extracted, so that Paradise withdrew from him.

52. Thus the devil by means of the serpent brought his poisoned ens on to the tree, and there he introduced his spume and crafty will, before the time of the creation of the [present] earth, into the attraction of Nature and her spiritual being. This ens in the attraction of Nature, at the beginning of creation, entered also into the creature, as indeed we are to consider of in all poisonous worms and the like. We are not to think that the devil has created them. No; he has been a poisoner of Nature, in the way in which he has poisoned his own nature and the human nature. But the Fiat has created them, every property of the divided attraction in its own identical form. According as the will in the attraction was in the working figure, so was the creature made.

53. For the speaking word in the property of every attraction brought itself into an image. The serpent was near the devil in the attraction of Nature, for he had introduced his poisonous will into it when as yet it was not a worm. But one must make a distinction between earthly creatures and those that are eternal; for the devil belongs to the eternal attraction, that is, to the Eternal Nature, and the serpent belongs to

time. But time has been spoken forth from eternity, and therefore they are separated from each other.

54. This poisonous subtle vermin, or the spawn of the devil, did the devil present to Eve on the tree, that she should become enamoured of its subtlety and make herself monstrous, as indeed came to pass. When Eve lusted after the cunning subtlety, the devil with his desire, with the serpent-monster, glided into the craving of Eve, viz. into soul and body; for Eve became desirous of the cunning or the subtlety, that her eyes might be opened and know evil and good. Thus the devil introduced into her the serpent's ens in a magical manner, in the way in which false magic uses incantations and enchantments, and introduces into man, into his body, an evil poison. And therefrom Eve got the will to be disobedient to God, and adventured it, and did eat of the tree of terrestrialness, in which evil and good were manifested. And indeed, still at the present day, after the fall, we eat nothing but such fruit. And when she eat, and did not fall down immediately and die, she gave also unto Adam, and he did eat thereof; for Adam had already plunged into it [by desire] when he stood in the image of God, but had not yet carried eating into the body.

CHAPTER VII

OF THE ANIMAL MANIFESTATION IN MAN. HOW THE EYES OF ADAM AND EVE WERE OPENED, AND HOW THIS IS FUNDAMENTALLY TO BE UNDERSTOOD.

1. IF we consider the image rightly in its magical ground, and how it is that in the *spiritus mundi* a counter-part is formed of all things, as is seen in a mirror, in water and in a shadow, we shall soon fathom how all beings have their origin from a sole and single Being, and how all creatures are contained in the *spiritus mundi* or in the expressed word of God. We may indeed with reason say that all creatures were contained likewise in Adam. Not that they proceeded out of Adam and entered into creaturely being; but in the eternal essence of the soul, where the Word of God forms itself into a natural and creaturely ground, in this ground lie all the properties. And Moses attests that man was to rule over all creatures; but now, after the fall, they rule in him.

2. For when the soul was in the temperament, the spirit of the soul's will penetrated through all the creatures, unimpaired by any of them, for none could lay hold of it. As no creature can take hold upon the sun's power and light by its own will, but must suffer them to penetrate it, so it was with the spirit of man's will. But when he was taken captive in the poison of the serpent, in the will of the devil, he became an enemy to all creatures, and lost this power.

3. The creatures also obtained dominion in him, and elevated themselves in him, as is plainly to be

seen that many a one lives in the property of a subtle serpent, full of evil cunning and poisonous malice; another has the property of a toad in him, or of a dog, cat, basilisk, lion, bear or wolf, and so on, through all the properties of beasts and creeping things.

4. They have indeed outwardly the first figured form in themselves, but in the property sits an evil beast. The like is to be understood concerning the good tame beasts, so that many a one lives in the property of a good beast. And there is no man begotten of Adam's seed, who in the earthly body has not the property of some beast in him,—one man an evil beast, and another man a good beast.

5. Now it is to be understood in connection with the fall that all the qualities in the *spiritus mundi* manifested themselves in man, all the fiery enkindling according to heat and cold, as well as all the other qualities; further, the property of the whole of Nature was manifested in him according to evil and good. For as soon as they began to eat of the earthly fruit and take it into the body, the temperament fell asunder, and the body was manifested according to all the qualities in the *spiritus mundi*. Then heat and cold came upon man, and penetrated into him; moreover, all the properties of Nature, wherein lies the creaturely ground, compacted themselves in him into a contrary will, whence sickness and also death by dissolution arose.

6. And through that Morsel he died as to the kingdom of God, and awoke to the kingdom of Nature. He was transported out of impassibility into passibility, and became by the outer body an animal of all animals, that is, he became the animal image of God, in which the Word of God manifested itself in an earthly image. Thus man became by the outer body

a master and sovereign of all animals, and yet was himself but an animal, though of a more noble essence than an animal. He had nevertheless an animal in his property.

7. And in that hour there was opened in man a gate of the dark world in God's wrath, namely, hell or the gulf of the devil, and at the same time the kingdom of phantasy became manifest in him. The angry God (so called according to the kingdom of darkness) was revealed in him, and took him prisoner according to the soul's essence in the creature. The ground of the soul's essence cannot be broken, but only the creature as springing from the first three forms, salt, sulphur and mercury, that is, the Eternal Nature, and also the temporal nature in the *spiritus mundi*. The temporal nature was brought into this earthly quality, and the Eternal Nature was brought into the wrath of the dark world, as a neighbour to the devil.

8. When these states of bondage were about to be broken in the two natures at the death of Christ, the earth trembled thereat, and the sun was darkened; to indicate, that as the eternal Light was now born again, the temporal light must cease.

9. To consider this correctly, as to what of man died at the fall, we must not only regard the temporal death, in which man dies and corrupts; for that is merely the animal death, and not the eternal death. Neither must we be blind and say, that the soul died in its creaturely being. No, that could not be, for what has issued from the Eternal admits no death; but the image of God, which was imprinted in the creaturely soul as the divine ens, was eclipsed when the wrath of fire awoke. For in God there is no dying, but only a separation of principles, in the way that we see night swallows up day into itself, and day

swallows up night, and thus one is as it were dead in the other, for it cannot manifest itself.

10. To understand this through a similitude: If the sun were to perish, the *spiritus mundi* would be a mere harsh hostile nature, and there would be perpetual night; and then the four elements could not operate or inqualify in their present characteristics, and no fruit would grow, nor could any creature live in the four elements. So in like manner Adam and his Eve died to the kingdom of the power of the divine Sun, that is, to the divine nature and will, and awoke to the fierce wrathful nature, inwardly as regards the soul and outwardly as regards the animal property.

11. The soul's will, which springs from the unfathomable will wherein God brings forth, did not die; for nothing can destroy it, but it remains eternally a free will. But its creaturely form, that is, the soul which was formed by the Spirit of God into an image from the eternal Nature, that image did lose the holy ens wherein God's light and love-fire burned. Not that this ens became a non-entity, although it became imperceptible and a non-entity to the creaturely soul; but the holy power, viz. the Spirit of God, which was the working life therein, concealed itself. Not of its own purpose; but the eternal Desire, that is, the unfathomable will to the soulish creature, went out from the love-will into its prickly property of the soulish nature.

12. God withdrew not himself from the soul, but the scientia of the free-will withdrew itself from God; just as the sun withdraws not itself from the thistle, but the thistle withdraws its prickly desire from the sun, and brings it into a prickly being. The more the sun shines upon it, the stronger and more prickly does

the desire of the operating will become; and so also it is to be understood with regard to the soul.

13. God dwells through all things, even through the darkness and through the devils; but the darkness apprehends him not, nor does the devil or the godless soul. Dost thou say, why so? Because the creaturely will to true resigned humility (putting oneself under obedience to God) is dead, and there is only a thistly and thorny will in the life of the creature. Thus the thorny will keeps the noble scientia of the eternal unfathomable will of the unground concealed or imprisoned in itself, and they are in one another as day and night.

14. The creaturely soul took the form of night. The *spiritus mundi*, which in the beginning was in equipoise in the body of man, had its subsistence in evil and good, just as all temporal things have. But the devil's thistle-seed had entered into it, in which lay temporal death, and there was nothing there but an animal of all animals. The equality proper to the formed expressed word stood in enmity and contrary will; the angelic image was wholly destroyed, both in respect of the soul and the senses. As we see even to-day that the senses continually in the animal will compact themselves into self-love, and with great difficulty come so far as to love God and equality; but they are always soaring aloft and wishing alone to possess everything, and would fain be the fairest child in the house, whence pride, covetousness, envy and hatred arise. All this implies the being of the serpent and the devil's introduced property, which cannot inherit the kingdom of God.

15. To the aid of this creaturely soul there came, out of pure grace, the living ever-speaking Word, the property of the highest Love, and spoke itself again

into the deadened ens of the heavenly world so as to make it an effectual working life. As the devil's word had been spoken into the soul, so the Word of the love of God came and spoke itself again into the deadened ens, signifying thereby that it was a goal of an eternal covenant of grace, wherein God's love in the name Jesus was to destroy the devil's works and introduce again the living holy ens in the name Jesus into this inner or inspoken word; which was accomplished in Christ's incarnation or becoming man.

16. And here we are to understand the foreknowledge or seeing by which the Spirit of God before the foundation of the world has seen this fall in the property of fire and of wrath in Nature, and provided the holy name Jesus with the highest Love-ens therein as a regenerator. For the one root of the ens that springs from the divine Love, namely, the ens of the heavenly world, the true image of God according to the property of the divine holiness, disappeared in Adam; and in this one image, which in Adam was eclipsed, God had embodied the goal of his eternal holy will in Christ. Into this same image did God's holy Word speak, when the poor creaturely soul had become blind as to God, and say: The seed of the woman shall bruise the serpent's head. And by this voice that was uttered within it, the poor soul again obtained divine breath and life. And this same voice was in the human life (as a figure of the true image in this goal of the covenant of God, which he had seen in the divine ens before the foundation of the world) propagated from man to man as a covenant of grace.

17. The inward speaking of the devil, from which an evil will arose, first took place in Adam when he was man and woman, and yet neither of them, but an image of God; and it penetrated from Adam into

Eve, who began sin. Therefore now came also the inward speaking of God and penetrated into Eve, as into the mother of all men, and set itself against the fountain of sin which had been initiated by Eve in Adam. For in Eve lay the tincture of light and of spiritual water : in her did the holy tincture in the Word or in the name Jesus embody itself, as it had to break the animal matrix and transform it into a holy matrix.

18. For it was not by Adam's fire-tincture that this was to be done, but by and in that part of the Adamic light-tincture wherein love did burn, and which was separated into the woman or into the mother of all men. Into this part God's voice promised to introduce again the living holy ens from heaven, and to generate anew in divine power the faded image of God which stood therein.

19. In the third chapter of John, verse 13, Christ says he was come from heaven, whereby is understood the primal Essence, for the Word needs no coming ; it is there before, and needs only to move itself. Now, all men by the corrupt soulish property lay in the seed of Adam ; and, on the other hand, all men lay in the matrix of Venus or in the female proprium, namely in Eve. And in Eve, as in the matrix of love from the being of the heavenly world which disappeared in Adam and Eve, God established his covenant and brought his Word thereinto, that the woman's seed (*i.e.* the heavenly seed which the Word was to re-introduce, and in which God and man were to be again one person) should bruise the head of the power of the serpent's spawn and the devil's will, and destroy the devil's works, which he would effectuate in soul and body.

20. Understand it aright. The first man as created

in Adam, that is, the part derived from the being of the heavenly world, and, secondly, the part which in the Word of God was to be introduced and become one being with the human or third part: he it was that had to do it, as God-Man and Man-God. Not a wholly strange Christ, but the same Word which had formed man out of itself into an image of God. Accordingly the formative Word and the formed word had to do it in the power of the Holy Spirit. The heavenly ens in the Word, as the temple of the Holy Spirit, was in the woman's seed to take unto itself a soulish seed, and also a corporeal seed from Adam's being out of the *limus* of the earth; in manner as God has taken the world unto himself, and yet dwells in heaven in the holy being.

21. Hence the Word received inwardly the deadened holy ens into its living ens, and in its power made the deadened ens alive; and the soulish and corporeal nature of the inner and outer world was suspended to the same ens, as Nature is suspended to God, who manifests himself through it. So likewise here the holy Word with the holy ens desired to manifest itself through the soulish and corporeal nature, and to tincture the soul again with the highest tincture, and to destroy the devil's robber-hold that he had built up in the wrath of the Eternal Nature: all which was fulfilled in the process of Christ.

22. Now, tell me Reason, Where does the deliberate will of God to harden man originally arise? Where is the purpose by which God has ordained one aggregate of people to eternal damnation, and the other aggregate to eternal life? For in Eve sin began, and in Eve also grace began, before she was pregnant with child. They were all involved in Eve in the same death, and all likewise were comprised in the one

covenant of grace in life. As the Apostle says (Rom. v. 18): As sin came from one and pressed upon all, so also grace came from one and pressed upon all. For the covenant had for its object not only a part taken from Eve, but the whole of Eve; except the works of the devil, which he had introduced into her: these were to be broken to pieces by Christ.

23. No soul could be born from the devil's introduced being, for the Word of God with the covenant intervened. Thus the covenant penetrated from Eve's soul into Adam, that is, from the tincture of light into Adam's fiery tincture. For Adam and Eve were in the Word one man; hence grace pressed upon this one man Adam and Eve.

24. Where is then the divine and eternal purpose of which Reason speaks? It aims at proving this purpose by the sacred Scriptures, and understands them not. For the words of Scripture are true, but an understanding must go with them, and not an outward imagining in which men exercise their fancy about a strange God who dwells alone far off and high up in a heaven.

25. We will point out to Reason in a brotherly way how Scripture is to be understood when it speaks of the purpose and election of God; and we will give to Reason the true understanding, as to how election takes place and what the purpose is. Not with intent to contemn anyone thus in his formed opinion; but for a better knowledge and Christian union in the understanding do we explain the Scriptures, to which end this book is written.

26. Now, in order to understand it, we will contrast the first and second Principle (*i.e.* (1) the kingdom of Nature for the divine manifestation, wherein hardening and God's wrath are understood; and (2)

the kingdom of Grace, as the true divine being), and see how the cause of hardening originally arises. And along with this we will examine the passages of Scripture which appear to be contrary to one another, that every one may see the ground of his opinion. But we will not bind ourselves to any opinion, to please any man. On the contrary, we seek to establish the foundation, and that in love, for a brotherly union of the opinions of all parties.

27. When Adam and Eve had fallen, they were blind as to the kingdom of God, and as it were dead; and there was no possibility in them of doing anything good, that is, by reference to the soulish and corporeal creature. But the attraction of the unground which springs from the Father's property, where a soul was formed in the fiery word, was unbound, and neither evil nor good, for it is the one will. In this eternal will God the Father brings forth his Son, though apart from the bringing forth (or the divine power) he is not called Father or God, but the eternal unfathomable will to something. And in this will is to be understood the birth of the Holy Trinity, as well as the origin of nature and the beginning of all beings.

28. The same will is the eternal beginning of the divine wisdom, *i.e.* of the intuition of the unground, and is likewise the beginning of the Word, viz. of the speaking forth of fire and of light. The speaking, however, does not take place in the will of the unground, but in the comprehension of the scientia [power], where this will comprehends itself in the place of God, in the triad of the engenderment. There the Word of power speaks itself forth into a distinctiveness of the power; and in this distinctiveness of the forth-speaking power, the image of God, viz. man,

has been seen from eternity in the Divine power and wisdom, in a magical form, without creaturely being. And in this seen image the Spirit of God has loved himself in the highest love, which is the name Jesus; for it was a figure of his likeness in power and bringing to birth.

29. But because God's love would not have been manifest without the eternal Nature, that is, because the fire of love would not have been manifest without the fire of wrath, therefore the wrath-fire in its ground of Nature was the root, and the love-fire was the manifestation of the wrath-fire, in manner as light comes from fire.

30. When the light in the creaturely eternal natural soul became extinct, the creaturely soul was merely a source of God's wrath, that is, a fiery nature. Now, God's love (or the holy name Jesus which is the One) had incorporated itself in the eternally seen image, in the scientia [desire] of the speaking forth, that is, in the human eternal image for which the creaturely soul was created. And in this incorporation man was chosen in Christ Jesus before the foundation of the world. But when the creaturely natural soul fell and lost the light, the Word of power (which had formed the soul in the fiery enkindling) spoke itself into the ungrounded will to the creature.

31. From eternity the name Jesus lay in man, viz. in the likeness of God, in an immovable love. For had it been mobile, the image would have had a real life; but thus the true life was only in the Word of power (John i. 4). But when the soul lost the light, the Word inspoke the name Jesus in the mobility, into the deadened ens of the being of the heavenly world.

32. Adam before his fall had the divine light from

Jehovah, that is, from the one God in which the high name Jesus stood hidden. Not that it was concealed in God, but in the creature, that is to say, in the attraction to the creature. But in the time of need when the soul fell, God manifested the riches of his glory and holiness in the unfathomable will of the soul, viz. in the eternally seen image; and embodied himself with the living voice of the Word, passing out of the divine love-fire into the eternal image, for a banner to the soul, towards which it should press. And though to force a way in were impossible to it, for it was as it were dead as regards God, yet the divine breath penetrated into it and exhorted it to stand still from its evil working, so that God's voice might begin to work again in the soul.

33. The point is this, that God's voice in Eve inspoke itself into the seed of the woman. For the true woman from the being of the heavenly world, when she was still in Adam according to the tincture of light, was virgin Sophia or the eternal virginity; in other words, the Love of the man, which was in Jehovah, was made manifest in Adam. And now it was manifested in the voice of the inner speaking in the name Jesus, which had unfolded itself out of Jehovah in consequence of this covenant: that the name Jesus would in the fulness of time introduce the holy ens of Sophia, *i.e.* the heavenly holy ens from the love, by which the love is enclosed, or in which the fiery love is an ens, into the deadened ens from Jehovah.

34. Again, that I say the ens from Jehovah was deadened at the fall, that is true, and is the very death in which Adam and Eve died. For they lost the right fire, and in them awoke the hot and cold fire of enmity; and in this fire Sophia is not manifest,

for it is not the divine but the natural fire-life. And in this natural fire-life of the soul appears the distinction between God's love and wrath.

35. The natural fire-life without the light is God's wrath, which desires only to have what is like itself. The same hardens the soul, and brings it into a strange will of its own, contrary to the property of the love-fire. And yet there passes not into the natural soul some manner of strange will in the form of a wrath-fire, which occupies the soul; but it is the special fire of that of which the soul is a being.

36. The fierceness of the individual nature hardens itself by compaction of the abomination in the first three forms, that is, in the property of the dark world, which is manifested in the false desire; and secondly it hardens itself from outward contingencies, which the false longing springing from the fiery desire takes into itself. Just as Adam and Eve hardened and poisoned themselves with the introduced craving of the serpent, whereby immediately this introduced poison began to hunger after such a property as itself was, so that one abomination produced another. As the Apostle Paul says (Rom. vii. 17) regarding it, that it is not he (Paul) in the spirit of Christ that wills and effects sin, but it is sin in the flesh, that is, which is in Nature; namely, the manifest wrath of the eternal and temporal Nature, as well as what the bestial lust may introduce into the flesh, this it is that does it.

37. Understand me correctly thus: The first and most inward ground in man is Christ, not according to the nature of man, but according to the divine property of the heavenly nature, which He has begotten anew. The second ground of Nature is the soul, understand the Eternal Nature, and in it Christ manifested himself and assumed the same. The third

ground is the created man composed of the *limus* (matter) of the earth, with the stars and elements.

38. In the first ground, which is Christ, is the working life in the divine love; in the second ground is the natural fire-life of the creaturely soul, wherein God calls himself a jealous God; and in the third ground is the created world of all the properties, which in Adam was in equipoise, and fell asunder at the fall.

39. In the first ground is God Jehovah, who gave the men which in the beginning were his, to the name and manifest power of Jesus, as Christ says (John xvii. 6): Father, the men were thine, and thou gavest them to me, and I give them eternal life. First they were in Jehovah, in the Father's proprium; now they are in the Son's proprium, according to the inward ground of the kingdom of heaven. For the inward ground is the inward heaven; it is the Sabbath, viz. Christ, which we ought to keep holy, that is, rest from our own will and working, in order that the Sabbath Christ may work within us.

40. The second ground is the kingdom of the Eternal Nature according to the Father's property, wherein is understood God's wrath and the dark world, over which God has made his Son a judge; for Christ says (Matt. xxviii. 18): All power has been given unto me in heaven and on earth by my Father. In these words is included also the judgment of all things.

Here follow some questions and the answers to them, for the understanding of the Bible passages concerning Election and the hardening of man.

41. Jesus says (Matt. xi. 28): Come unto me, all ye that labour and are heavy laden, and I will refresh you.

42. Now the question is, Why all are not weary and heavy laden, and come for refreshment? Answer: Christ says (John vi. 44): No man can come to me, except my heavenly Father draw him.

43. Question: Whom does the Father draw to Christ? Answer (John i. 13): Those that are born, not of flesh or blood, nor of the will of man, but of God.

44. Question: Who are these? Answer: These are they who are born of grace, these he chooses for himself.

45. Question: What is grace? Answer: It is the inward ground, viz. Christ, who as a principle of grace gave himself again to the deadened inward ground. Those who are born anew of that inward ground, namely, of Sophia or the heavenly virginity, are members of Christ's body and a temple of God. These are chosen to be children; the others are hardened, as the Scripture says.

46. Question: How is it that they are hardened? Answer: They are all dead in Adam, and cannot without the grace in Christ have or obtain the divine life.

47. Question: Can then the creaturely soul in its own power and will, in its selfhood, take to itself nothing of this grace? Answer: No, it cannot; for it depends not on any man's own willing or running, but on God's mercy, which exists solely in Christ in grace (Rom. ix. 16).

48. Question: How then does mercy enter into the soul, and the soul come under the election of grace? Answer: As said above, Those that are born, not of flesh or blood, nor of the will of man, but of the blessed seed of the woman, that is, of the inward ground: in such case the soul draws Christ into itself. Not on

the basis of an assumed outward grace, as Reason says, declaring that God receives in Christ the sinful man who lies dead in sin, through the predetermined election of grace, in order that he may make known the riches of his grace (Rom. ix. 23). No, this avails not; for the Scripture says: Except ye turn and become as little children, and be born anew of water and of the Spirit, ye shall not see the kingdom of God (Matt. xviii. 3; John iii. 5). The indwelling, inborn grace of childship alone avails; for Christ says: That which is born of the Spirit is spirit; and that which is born of the flesh is flesh. And Paul says: Flesh and blood cannot inherit the kingdom of God (1 Cor. xv. 50).

49. Question: Now it may be asked: How is then this inborn filial birth, seeing that in Adam all are dead? Accordingly some must be chosen and born children of God of a set purpose, while the others remain hardened in God's purpose. What can the child do, if God will not have it? Here we have the knotty point, about which the dispute is.

50. Christ says (Matt. vii. 18): A corrupt tree cannot bring forth good fruit, neither can a good tree bring forth evil fruit. Now, if we would fathom this, we must examine this tree of knowledge, which is evil and good, and see what fruit it bears, and from what kind of essence each fruit grows; in this way we shall attain our object. Thus we see that every power contracts into a being and will.

51. The Scripture says (Wisd. xi. 22): God has shut up all things in time, number, measure and weight, according as they have to go. But it cannot be said of man that in the beginning he was shut up in time, for in Paradise he was included in eternity. God had created him in his image; but when he fell,

then there laid hold of him the confining bounds of time, in which all things are found in number, weight and measure. This clockwork is the expressed formed word of God according to love and wrath, and in it lies the whole creation together with man according to nature and creature.

52. Now the name Jesus manifested itself in this expressed word, in the Father's property, as all power was given unto him in heaven and on earth. Hence all is his, both bad and good,—not through the possession of its peculiar property, but as a salvation to the good and a judge to the bad. And all things are set in opposition to one another, love against wrath, and wrath against love, that the one may be manifested in the other for the day of separation by the judge, when he shall separate all things. For, if he were not Lord over all that is bad, he could not be a judge of the devils and the godless.

53. Thus the tree of knowledge stands in great anxiety in process of birth. On the one hand it is Christ, and on the other it is the kingdom of Nature in the wrath of God the Father according to the property of the dark world and the fire-world. The fiery world gives being to the spirit-life; and Christ in the love gives being to the essence of the fruit, and tinctures the wrath, so that it becomes a kingdom of joy in the Being of all beings.

54. And in this lies the subject of dispute. Into what kind of ens the centre of nature, viz. the will of the unground in the eternal Father's property, formatively introduces itself,—whether into the grace of Christ in Sophia, or into the might of the wrathful fire for phantasy—a corresponding image stands in accordance with the soul. And here the Father gives the soul to his Son Christ. For in the Father's pro-

perty is the fashioning of the soul, and in the Son's property is the noble fashioning of Sophia as the eternal Virginity in Christ. Now it depends on the will of the ungrounded being out of nature towards the soulish creature, as to what sphere this latter shall separate itself: whether into selfhood as Lucifer did, or into engenderment of the holy triad of the Deity; that is to say, that it commits itself to God, or wills and runs of itself.

55. Now upon this is the election. It is as St. Paul says (Rom. vi. 16): To whom ye yield yourselves servants to obey, his servants ye are to whom ye obey; whether of sin unto death, or of obedience unto righteousness.

56. Reason says: What can a child help it, that it becomes a thistle before it has got its life and understanding? Answer: What can God's love in Christ help it, that Adam went out of the temperament into the tree of knowledge of good and evil, that is, into combat and strife? He had freewill; why did he break it against the will of God within him? why did he become disobedient to God?

57. Reason goes on to say: Do then all men come into the world in such a circumscribed comprehension? Answer: No, by no means so in consequence of God's purpose, but in consequence of the fountain of the actual sins of parents and ancestors. For God says in Moses (Exod. xx. 5, 6): I will visit the sins of the fathers upon the children unto the third and fourth generation; but to them that love me I will show mercy even to the thousandth generation.

58. Here we have the true ground of the thistle-children and the hardening, which is, that the parents introduce the devil's malice into flesh and blood, into the mystery of the formed expressed word of God,

namely, as falsehood, lying, pride, covetousness, envy, rage, and also often heavy curses, which, upon cause given, have by the wishing of another obtained entrance into their bodies and souls. And if such an individual has been the cause of them, they remain in the tree of his life. And then are born therefrom such twigs as cannot attain the being of Christ, but are born only from the parents' flesh and blood, in the will of the man and woman, where the soulish element passes into a thistly nature, often into the property of a serpent, a dog, or some horrible beast.

59. Upon these thistle-children, who on earth neither will nor do anything that is good, is set the election [to hardening]. And though the parents often still retain or have in themselves a spark of the divine being, and at last enter into repentance in order to the new birth, yet in the meantime such thistle-children are begotten.

60. Further, there is a very great difference among those whom the divine call lays hold of in the working tree of life; for Christ says: Many are called, but few are chosen (Matt. xx. 16). The call is to be understood as follows: Christ himself is the call, and he calls unceasingly in the essence of the tree: Come unto me, all ye that labour and are heavy laden. He stretches out his hand the whole day to a disobedient people that will not let themselves be drawn, and will not suffer his spirit to reprove them, as the Scripture laments.

61. Now, the call extends to all men, it calls them all; for it is written: God willeth that all men should be saved (1 Tim. ii. 4). And again: Thou art not a God that willeth what is evil (Ps. v. 4). God willeth not in his own will that a single thistle-child be born. But his wrath according to Nature lays

hold of and appropriates them. Yet it is the case that the divine call also has somewhat of a hold, and strikes root too, so that in many a one there exists a spark of the being of Christ, that is, of the divine hearing of God's voice. God allows such people to preach and teach, and reveals his will to them. For they are those that are heavy laden with sin, and lie half dead at Jericho. For them Christ has instituted baptism and the Supper, and is always calling, Come, come and labour in my vineyard; take my yoke upon you (Matt. xi. 29); namely, the corrupt nature of the formed expressed word, which in Christ has become a yoke, and in which are contained the sins of men.

62. Concerning them Christ says: Unto one was given one talent, to another two, to the third three, to the fourth four, to the fifth five, with which they were to trade and get gain (Matt. xxv. 14, 15). Now, such a one as hath in him but a little spark of God's voice, may, if he will, become active therein and bring it into a great tree. For to such he gave power to become children of God (John i. 12): not in their own will or ability, but in the ability of this little spark. For the soul rests there, and the drawing of the Father in the soul to Christ takes place there. For as soon as the soul tastes the grace of God, the Father's will in the unfathomable attraction hastens to the fountain or Christ. And though the kingdom of God is at first little, like a grain of mustard seed; if the soul do but receive it and work therein with its fiery desire, it grows at last as big as a bay-tree.

63. But the soul which will not adopt it, but enters into the lust of the flesh and wantonizes with the devil, of such a soul Christ says: He who hath not, that is, he who hath somewhat and will not work

therein, from him it shall be taken and given to him who hath much (Matt. xxv. 29). But he who hath, to him shall be given, that is, he who worketh in that little, to him shall be given. And in this connection it is said : Many are called, but few chosen.

64. For many of them have the pledge of grace, but they tread it under foot and disregard it : some on account of outward contingencies, and others on account of the coarseness of the bestial property. For Christ disseminates his voice in his word, as a sower sows his seed. It is disseminated into all men, into the wicked as well as the righteous. Now, when the seed is sown, it depends on the quality of the ground where the seed falls. If it fall on a hard road, that is, into a bestial property where in the flesh a coarse beast sits, then it is trodden down by the coarseness and unheedingness. But if a covetous beast, as a dog, wolf or the like, sit therein, then the cares of covetousness lie in the way and choke the seed. But if it fall into a lofty temper and disposition, which sits in the might and honour of the world, then pride has put itself in the way. This seed has fallen upon a rock and yields no fruit. But if it fall into a good ground (*Vernunft*), where in the property is a Man, that is, a true humility, then it is seized ; and such a one forms a good soil. For God's essence is humility, and hence this property is a likeness to Him. There the seed springs up and bears much fruit.

65. Therefore we are to consider Scripture correctly when it says : Many are called, but few chosen. Scripture means this as follows : Very many, in fact the greatest number, have been laid hold of in the divine call, and could attain to filiation or sonship ; but their godless life, to which they give themselves

up and in which they are corrupted by outward contingencies, hardens them. Hence a child is often more blessed than an elder person; and Christ also says: Suffer little children to come unto me, for of such is the kingdom of God. Christ has received them into his call or covenant. But when man comes to years, and steps aside from the divine call, and surrenders himself to the devil's will, and nevertheless comforts himself with a grace-childship appropriated from without, as Babel does, and says: Christ has done it, He has paid, I need only comfort myself therewith and accept of it; his grace is imputed to me as a gift; I am saved in the divine purpose without any works of my will. Certainly I am dead in sins, and without him can do nothing that is good, unless He draw me thereinto; but He will make known his purpose in me, and make me a child of grace by his power of adoption from without, and remit my sins. Even though I live wickedly, yet I am a child of grace in his purpose.

66. Of such the Scripture says: Let their way become a snare and a trap (Ps. lxix. 23). He causeth their light to go out in the midst of the darkness, and hardeneth them in their own folly, for their ways are harmful. Upon these passes the election [to hardening]; for they were originally called, and are still continually called, but they will not come.

67. Thus Christ says: We have piped unto you, and ye have not danced (Matt. xi. 17). And again: O Jerusalem, how often would I have gathered thy children together, even as a hen gathereth her chickens under her wings, and ye would not! Thou hast been laid hold of in the call of God, and thou hast turned away therefrom into thine own will.

68. Then saith Reason: They could not. Answer:

Why could they not, seeing they were called? They cannot who are not included in the call; but who shall say which they are? The devil within them will not; he taketh away the word out of their hearts, lest they should believe and be saved, as Christ says; hence in the election they are rejected. For the election passes over them at the time of harvest. When the measure of iniquity is full, then, in the winnowing, the chaff (being too light in weight) remains behind.

69. It is as Christ says: The kingdom of heaven is like a man which soweth good seed in his field; then cometh the enemy and soweth tares among the wheat (Matt. xiii. 25). And when the tares grow up they choke the wheat, so that it cannot grow and bear fruit. So likewise is it with man: Many a soul is a good grain, but the devil's tares destroy it.

70. Thou sayest: That cannot be, because Christ says (John x. 28): My sheep are in my hands, and no one is able to snatch them from me. Answer: All this is true, but observe: Only so long as the will of the soul remains in God is the devil unable to snatch them out of his hand. But if the soul break itself off from the will of God, then the motion of the unfathomable will (wherein Christ dwells) is obscured, and Christ in his members is crucified and slain, and the temple of the Holy Ghost is converted into a temple of prostitution in the soul. We are not to imagine that Christ is slain; but his temple, or a member of him, is slain. And here is the separation of the election.

71. The election is the Spirit of Christ, which thereupon passes over such a soul, for his voice is no more in the soul; the soul no longer has divine hearing, for

it is out of God. And hence Christ says: He that is of God heareth God's words: ye therefore hear them not, because ye are not of God (John viii. 47). They have lost the divine voice within them, and have received the devil's voice for the great judgment.

CHAPTER VIII

OF PASSAGES OF THE HOLY SCRIPTURE. HOW THE PASSAGES IN QUESTION STAND OPPOSED TO EACH OTHER, AND HOW THEY ARE TO BE UNDERSTOOD. AND, SECONDLY, OF THE TREE OF LIFE AND THE KNOWLEDGE OF GOOD AND EVIL.

1. WE will present the high mysteries under a figure for the weak to reflect upon, and show how the children of God and also the children of perdition are generated from their origin, and then how they are during the period of their life on earth.

2. Consider a tree, which grows from its ens and seed. In this seed is contained the tincture of growth together with the principle of the *corpus* or wood: all the four elements are contained in it, together with the *astrum* and the virtue of the sun.

3. The seed falls into the earth, which receives it; for the earth too is a being of the *astrum* and elements. And the *astrum* and elements are a being of the *spiritus mundi*; and the *spiritus mundi* is *Mysterium magnum*, as the formed expressed word of God from out of the eternal Speaking. And in the eternal Speaking is understood separability for love and wrath, viz. for fire and light.

4. The element of separation pertaining to the Speaking is the eternal Nature; and the Speaking in itself is God's Word, which has its origin from the power in wisdom. And wisdom is what is breathed forth from the triad, and is God's discovery, in which the unground finds itself in a ground. And the dis-

covery is the one eternal will, which brings itself in itself into a scientia [centrum], to a begetting of the Deity which itself is. Thus we see how what is inmost has effused itself into something that is external; and just as the internal has its mode of generating and working, so likewise has the external such.

5. And three Principles are to be understood in this omnipresent generating process, wherein also there are three kinds of life, and yet they are united together as one. But each of them is in its own property manifest to itself, and not to the others. If, however, these three kinds of life are manifest together in a thing, in such a way that one sees and comprehends the other in itself; then that thing is divine, for it is in the temperament.

6. One life is the fiery or the natural life; the other life is the lightful or the giving life; and the third is the sounding or the feeling, moving life. The fiery life furnishes divisibility, the lightful life furnishes being and substantiality, and the sounding life furnishes power and will, that is, in substance it produces growth, and in the life of fire and light a rational nature of sensibility.

7. The first Principle is the fiery life and the first revelation of God, and therein Nature is understood. The second Principle is light, in which the holy life of the understanding together with the original state of existence is understood, and is called God's kingdom. The third Principle comes from the power of essence, and has its beginning from the power of fire and light, from the fiery outbreathing of fire and light into a form, which is *Mysterium magnum* wherein all things lie; and yet this form is not an image, but an ens. It is the *spiritus mundi,* which the fiery life in the hungry desire seizes, and brings into a separa-

tion of working powers, and takes form itself therein. That is, the fire-life seizes the given substance of the light, and in it draws itself up into a form; as is to be seen in a seed, and also in the four elements, which are all only a *corpus* of the *spiritus mundi*.

8. And it is to be duly understood that the *Mysterium magnum* to evil and good exists in everything. This Mysterium is in itself good, and no trace of evil is to be found in it; but in its process of unfolding, since it is carried into divisibility, it becomes a *contrarium* of qualities, in which one overpowers the other and rejects it from fellowship. Here we understand the great mysteries of God, how it has been with the whole creation.

9. Consider the germ of a tree. In this germ, according to its proprium, lies the *Mysterium magnum*; for the entire tree together with the root and fruit is contained in it, and yet neither becomes manifest while they are but a seed. But when the seed is sown in its mother the earth, they become manifest, and begin to shoot forth in the fiery enkindling. Now the earth could not enkindle the ens in the germ, in which the first three forms (salt, sulphur and mercury) reveal themselves, if the sun, viz. the light, did not previously enkindle it; for these first three forms lie in the earth shut up in the cold fire. But if the sun enkindle the earth, then the hot fire from which the light of nature arises is evolved, that is, it is evolved in the earth, and into that evolving the germ is received. Namely, the power of the earth receives there in the germ its dear son, which is born from it, and receives him with joy, for he is more noble than his mother in his ens or being.

10. Now, we are to consider the soil of the earth, as to whether the first three forms, at the place where

the germ is sown, are similar in their working manifest being to the germ in its quality. If this be so, then they receive the germ as a dear son with joy. So too, in return, the ens of the germ gives itself up with great desire to its mother the earth ; for it finds its true mother, out of whose proprium it was born. In like manner the ens of the earth finds a true very dear son in the ens of the germ, and one rejoices in the other, and growth begins.

11. If, however, the ens of the earth at the same place be unlike the ens of the germ, then the earth receives it indeed, but only as a stepson. The earth introduces not her joy and desire into the germ, but leaves the stepson untouched. He may suck for himself being from his true mother, which is very deeply hidden in that place. And from this hiddenness many a germ perishes, before it can reach its true mother as belonging to its property. And though it receive being from what is dissimilar, yet it is in great danger ere it can transform itself with its essence into a different ens, and never becomes so good and strong a tree as if it had been sown with its germ in its true mother. For the contrary ens is always repugnant to it, and the essences are in conflict, whereby the tree becomes humpy and crooked, moreover bears scanty and (if externally an evil constellation come upon it) often bad fruit, and even withers and dies. For if the ens of the earth mix with the adverse constellation and receive it, then the earth rejoices in the property of that constellation, for they are of the same quality of will, and desire in their conjunction to bring forth a new son. Thus then the tree is forsaken by the ens of the earth, and perishes ; or yields bad and scanty, or no fruit.

12. Now, if we consider the growth of this tree, we

find the hidden ground of all mystery. For first it takes to itself the ens of the stepmother and gives up its own ens to the stepmother, who receives the ens of the seed, but not with such joy as if it were a similar ens. She draws indeed to herself the ens of the seed, in which conjunction the root originates; but there soon appears a contrary will in the first three forms of the matrix, whereby the root becomes knotty and bent.

13. In this conflict fire is enkindled in the ens of the seed by the power of the sun, in which enkindling the great Mystery in the *spiritus mundi* becomes manifest. This is laid hold of by the ens of the sun, which rejoices in the same; for the power of the sun becomes essential in it, and draws the ens of the seed upward from the root to itself, that fruit may be produced therein.

14. The sun gives itself with its power without distinction. It loves every fruit and growth, and withdraws itself from nothing. It wills nothing else but to draw up a good fruit in every herb or plant. It receives them all, be they evil or good, and gives them its love-will. For it cannot do otherwise: it includes no other thing than what it is in itself.

15. But we must rightly consider how the sun is also a poison to what is evil, and a good to what is good; for in its power arises the vegetative soul, and in its power it also perishes. Understand this as follows: If the first three forms of Nature in the root of the tree are of like will with the matrix of the earth, then the earth gives its power and sap to the root with great desire, the power of the sun rejoicing therein and hasting unto growth. But if the earth and root be contrary to each other, then the earth's power and sap is withheld from the root. And if

then the sun with its rays of light enkindles the root and the tree, the first three forms become inflamed therein in their malignity, and burn the ens of the sun and dry up the water, and so the stem or branches wither. But if the first three forms can obtain the sap of the earth, they remain in the sphere of equality and rouse not one another in conflict, but are in unison with the sun's rays of light. As we see likewise in the Mysterium in the *spiritus mundi,* when the fiery property climbs up, so that the sun can enkindle it, that then a parching heat arises, so that herbs and grass are pressed down.

16. Further, we see in this figure how the growth of the branches takes place. When the stem springs up, conflict in Nature springs up with it. For when Nature becomes kindled in her temperament [state of harmonious accord], she remains continuously in separation. The power of the sun is always striving to cast off the malignity of the first three forms, while they push on in their own will; and in consequence of this separation and sunderance the twigs press forth from the stem. In winter the cold locks them and their struggle up; and when spring comes, if they can but obtain heat, they enter again into conflict, and the struggle again presses forth into branches and twigs; as indeed in every tree its year's growth is thus seen.

17. We are now to consider the inward ground and the shooting forth of the branches. For we see that one branch grows big and bears fruit, and another withers. This is understood by reference to the divisibility of Nature through the *spiritus mundi,* where the properties are each of them desirous to embody itself in a selfness in the ens of the tree, and abandon equality. Now, this selfness, rising out of the general equality in

its pride, presses forth in the power of fire above the others, and will not remain in the sun's will in the temperament; and we are to consider how it draws up the temperament in it, and extinguishes it when it is forced out from the stem. For that scientia in that proprium has disposed itself into particular will; and such seek in pride to press forth sooner than the others in the equality, and have not power enough. If then a strong constellation of the firmament penetrates from without into these proud twigs, and sifts and tries them to see whether they belong to the equality, they are poisoned and wither away, for they are apostate twigs. Moreover, the sun's heat in the *spiritus mundi* dries them up.

18. But the other branches come from the temperament, from the powerful drawing-out of the sun, as the sun rejoices in the properties and tempers the properties, and is drawn out in them. These branches the sun in its power makes to grow, for the properties are rooted in its will. We see further how the properties of Nature in the branches, when they are full-grówn, are corrupted by outward influences, as by the stars, and also by impure air when the sun cannot reach them with its rays, so that they become humpy, crooked and hunched; and many a branch is thus hardened and thrown off, so that it withers away.

19. And as it is with the origin and growth of the tree, so it is with the origin and growth of man. Although man in the proprium of nature and of light is higher than the plants of the earth, yet all is included in one order, for it proceeds from one ground, namely, through the expressed word of God, wherein the divine Speaking in *Mysterium magnum* co-operates. But man in his being of the body is a degree higher than the earth and its products, and by the soul is

higher even than the *spiritus mundi.* Apart from this, however, everything at its origin proceeds from one ground, yet divides asunder, and forms itself into special beginnings in the world of creation.

20. God's one purpose is his ever-speaking Word, which he speaks forth through wisdom out of his power in the scientia into separability for his manifestation. He has no other purpose in him, nor is it possible for him to have other purposes; for if that was so, there would have to be something before him whereby he might take occasion to form a purpose.

21. Accordingly, the Speaking of his power for his self-revelation constitutes the one divine purpose; yet it is not a purpose that has a beginning, but a purpose which generates. The Word's purpose consists in the separability and formability of the one divine power, and this separability and formability the one God in his triad has spoken forth from eternity into a beginning by the Word, as into a being of all the propria of the separability, in which all the separables are united in each other. And what is thus spoken forth is *Mysterium magnum,* and a true single purpose of the Word.

22. The Word desires nothing more than to manifest its holy power through the separability; and in the Word the Deity becomes manifest in the separability by fire and light. And these two, viz. the Word and *Mysterium magnum,* are in one another as soul and body; for *Mysterium magnum* is the being of the Word, in and through which the invisible God in his trinity is made manifest, and is revealed from eternity to eternity. For of whatever the Word is in power and sound, of that is *Mysterium magnum* a being: it is the eternal essential Word of God.

23. Understand us aright. The spiritual sounding

Word is the divine Understanding, which has by *Mysterium magnum, i.e.* by the eternal being of the Word, spoken forth itself into a form, as into a beginning and time. And the separability, which is contained in *Mysterium magnum* in a working being, has the ever-speaking Spirit made manifest, that there may be a moving, grasping, generating life; and this life is the *spiritus* of the external world. Its motion is the creaturely life, the four elements are its being, and the separation in the *spiritus mundi* is the constellation in which the vegetative life stands.

24. This eternal *Mysterium magnum* has in the beginning of its separability, through the speaking forth of the Word of the Deity, been divided, that is, the subtle ens has been separated from the coarse coagulated ens. The subtle ens is the firmament, namely, a quintessence; and the coarse coagulated ens is the offcasting, the same is earth, stones and metals. The offcasting has taken place that there might be a purity in the *spiritus mundi*, that is, a shining sensible life. The offcasting again is of a twofold character, namely, (1) a subtle quality springing from the power of the light in the Word, and (2) a coarse quality according to the compaction of the darkness in the origin of fire. By the coarse quality is understood the earth, and by the subtle quality is understood the power in the ens of the earth, and from this power in the separation have herbs, trees and metals their growth. All flesh likewise comes from the subtle ens of the earth. All that belongs only to time, and is found in the life of the *spiritus mundi*, has its body from the ens of the earth.

25. This *spiritus mundi* with the firmament of its scientia [power], and with the subtle *corpus* of fire, water and air, along with its fixity of earth and what-

ever is included therein: this is the life and being which has been spoken forth from the inner eternal Mysterium or from the inner essential Word of God. This eternal Word of God dwells and works in holy power in the inward ground, and with the beginning of this world has through the inner mysterium spoken forth itself into an outer mysterium. And from this outer mysterium the whole creation of the external world has proceeded, and is enclosed therein as in the womb of its mother, where the eternal Word with the separability has brought itself out of the powers into a figurate life.

26. This external mysterium of the formed word is shut up with its generating life in a wheel, like a clockwork, where the properties are in process of wrestling for the primacy. Now one is atop, at another time the second, third, fourth, fifth, sixth and seventh; and indeed thus is to be understood the issuings of the seven properties. At one time the *spiritus* in fire gets the victory, whereby heat arises; at another time the *spiritus* in water prevails, whereby it rains. At other times the *spiritus* in air conquers, whereby wind rises; and again at other times the *spiritus* in what is earthy prevails, whence cold results. What one property builds up, the other pulls down; one property is giving, the other hardens the giving, so that it is corrupted; one gives good being and will, the other gives evil will and hinders the good, that one may be manifested in the other.

27. Into this external mysterium of properties, wherein is understood the separation of the expressed word, God has inspoken the light of nature out of *Mysterium magnum* by and through the power of the eternal Light, so that in every evil being there exists a good principle, namely, a good power springing

from the holy Word, and that no badness is found alone without goodness.

28. Further, God has given the sun to the properties of the external world so as to make a working life, that all things may form or comprehend themselves therein and pass into a common state of struggle, in which they may grow and bear fruit. And though the light of nature from the divine power co-operates in everything, as well as that the sun from without penetrates and introduces itself into all living and growing things, yet the fiery property in the fierce wrath is so strong that the properties become impressed with hardness through the power of the darkness, so that many creatures and plants necessarily have to live in what is bad; for the hunger in the dark impression is so strong that it holds all creatures under its power.

29. This working being in the properties along with light and darkness, wherein the whole creation is comprised, is the one purpose of God's Word, which is, to generate lives and creatures, and bring the expressed word into a figurate existence, so that every power in the separability may stand in a life and image, both according to the property of the light-power of the holy Word, and also according to the properties of the fire-power. The light, however, is given to all things for a temperament. We must not conceive that the light only shines upon the being from without; on the contrary, it co-operates with every being, co-working in all that lives and grows.

30. No creature ought therefore to complain of its creator, that he has created it for evil; but it is the fierce wrathfulness in nature which hardens a thing and impedes the power of the light. Secondly, the curse is a hindrance, so that the holy tincture of the

holy ground of the speaking Word in the eternal Light has (because of the devil's, and man's, and the creature's vanity) retired into itself, and gives itself only to that which brings itself into an image of the light-power, and will not work with that scientia [will] which gives itself up to the fierce wrath of the darkness. The reason is this : the darkness would otherwise lay hold of the holy power and introduce it into its own malignity. And thus it is as Scripture expresses it (Ps. xviii. 26, 27) : With the perverse thou art perverse, and with the holy thou art holy. As the sun has to suffer the thistle to swallow up his good ens into its prickly selfness, and make use of his ens for its own prickles ; so the highest tincture wills not to give itself to the false form of the scientia, where the eternal unfathomable will is transmuted into an image of the dark world's property.

31. The other purpose of God, that is worked out by the speaking Word of God, wherewith God has willed to reveal himself through *Mysterium magnum*, is the most precious name Jesus. After having turned from God to the creature, man had lost the voice of God. This voice God again inspoke into him in grace in the woman's seed with the implanted name Jesus, as with the second purpose springing from the divine ground.

32. The first purpose with regard to nature and creature belongs to the Father's property. The second purpose, namely, to redeem nature and creature from the curse and from pain, is the name Jesus, or the highest tincture of the divine power, that is, to reveal the same through the formed expressed word in the proprium of the good, which is kept a prisoner in what is bad.

33. This name Jesus, as the purpose of his love,

God has inspoken into the mother of all men and as a living power embodied it in an eternal covenant, and has fulfilled this covenant by introducing the Divine being into human quality. So that now as all men bring with them into the world the curse and corruption, in which they are all children of the wrath of God and are shut up under the curse, in like manner all bring with them into the world the covenant of grace in the encorporate name Jesus. And this covenant has God in Christ confirmed with the seal of baptism, but to them of old time God confirmed it with circumcision.

34. Know, then, that God has through his Word revealed no other purpose than the ground of creation or the nature of separation, wherein purposes conducive to badness take their rise. There the attraction of the unfathomable will in the fiery separation brings itself, as to one part, into the power of light; and, as to another part, it brings itself into the fiery property of painfulness; and, as to a third part, it brings itself into phantasy according to fire, light and darkness, viz. into the selfhood of pride, as Lucifer and Adam did. But whatever is separated into the power of light is good; and whatever in the temperament remains in the fiery separation, to that the highest tincture of power unites itself; but to the other constituents in the sphere of the separation the tincture of the sun and the *spiritus mundi* unites itself.

35. Upon this basis we will develop the simile of a tree in reference to man, proceeding from the planting of it to good and evil. And we will show what the purpose of God is,—both the drawing of the Father in good and evil, as well as Election in regard to men; and then we will compare this with passages of Scripture.

36. Man was in the beginning brought out of the purpose of the eternal and temporal nature into an image consisting of the speaking and forth-spoken word, in which lies the speaking Word of separability itself. For he is by the external body a being of the four elements, and by the external life he is a being of the *spiritus mundi*. But by the inner body he is a being of the eternal Word of God, namely, of the highest Mysterium of the essential powers of God. And by the inner spirit he exists in two properties, as follows: The creaturely soul is of the Father's nature, belonging to the eternal separation of the Word of God into light and darkness; and this property gives the creaturely soul's selfhood, as arising out of the ground of the eternal will. The other property is the true Divine property in the power of the light: that is, Christ, in whom the name Jesus was revealed. This property is the true eternal purpose of God before the foundation of the world, when the soul was not yet a creature, but merely an ens in the great Mystery.

37. This other property was in man, in the beginning before sin, made manifest in Jehovah. But when the soul broke itself off therefrom and turned to the creatures, the creaturely soul became dumb as to God. Then the purpose in the holy name Jesus manifested itself as a gift of grace, and entered into the light of life. This gift of grace belongs not to the creaturely soul's selfhood; the latter possesses it not as a natural right, nor ever obtains it as a natural right; but it dwells in the soul in a special centre, and calls to the soul, and offers itself to it, that it may reveal itself in it.

38. The soul should stand still from the imagination of the earthly creatures, and not introduce into its fire-life earthly being, from which a false light

arises; and then this divine purpose in the highest tincture will reveal itself out of the holy love-fire with the holy light. As fire through-glows iron, so that the iron seems to be pure fire; so likewise the love-fire of this purpose of the gift of grace transforms the soul into its own property, and yet the soul retains its nature, as iron retains its nature in fire.

39. Every child born of the seed of man and woman has this gift of grace confronting it in its inward ground in the light of life. It offers itself to every soul, and during the whole period of man's life reaches forth its desire towards the soul, and calls it, saying: Come hither unto me, and go out from earthly imagination in the wrath, and from phantasy.

40. On the other hand, there exists in every soul, as soon as its life begins, the fierce awakened anger of God in the essence of the separation, wherein is also the introduced poison of the serpent and the devil's desire.

41. Thirdly, every seed of the body according to the outer world is under the dominion of the *spiritus mundi*, and depends on the constellation. According as the great clockwork at the time [of procreation and birth] stands in figure, such a figure does the *spiritus mundi* give to the seed or to the proprium of the external life, such a beast does it imprint in the external life's property. For the *spiritus* of the outer world that springs from the elements can give nothing but a beast. And such beast arises for this reason, that in man lies the whole creation, and that at the fall he brought himself out of the temperament into earthly desire and imagination, so that the *spiritus mundi* with its separation became manifest in him.

42. And therefore now always at the beginning of every child's life the *spiritus mundi* separates itself

into such a figure. According as the constellation is in its orb, such a figure does the *spiritus mundi* make in the proprium arising out of the *limus* of the earth, that is, in the four elements, whereby many a man from his mother's womb is, as to the outer man, of the nature of an evil poisonous serpent, or of a wolf, dog, toad, cunning fox, haughty lion, filthy swine, proud peacock, or again, of the nature of a mettlesome horse or other good tame beast, all according as the figure is in the *spiritus mundi*. In like manner this constellation pertaining to the external purpose of the formed word engrafts into some good reason and senses, superadding honour and worldly prosperity; and into some it engrafts misery, misfortune, folly, malice, knavery and an evil will for all manner of vices, whereby many a man, if he do not continually slay the earthly implanted beast and break the evil will with the divine gift of grace, falls into the hands of the hangman.

43. Now consider, O man, this is brought to thee by the external purpose of the formed and expressed word, wherein is evil and good, and in which the essence of the seed in the beginning of the life separates itself into a proprium. And here we have the drawing from the Father's property to evil or good. Into whatever being the life has constellated itself, that constellation is attracted to its likeness, like will always dwell with and in like. As for instance, a devout man likes living with devout people, a mocker with mockers, a thief with thieves, a glutton, drunkard, gambler, lecher with people like themselves; and thereunto their nature which springs from the property of the wrath of God draws them. So too the actual sins of the parents enter into the proprium, for every child is born out of the seed of the parents.

As the parents are, such is also the child. But the child often transforms the constellation by force and brings it under its power, if it be strong.

44. That is the drawing of the external life, regarding which God says: Whom I harden, I harden. Accordingly the external man is hardened; and devout as well as sensual men are drawn to humility and pride. That is God's purpose according to his wrath, which man has awakened in himself. For it is the external generating word of God, and through it God deals with the external creature as he lays hold of the latter in his clockwork. And by means of this clockwork he also reveals his glory, both according to fire and light, according to understanding and folly, that the one may be manifested in the other, and that it may be known what is good.

45. But this clockwork of the expressed word is not God himself; it is only an image of him, as the external essential word in which he has enclosed the creation, and from which he has produced it. For no creature can arise from purely divine quality, for such quality has no ground nor beginning. And it cannot be formed into any beginning save by the Word of power, or by and through the separation of the Speaking; as the Speaking must pass into the condition of nature, else the Word would not be manifest.

46. Now, the inner proprium of the soul lies in the first created constellation, in the eternal original ground; it is not formatively introduced into the external animal constellation. For the soul's essence has one form, as it were a magical fire-source, and separates itself in the life itself into the figure of the body. It contains the principle of the eternal nature, and is capable of good and evil; for it is the cause of fire and light, but is grievously and rigorously im-

prisoned in sin. For here lurks original sin in the centre of nature, wherein the devil has got an abode. Here too are the inherited sins from parents and grandparents, like an evil poison, regarding which God says, He will visit them upon the children unto the third and fourth generation. And here also are the parents' well-doing and God's blessing, which pass upon the children (Ex. xx. 5, 6). These properties, moreover, constellate themselves into a figure after their kind, by which the soul figurizes itself either into an angelic or diabolic image.

47. And here appears the difficult argument, as the Election of God sees what kind of angel will be formed there. And yet no resolution or decree [of unalterable predestination] has been made about it. For the gift of grace lies in the inward ground, and unites itself to the centre of the ungrounded principle of the soul, namely, to the will of the eternal Father. There Christ makes supplication for the poor imprisoned soul, as the Scripture says; for the soul lies in the bonds of God's wrath, and is hardened in its sins. There the life draws itself through death, and scrutinizes the process to see if there be present any good spark that is susceptible of the divine power; and in that case it is drawn. For Christ desires to become manifest, and the fierce wrath of Nature also desires to become manifest. Thus these two purposes in the formed word are at strife about man, viz. about the image of God. The kingdom of grace in light desires to possess it and manifest itself in it, and the kingdom of nature in the fierceness of fire in the separation of nature also desires to possess it and manifest itself in it. And these two are contained in the formed word, namely, the Father's property in the fierce wrath and the Son's love-property in the light.

48. Now mark the forementioned figure of comparison of a tree. The woman is the soil, and the man is the grain that is sown for the formation of a human tree. Then says Reason: God conjoins them as he chooses to have them. Answer: Yes, certainly! but by his purpose which he has framed into a government in the word through the great clockwork of nature. The constellations [the state and attitude of the forces of nature at the time of procreation and birth] draw them together; but most of them are drawn together by their own will, as the human will, issuing from the eternal ground, constellates itself, whereby the external constellation is broken.

49. This is seen in the fact that those who are rich constellate themselves with the rich, and those who are noble with the noble. Otherwise, if the constellation of the *spiritus mundi* were not broken, many a poor maid-servant would be conjoined with a nobleman, who in the *spiritus mundi* do outwardly constellate with each other. But the self-framed human soulish constellation from out of the high ground is mightier than the constellation in the *spiritus mundi*. Therefore it goes for the most part in accordance with the constellation of the soul, which surpasses the outer world in might and ascendancy; like as it depends on the sower as to where he sows his grain, though another soil were better fitted for it.

50. But if the soul give up its will to God and does not constellate itself in such orders, but commits itself to the purpose of God, then is the masculine and feminine tincture comprehended in the Word and constellated in the right divine order, as regards the soul in the *Mysterium magnum*, and as regards the body in the *spiritus mundi*. Then a love is awakened according to the true likeness of the properties; and if a

man follow it, he regards not wealth, nobility, or beauty and talents. In this way his own constellation, which he has from Nature, obtains the true real likeness, and is a soil that is agreeable to and one with the grain. Therefore strife does not so easily and readily rise in the fruit, for the soil and the grain exist together in what is like; and under these circumstances the inner and outer sun can constellate together more favourably in the fruit.

51. But we see how it goes in the world, what Nature brings and binds together. Thus two young people often constellate together in the highest love (which is accomplished by the great purpose of the true constellation in the *spiritus mundi* as the formed word), and it is broken by parents and friends on account of poverty or high station. As indeed God says to Noah: Men will not suffer my spirit to draw them, but they take wives and lie with the daughters of men according as they are fair (Gen. vi. 2, 3), rich and noble; all which is man's invention and devising. From thence come mighty men and tyrants, to whom God opposes the flood of his wrath in their self-framed constellation, and hardens their will. Accordingly, on account of riches or high rank, many people are coupled and forced together, who afterwards get to hate each other, and all their days wish in their hearts for death and separation.

52. These people have to bring together their tinctures in the seed into a conjunction to make the human life of a child. The woman is the soil, and the man sows the grain. Now, if the two tinctures shall enter into each other and be transformed into one in the feminine and masculine seed, the ens will be introduced into a joyful likeness. But if they are unlike each other in will, the soil receives with the

grain a stepson. The soil must indeed receive the grain, for the latter intrudes into it and draws the ens out of the soil into itself, but the soil gives not its good will to the grain. Hence the ens of the seed must seek its likeness in the feminine seed; but this likeness lies too deeply shut up in the constellation, and may hardly be reached; whence sterility arises and the loathing of Nature. And though it happen that the grain become rooted in the feminine tincture of the soil, yet the external constellation in the *spiritus mundi*, in the true order of the formed expressed word, is adverse to it; for it stands not in the figure of the kingdom of joy in the great clockwork of Nature, but at once carries its hostile rays out of the *turba magna* into the formation of the creature, whereby many a fruit perishes before it has life.

53. Now, what kind of working there can be here in the centre of Nature for the production of life, I present for Reason's consideration, as well as how Nature in its contrariety becomes hardened. What sort of soulish fire Nature awakens and generates in itself is carefully to be considered; in reference to which the Scripture says: God's wrath hardens them, lest they should obtain the true holy light. For of whatever property the soulish fire is, a corresponding light arises therefrom; and the life then lives in the soulish light. Therefore the Scripture says: With the holy thou art holy, and with the perverse thou art perverse (Ps. xviii. 26, 27); such as the people is, such a God do they have.

54. The light of nature, wherein the voice of God in Paradise incorporated itself again in the woman's seed (in which seed Christ was conceived and born), dwells now in the most inward ground, and should be revealed through the enkindled fire of the soul, and

enter into the creature and be operative. The soul should stand still to the Spirit of Christ, that he may work in it, and yet it (*i.e.* the soulish proprium in which the soul's fire burns and attains to life) has its being in the fierceness of strife.

55. Here we have the drawing in the Wrath and also the drawing of Christ through the light of nature, and in this connection it is rightly said: To whatever the scientia [drawing] of the unfathomable will from the ground of the Eternal Nature in the soulish proprium turns itself, and gives itself up in obedience as a servant, to that it is servant: either to the wrath of God in the fierceness of the Eternal Nature, or to the life of Christ in grace, as St. Paul says (Rom. vi. 16).

56. Reason says: The soul's essence cannot do this, it must suffer what God does with it; moreover, it is corrupt, and inclined towards wrath. Answer: Indeed it cannot in its selfhood; but Christ, when he assumed the soulish proprium, broke down the wrath and the *turba* of the false will by love, and introduced his love into the creaturely word, and gave it to the soul's ens for a helpmate. It depends merely on which property surpasses the other, whether the property of the light-fire or the property of the wrath-fire, that is, God's love or his anger. For the ens of the soul has as yet no understanding, but it possesses the ground of will from the unfathomable eternal will, for generation of the place of God, where the Father's unfathomable will begets the Son or power.

57. In this unfathomable will is the soul's ens, and God requires from it that it should generate divine power. And whereas after its fall it cannot do this by its own ability, he has incorporated into it the kingdom of his grace and revealed the same in the

name Jesus. Now if the soul's unfathomable will unite itself to the Spirit of Christ in the inward ground, then Christ lays hold of it and draws it up into himself. There the ability [to generate divine power] originally arises; for the essence of the wrath is shattered by the embodied voice of the divine love, and the Spirit of Christ presses through the light of nature in the soulish proprium and acts on this proprium, just as the light of nature works in the earth in the seed of a tree, and forces its way in, that the seed may take root.

58. And this penetration of the Spirit of Christ into the ens of the soul is the divine call, in reference to which the Scripture says: Many are called. For thus are they called in the soulish ground, before the soul has life.

59. Question: But why does Scripture say *many*, and not *all*? Answer: Christ stands related to all men, and calls them all; for the Scripture says: God willeth that all men should be saved (1 Tim. ii. 4). But they are not all susceptible of the call, for many an ens is rather devilish than human: such a one has the wrath overpowered and hardened.

60. There then the light shines in itself in the darkness, and the dark essence of the soul has not taken hold on it. In the presence of such a soulish essence the call passes by; for the soul's proprium is involved in darkness. The light certainly penetrates it, but finds no being of love therein, in which it might kindle itself. Therefore the ens of the creaturely soul remains out of God, dwelling in itself, and Christ likewise dwells in himself. And yet they are near one another, but a Principle separates them, like the great gulf in the case of the rich man and poor Lazarus; for they are to one another as life and death.

61. As regards these we are to understand that God makes known his wrath and hardens them, yet not in consequence of a foreign or even a divine will or purpose; but in consequence of the fact that he has brought his Word into nature and separation. Not that the holy will of God withdraws itself from them, so that they must necessarily remain hardened, as Reason erroneously supposes; for it is in them, and would fain have them and manifest itself in them, viz. in the image of God. But the fierce wrath in the centre of nature, where the will of the unground separates itself into darkness, has laid hold of them, and filled the shattered gates of the Divine love with the abominations of inherited sins.

62. The contrary constellation of disparity helps to bring this about, as husband and wife in their two wills sow only hatred and curses against each other, and nothing but death's will in one another. They put their vital tincture into a hostile will, and in the mingling of their seed come together in bestial lust. Neither will is faithful to the other. They mean only poison and death, curse each other at all hours, and live together like cats and dogs. Now as their life and constant will is, so is their soulish tincture in the seed, and therefore Christ says: A corrupt tree cannot bring forth good fruit; for in their tincture contained in the seed there is already hardening. What can God help it, that the parents plant a thistle?

63. But thou wilt say: What can the child help it? Answer: The child and the parents are one tree; the child is a branch in that tree. Listen, Reason: When does the sun change a branch on a sour crabtree, so that it becomes sweet? Shall then God for the sake of a thistle act contrary to his purpose as presented in his expressed word and will? The kingdom of

darkness also requires creatures; they are all of use to God: The wicked is to him a savour unto death, and the holy a savour unto life (2 Cor. ii. 15, 16).

64. Therefore the will to perdition originally arises in the root to the creature, and the will to the holy life has its origin from God in Christ; and these two are in one another as one thing, but are understood in two principles. While both are in action in the creatures, they are drawn by both. But if Christ can find no place for his rest, then the devil possesses the place where Christ should work.

65. And it is in this connection that Christ says: Few are chosen (Matt. xx. 16). Why? Many of them still have a spark of the good ens in themselves, wherein Christ works, and calls and warns them unceasingly. But the false ens is so great and strong, and draws a multitude of evil influences from without into itself and darkens the image of God, slays the good ens and will and crucifies the form of Christ, which Christ at his breaking through has sprinkled with his blood and redeemed by his death. This form does such a one crucify in himself by sin, and slay Christ in his member.

66. And when the master of the house comes in to see his guests at the marriage of the Lamb, he sees that this redeemed form of Christ, which was invited to the marriage, has not on a wedding-garment. Then he bids his minister of wrath, as regards this guest in Christ's place, to bind him hand and foot in the ground of life and cast him into outer darkness; there shall be wailing and gnashing of teeth, as Christ says in the Gospel (Matt. xxii. 12, 13).

67. This evil wedding guest, though he boast of Christ's name, is not elected to the eternal supper of the Lamb. They only are elected whose souls put on

Christ, and crucify and continually mortify the will of sin in the flesh.

68. Therefore Christ says: Few are chosen. For those only are chosen to be the children of God in Christ, who obey the voice of Christ in them, who in their good spark listen unto the voice of the bridegroom when Christ says within them: Turn and repent, come into the vineyard of Christ! This they accordingly receive, hear and do, and wait not till God falls upon the false will and breaks it by force, and produces salvation, Reason erroneously adducing passages respecting Election, opposed to any parables contained in the words of Christ.

69. Christ said to his disciples, when he offered them his body for food: Take, eat; take and drink, this is my flesh and blood (Matt. xxvi. 26-28). He bade the soul reach out and take it. So likewise in the inward ground, when he offers himself to the soul in the light of life, he says: Come unto me, and I will refresh thee; receive me, open wide thy desire towards me and unclose the door of thy will, and then I will make my abode with thee.

70. He stands before the door of the soul's ground and knocks; and the soul which opens to him, to that soul will he come in, and will sup with it. His calling and knocking is his drawing and willing; but the soul has also an eternal power of willing and an unfathomable will.

71. In sum, the soul is the eternal Father's natural fire-will, and Christ is the eternal Light's love-will; these are in one another. Christ desires to take form in the soulish creature, and in like manner the fire-will desires in its selfhood to fashion itself. Whichever conquers, on it the formation depends. This conflict of formative power commences at once in the

seed, along with the forming of creatures, by the disparity between the seed and the soil, many a twig through the contrariety and hostility of the tinctures immediately becoming a wild thistle. And yet the light of nature (in which Christ dwells in the inward ground) withdraws not itself from such a thistle child until the will of the soul itself in its natural light darkens itself with the poison of wrath.

72. As strife in the root of a tree is kindled in a contrary soil, whereby the twig that springs from the root perishes before it grows up ; and as the sun with his light and power comes to the aid of the twig as soon as it sprouts up out of the root : so likewise Christ comes to the aid of the soul as soon as it comes out of the womb, and also assists it from without on account of evil accessions, and has instituted in his covenant a bath of regeneration by baptism, in which he shines on little children with the eternal Sun, and thus acts on them and pours himself into them in his covenant, in order to see if the soul's essence be capable of the offered grace.

73. Afterwards, when the soul attains to reason, he draws and calls it by his revealed word out of the mouth of the children of God, and offers himself to the soul during the time of the whole external life, and is sounding every day and hour with his word and power in the soul, to see if it will stand still from the animal imagination, that he may generate it anew.

74. As the power of the sun in the essence of the wood in a tree is drawn up along with it and tampers the property of the strifeful nature, so also Christ with his power from the inward ground turns unceasingly to the soul and tempers the forms of life, that they should not separate into contrary will and

enmity and go out from equality into false desire, by which false desire the proprium of the soul introduces the source of poison into itself.

75. And as the stem with its branches becomes humpy and crooked by the inward strife of nature and by the external influences of the constellations, so also the soul by the internal opposition which is found in the dissimilarity of the natures of father and mother, and by the outward influences of the world's wickedness, brings itself into a misshapen figure in the sight of God.

76. Then the wedding-garment of baptism is changed into a bestial distortion, and the Election passes over it, so long as the soul has in itself this deformed monstrous image.

77. This monstrous shape prevents the ens or being of Christ from producing fruit to the praise of God. For the devil continually sows his desire in this frightful distortion, so that false young twigs grow from it with a false apostate will, which bring themselves into pride in the devil's will and break out from humility, like young twigs sprouting forth from a tree break out from the co-ordination, and will be distinct separate trees. And when they have broken out, they are in the constellation of the world; and then the constellation of the firmament sifts them by means of subtle individuals, and leads them from one curiosity into another. At one time pride strikes in, at another time covetousness, at other times envy, anger, lying and deceiving, and all that rules in the world. There the young proud twig strives to climb up in arts, and burns itself in everything. Now if the divine Sun shines into it and seeks to come to the aid of the apostate twig, and the fiery life be sensible of this, then the latter soars aloft like Lucifer,

ascribes to itself wisdom and understanding, and despises what is simple. From thence come the reason-wise people, who are full of pride and self-honouring desire, and only burn themselves by the light which shines in them of grace, and use it for the lust of the flesh. Christ has therefore to be a cover for their wickedness.

78. All these are false twigs, and the Election of harvest-time passes over these. For they have been called in Christ's spirit, he has given himself to them, worked with them and illuminated their reason, yet they have not been born of Christ's spirit, but in the pleasure of the world. They have trodden Christ under foot and never ministered unto him. Christ has been to them hungry, thirsty, sick, in prison, naked and wretched, and they have never ministered unto him. His name indeed has moved in their mouth, but their soul has always turned to its own desire of the world and the devil. They have left Christ unnoticed, and held the light to their own wickedness.

79. They have gone out from the stem of harmony and equality, and have not grown up in the true Sun which is Christ and been born of God, but in their own nature which is self-will; therefore their fruits are mere futilities. And though they become great people in the world, and learn many arts and languages, yet all this has sprung from the vanity of Nature, and all their works are in the sight of God as a stained and polluted cloth.

80. But the soul which has its origin in a good soil, by reason that the parents place their will in God and walk in the true bond of love as in the true constellation, and put their hope in God, since Christ in them works, lives and has being: from these flow rivers of

living water, as Christ says. And though the Adamic corruption is in their flesh, and moreover an evil constellation often falls into the flesh as into the source of sin, yet Christ remains in the inward ground of the soul in them.

81. Now the soul is born from the soul, and the body from the seed of the body. And though the external seed be earthly and evil, and in such a constellation be poisoned, yet Christ possesses the soulish ground in the inward centre; there is and remains in the ens of the soul the Ens of Christ, and in it the soul is conceived and born.

82. And in this connection Christ says: He that is born of God, heareth God's word (John viii. 47). But to the proud Pharisees he said: Ye therefore hear not, because ye are not of God. That is, though they carried his word and law in their mouth, yet their soul was not born in the Divine ens; though they had the light of nature, yet it shone from an alien fire: there Christ did indeed shine through, but they were not capable of receiving him, for their ground was false.

83. And a good seed is also sometimes sown in an evil soil, yet the ground of the seed still remains good. But when a false grain is sown in an evil soil, there grows from it what is like to its own nature. And as a good grain must frequently be set in an evil soil, and even bears fruit unless outward influences destroy it, so likewise a seed of faith is often sown from one tincture, either of the husband or wife, and the other sows his or her poison in it, whereby the outer man becomes unruly and inclined to what is bad. But the inward ground still remains good: it does indeed quickly do something that is evil, but this it speedily repents of, and it enters into abstinence therefrom.

84. Moreover, many a one is thus as to one part poisoned by the fountain of sin, in such a way that he has in himself an evil inclination to stealing, rapine and murder; further, to lust, calumny etc. But the other part in the Ens of Christ is perpetually drawing him away from it. And though, owing to the devil's assaults, he in weakness transgress, yet the Divine ens comes to his aid if he continue not in sin or death: as happened to the thief on the cross, Mary Magdalene and other great sinners.

85. For there is no man who has not in the flesh a source or fountain of sin springing from the itch of his own brutish animal flesh. And as a tree has to grow up in conflict and contrary will, seeing that what is hostile falls upon it on all sides,—now heat, now cold, now wind oppresses it, so that it is ready to break, and at another time a poison from the stars falls upon it,—yet it grows up nevertheless in the power of the sun and in its own inward light-ens of nature, and bears good fruit which has not the taste of the earth; on the contrary, the noble tincture has thus brought itself into a good savoury *corpus*. So likewise is it with man.

86. The Divine ens, which is spiritual, cannot become manifest save through the strife of nature. It sows itself in the soulish ground of the eternal nature, and gives itself to the struggle of the separation of fire, whereby it receives its light, and brings itself out of the fire into the power and properties of the love-desire. In the fire of the soul it receives properties and will; for in God it is one only, and merely a single will. This will is the eternal good, but thus it is not manifest to itself. But in the fiery separation of the soul it is manifested to itself, so that the power issues in many powers of working

virtues into a shape and form : just as a tree through strife becomes manifest with its branches and fruit, so that we see what was contained in the mystery of the seed of the tree.

87. And therefore the divine power unites itself to the soul of man, that it may grow up therein and may manifest its virtue in the fiery separation, where evil and good work with each other. Thus the Spirit of God in Christ exsurges in the good, and works so as to produce fruit, *i.e.* divine form. Now this cannot take place unless the soul's fire eat of the Divine ens in itself, by which fiery appropriation a true power goes forth in the light of nature.

88. The fire of the soul must have the proper fuel, if it is to give a good and powerful light ; for through the soul's fire God's Spirit in its power becomes separable and manifest in the nature of the soul. In the same way as light becomes manifest through fire, and air through fire and light, and from the air a subtle water proceeds, which becomes essential after its issuing forth, and from which the light draws power again into itself for its food. Hence Christ said (John vi. 53) : He that eateth not the flesh of the Son of man, and drinketh not his blood, hath no life in himself.

89. As a tree cannot grow nor bear fruit without the light of nature, which the sun, which penetrates thereinto, vivificates ; and as the light of nature, as well as the sun's power, could not become manifest and operative in the tree without the fiery enkindling, viz. the fiery ground of nature which is the soul of the tree :

90. So in like manner Christ cannot become manifest in man (though He is in him, and draws him and calls him, and presses into the soul), unless the soul

eat of the Divine ens, taking it into its fiery property. This ens enters with difficulty into the fire of pride, seeing that the latter would have to feed upon the water-fountain of the love-life and gentleness. It would rather feed upon sulphur and mercury, *i.e.* its own likeness. But if it do feed upon the water-fountain, then the spirit of love and humility, viz. the Divine ens, becomes fiery, and lays hold of the fire-root consisting of the first three forms (salt, sulphur and mercury), and transmutes them into itself. As a tincture falls upon a glowing iron and changes the iron into gold, so also here the soulish centre from the fire-nature of the Father is changed into a love-fire, and in this love-fire Christ becomes manifest and is born in the soul. And then from the soul's fire the right Divine air-spirit proceeds from fire and light, and brings its spiritual water out of itself, out of the light. This water becomes essential; and the power of the light eats thereof, and in the love-desire brings itself into a holy being, that is, into a spiritual corporeality in which the Holy Trinity dwells. And this being is the true temple of the Holy Ghost, yea God in his own revelation.

91. Therefore Christ said he would give us the water of eternal life, which would spring up in us into a fountain of everlasting life (John iv. 14). Now that is the case when the soul receives his Word, which is himself. Thus, he pours his essential power, which he has made manifest in our humanity, into the soul: this is its tincture, which changes its hostility of the fiery property into a fire of love. For there in the dead soulish property Christ rises from the dead, and the soul becomes a member of Christ's body and draws Christ to itself; indeed according to the property of love it is wholly implanted into Christ.

Hence Christ says: He that eateth my flesh, and drinketh my blood, dwelleth in me, and I in him (John vi. 56). Further: We will come unto you, and make our abode in you (John xiv. 23); that is, the whole God is manifested in this new birth in Christ in the soul, and produces good divine fruit.

92. As the power of the sun is manifested in a tree, and kindles the light in the ens of the sulphur-spirit, in the mercury, as in the resinous property in which the tree grows and bears fruit; so likewise God is manifested in his formed expressed word (viz. in man, into whom he has introduced his highest love-tincture in the name Jesus), and tinctures the fiery soul or the spiritual sulphur and mercury, in which the light of the Eternal Nature becomes manifest and shining, and in which Christ in his formed word is born, and grows into a glorious divine tree, and thus into the image of God, and bears an abundance of good divine fruit.

93. Then such a man speaks from God's Word. These are then divine fruits, in which God's formed word or the creaturely soul speaks forth the fountain of the divine Speaking from itself, and generates God's word in its speaking forth; just as the one God speaks forth and ever begets his Word from himself; and yet the Speaking remains in him, and contains the speaking and what is spoken forth.

94. And though the corrupt nature in the flesh of the earthly animal property clings to such a man and assails him, fighting against the soul, that harms him not. For the soul has now in Christ overcome the wrathful, corrupt, fiery property, and Christ in the soul continually bruises the head of the serpent's poison in the earthly flesh, works through the flesh and draws himself up in the flesh into a new body.

As precious gold lies and grows in a coarse stone, to which the coarseness must contribute although it is not like the gold; so also the earthly body must co-operate in bringing forth Christ in itself, although it is not Christ, nor ever will become so; nor is it of any use for the kingdom of God, yet it must be an instrument. Though it has a different, false will and desire, and is a stronghold of the devil, yet God uses it as his instrument. Concerning this Christ says that it is his yoke; that is, our earthly body, which he helps us to bear, is his yoke in us. This yoke the holy soul must take upon itself in patience, and suffer to pass upon it every misfortune from without, as well as the assaults of the flesh from the devil and the world's wickedness, and bow down under the crucial engendure of Christ, submit to his yoke, and take patience; and thus amid tribulation grow up with the noble Pearl-Tree of Christ under all evil ways and doings, and in accordance with the true and real Plant produce and bring forth nothing but good, holy, heavenly fruits. These fruits are not of this world, that is, not of the four elements according to the *spiritus mundi* from without, but as Paul says: Our walk and conversation is in heaven (Phil. iii. 20). And Christ says: I have chosen you out of the world, that ye may be where I am; and therefore the world hateth you, because it knoweth neither me, nor you, nor my Father. But be of good cheer: In me ye have peace, though in the world ye have tribulation (John xvi. 33). That is to say, in me, in the inward ground of the new birth, ye have peace with God; whereas in the outer flesh, in the world, ye have tribulation. But I will come again, and receive you unto myself where I am (John xiv. 3). That is, He will come again to man, who was formed out of the *limus* of the earth, and will receive him again into Himself, as into the new spiritual man, and retain him eternally. But he must first enter into the putrefaction of the earth, and lay off the serpent's ens together with the imprinted beast and all effected falsity: then He will come again to man, and awaken the Adamic body from death and take it to himself; and He will wipe away all tears from man's eyes, and turn them into joy.

95. Such, my dear Reader, is the true ground of the new birth, and in no other manner at all, as Reason supposes, which holds (1) that we are children of grace adopted from without, and (2) that we are freed from sin by a divine purpose. No; it is necessary to be born anew of the water aforesaid and the Holy Spirit.

96. The soul must in the drawing of Christ turn round from its own will, and bring its desiring will in relation to Christ's desire (which presses powerfully towards the soul's desiring will and penetrates into it by desire), and must open wide the fiery jaws or the spiritual sulphur-worm in the mercury of the spirit-life, and then the spirit of Christ penetrates into the essence of the soul. This is called faith and acceptance. It is not merely a matter of knowledge, taking comfort, soothing, flattering, and wrapping Christ's mantle round one outwardly, speaking continually about grace, and wishing to be children of grace in the malice and wickedness of the devil; but one must in the spirit of Christ become like a child at its mother's breast, that desires only to suck the breasts of its mother, nor desires anything more, for in the being of Christ alone grows the right new man.

97. But that Reason says: We shall only in the resurrection be new born and put on Christ in the flesh

—this is Babel, and implies no understanding of the words of Christ.

98. The body that comes from the earth shall put on Christ essentially only in the resurrection, but the soul must in this present time put on Christ in his heavenly flesh, and in Christ must the new body be given to the soul. Not as coming from the blood of man nor from the flesh, but as proceeding from the Word and the Divine ens into the deadened nature of the Divine ens, which lost its vitality in Adam and became insensible and inert as to God's working. It is in this body that Christ must be new born and become a God-man, and man become a Man-god.

99. Therefore, brethren, understand, on the one hand, that Christ is the divine purpose and the divine will in the operation of grace. Whoever is born of him and putteth him on, is chosen in Christ and is a child of grace. And, on the other hand, the purpose of God is to be found in the fiery will of the soul which arises from the centre of the eternal Nature, where light and darkness separate. There one part, as the coarse phantastic sulphur, enters into the centre of darkness; but the subtle pure part enters into the light. Now, into whatever the attraction of the unfathomable will to Nature severizes itself, in that does the will become a creature, either in the light or in the darkness.

100. The purpose of God proceeds entirely from the soulish ground. For the inner ground of the soul is the divine nature to the ever-speaking Word, and is neither evil nor good. But in the separation of fire, viz. in the enkindled life of the soul, this will separates either into God's wrath or into God's love-fire. And this takes place no otherwise than through the proprium which the soulish essence in itself is.

It is itself its own ground for evil or good; for it is the centrum of God, in which God's love and wrath lie undeveloped in a ground.

101. This then is the purpose of God, that he wills to reveal himself through the expressed formed word, of which the soul in the speaking of the separation is a being. There the coarseness becomes hardened in the inherited abominations as well as in the actual compacted horrors.

102. For there is no other will of God in the existence of this world, save that which is revealed out of the eternal ground in fire, light and darkness. The soul is in itself elected to be a child of grace when it is born of Christ from the Divine ens. And this is the single purpose of the divine grace, by which purpose God's grace in the soul is revealed. And the soul is likewise in itself elected to damnation by reason of its own nature, which is a false entity wherein no light can be born.

103. God's purpose which effects hardening is contained in the soul's own nature, and is the unfathomable will to Nature that manifests itself in every being, according as the being's proprium is. And thus we may conceive that with its immassing of the coarseness it has formed and separated itself into the dark world or hell. For the will which is in hell, and the will which is manifest in heaven, are in the inward ground out of the manifestation but one thing; for separation or distinction first appears in enunciation of the word. Heaven and hell are in one another as day and night, and hell is a ground of heaven; for God's wrath-fire is a ground of his love or the light.

104. Therefore, brethren, become seeing; never wrangle about the will of God. We ourselves are God's will to evil and good; the one that is mani-

fested in us, whether as heaven or hell, that we are. Our own hell in us hardens us, as it is, in fact, the same property ; and our own heaven in us, if it can be manifested, makes us blessed. All is mere futility that men have hitherto wrangled about for so long a time. *Christ has been found* : For this be unto Him eternal praise and thanks, and might, and honour, and riches, together with all power in heaven and on earth (Matt. xxviii. 18).

CHAPTER IX

Of opposition between passages in the Scriptures, or of the right understanding of Scripture.

1. Hath not the potter power, out of one lump of clay to make one vessel unto honour, and another unto dishonour? (Rom. ix. 21). Answer: The lump of clay indicates the great Mystery, in which the eternal God has expressed himself by the Word. There from one being two beings proceed: one in the fiery separation into darkness according to the grossness of the attraction, and the other in the light according to the Divine proprium. These two come from one ground; and likewise the false soul and the holy soul both come from Adam's soul, but one separates itself into light and the other into darkness.

2. This potter makes from every separation such a vessel as the separated matter is fit for. He takes not holy matter and makes therefrom a devil; but as the soul's ens is, so is also the will to make. God sits not over the will and forms it, as the potter does the clay; but he generates it through its own property. Now, wherefore should the godless man say: Why dost thou make me in such a way that I am wicked?

3. God produces a life from all things: from the evil ens he produces an evil life and from the good ens a good life, as it is written: With the holy thou art holy, and with the perverse thou art perverse (Ps. xviii. 26). No one, therefore, can accuse God of

having produced an evil life in him. Had the clay been better, he would have made for himself from it a vessel unto honour; but if it has to serve him unto dishonour, he makes for himself from it a vessel of his wrath.

4. For God's Word is the life, being and beginning of all things. But as the ferventness of wrath is also contained in it, this ferventness likewise brings itself into a life; for, who shall check it? Christ, however, has come from the eternal Word to be the auxiliary of man, and says: As truly as I live, I have no pleasure in the death of the wicked; but that the wicked turn from his way and live (Ezek. xxxiii. 11). But what can Christ do, if the soul's ens be evil and incompetent, and incapable of the Divine ens? God's wrath makes no will out of or beyond the creature. Moreover Christ says: All power is given unto me in heaven and on earth (Matt. xxviii. 18). He also says (John iii. 17): God sent not his Son into the world to condemn the world, but that the world through him might be saved. Now, if he hath all power, then there exists no other maker unto dishonour but that which arises in the ground of the soul from its own centre. This is, in fact, the angry God himself, who makes to himself from his essence an image which is his like. Therefore Paul says: Has not the potter power to make what he pleases? This potter is God in the speaking of his separability, whereby he manifests his glory.

5. Since Christ alone has all power, no other will to make besides him can be. Therefore the godless man is not entitled to say: God makes me wicked. But it is the God within him, in whose ground he has his subsistence, makes him whatever he potentially is able to become. The ground of his being, whereof

he himself is, forms the beginning. As soon as the life is born from this ground, the maker is in the life, that is to say, the angry God: this latter is then revealed to him, this God makes him.

6. As Christ introduces his will into his children, who are born in him, so does God's wrath do with its children, who are born from it. For in the soul God is manifested either in love or wrath. Nature is the soul, and the acting life is God himself, that is, according to the word of separation.

7. For the pure God apart from nature is not a maker of wills, for he is One only. But in his word, since it brings itself into separation, wills to evil and good take their rise. From every separation of the separated one there springs a will in accordance with that quality. Into whatever quality the unfathomable will has brought itself in the separation, a corresponding will arises.

8. Now, Adam has brought himself in himself out of the temperament into separation. Hence his twigs live in this separation, and therefrom comes a will: each of them obtains a will according to its nature. But the purpose rules, that is to say, the fiery word of nature and the love-word of grace. These two are the makers of the vessel unto honour and dishonour; and both of these are in man.

The highest gate. Of Cain and Abel; also of Ishmael and Isaac, and of Esau and Jacob.

9. The kingdom of nature is the ground of the speaking Word; for if there is to be a creature, there must first be nature. Now, the Word of God is the ground of all beings, the beginning of qualities. The Word is God's Speaking, and remains in God; but

the speaking forth or the outgoing of the Word (as the unfathomable will through the speaking forth passes into separation) gives nature and quality, and likewise a particular will. For the unfathomable will separates itself from the Speaking, and comprehends itself in separation in a self-speaking, as in an original will. From the one, eternal, entire will have qualities arisen, and from these the creation and the creatures.

10. Now this is the first purpose of God, in which the Word of power has established itself out of itself on its own account, that is, has brought the unfathomable incomprehensible Word of life into a comprehensibility wherein it can live. This comprehensibility is nature, and the incomprehensible life in nature is God's ever-speaking Word, which remains in God and is God himself.

11. The second purpose of the Word is this, namely, that the comprehensibility, or the self-comprehended will, shall suffer the incomprehensible one will of God to dwell in it; for the one life has put itself into comprehensibility, and would become manifest in the comprehensibility. The comprehensibility has to comprehend in itself the incomprehensible life, and make it comprehensible; of which we have an example in fire and light. For fire is nature or the comprehensible life, and it comprehends in itself the non-natural life or the light. For in the light the virtues of the non-natural life are manifested through fire. The light accordingly dwells in the fire, and the non-natural life in the light is brought into power, viz. into tincture, air and water.

12. Understand, then, that the holy life of God would not be manifest without nature, save in an eternal stillness, in which nothing were capable of existing without the speaking forth and the compre-

hensibility. If God's holiness and love is to be made manifest, there must be something to which love and grace are necessary, and which is not on a level with the love and grace. Now this something is the will of nature, which in its life rests upon contrariety: it is this to which love and grace are necessary, in order that its pain may be transformed into joy.

13. And in this transformation the holy incomprehensible life in the Word is manifested as a co-operating life in nature. For pain occasions the will of the unground (which in the speaking forth has separated itself into selfhood) to unite itself again to the holy unfathomable life, that it may be meekened. And in the meekening process it is manifested in the life of God; for it comprehends this life in itself, in its desire, and thus too the holy life of the unground is manifested in it.

14. And in this manifestation of the holy life in nature, the holy life is called *power*, and the comprehension of nature which comprehends it, is called *tincture*; for it is the power of the lustre of fire and light. And if this were not, then no fire would shine, for the particular will of nature does not shine. For the comprehension is a shutting-in, and is the ground of darkness.

15. In Adam the kingdom of grace or the divine life was manifest, for he stood in the temperament of the qualities. But he knew not that God was manifest in him, for he had known no evil. In like manner the particular will knew not what good was; for how should there be joy, if there be no knowledge of pain or sorrow?

16. That is joy, when nature or the particular will is released from its pain; and hence it rejoices in the good when this happens to it. But if it had it in its

own power to take this good, there would be no joy; for the particular will would live as it listed, and would have no hope if it were able itself to do everything. But if it cannot itself do this, then it rejoices in that which it experiences by grace, or in that which it hopes it shall experience. All joy rests upon the hope of grace, which it always experiences without ability of its own to do or to take.

17. And nature accordingly is in pain and conflict, that the grace-kingdom of love may be manifested in it, and that it may become a kingdom of joy through that which it continually experiences. For the life of God is manifested in it, and it thus obtains a holy tincture which tinctures the pain, and changes it into joy, as into an image of the holy life.

18. When Adam stood in the sphere of equality, he was not cognisant of it. He knew not what evil in nature was, nor did he know anything of the kingdom of grace, for both he and it were in the temperament. But when the free will introduced itself into the separation of the Word of power, the painfulness of the kingdom of nature became manifest in him. It was now necessary that the power of grace should also become moving in him, and this the kingdom of nature could not do, there being no possibility thereof in its particular will; for the particular will is comprehensible, and the kingdom of grace is incomprehensible. Hence the soul or the comprehensible will could not take anything into it of the incomprehensible life; but God would thus have remained hidden in this image, and would not himself have been manifest.

19. Therefore the incomprehensible holy life in its love spoke itself into the soulish comprehensible life, in order that it might have something that it would

have cause to love; and took form in the properties of the soulish nature so as to become a helper.

20. And this was the serpent-bruiser, who was to bruise the head of the serpent's introduced poison and of the will of painfulness by the love-desire. The same comprehension [of love] came to the aid of the kingdom of nature and put itself into figure; and nature now being hungry for grace suffered itself to be comprehended in an image of the natural soul and body.

21. And of this image Abel was a figure in the image of Christ, until in the fulness of time the same comprehension of the love put itself in motion once again, and comprehended itself in an ens of a being in human quality, so that the Godhead itself was a being in human being. This being indeed existed previously in Adam, but he was not cognisant of it. And when with the particular will of nature he brought himself out from this being, the soul became blind as to God, and lived only in itself.

22. Now if we will but see, and do not make ourselves blind, we have before us Cain and Abel. Cain must be the first, as he is Adam's image after the fall; for Adam had been created for the kingdom of God.

23. Cain represents the kingdom of nature, and is a true image of what Adam was in himself apart from grace. Abel is the image of what Adam was in the re-inspoken grace; and this denotes Christ, who was to give himself to a human nature and inspeak grace into the corrupt nature in Cain's image.

24. Accordingly Christ said that all power had been given to him by his Father, so that he had power to inspeak grace into the will of nature.

25. Now God has exhibited the figure in Cain and Abel, also in Ishmael and Isaac, and in Esau and Jacob, signifying that He would send Christ into the

flesh, whom here He had inspoken in power into Adam and Eve in the voice of his Word as a fountain of life.

26. It was His will to fill this power with human essence, which was accomplished in Christ. And to this man Christ, in the same power and voice, power had been given to cancel sin by his own voice, and to resuscitate nature in him to a divine life.

27. But if this was to be, it was necessary for grace in the power of love to enter into the contrariety of the painful nature, and give itself up to nature's particular will, that it might comprehend nature. And in this comprehension of the high love, nature was transmuted into the divine love-will, and died to the comprehended particular will; not as a dying in the form of death, but as a losing of the particular will, which took place in Christ in our humanity.

28. Now when the particular will loses its right, the inspoken Word becomes essential; and this cannot be until the self-will of the attraction (scientia) of the unground gives up its right. Otherwise, it draws the Divine ens into selfhood, and transforms it into its own malignity; as Lucifer and his following did, who were angels and had in them the Divine ens, wherein their light was a lustre, but the self-will springing from the attraction of the unground destroyed it.

29. Who shall now with reason say that the Divine voice of grace (which inspoke itself into the woman's seed) did not exist in Cain? What book of Scripture says so? Answer: *Not one.* For when God had not respect unto his offering, and Cain grew furious against Abel, as against Christ's figure which had separated itself from him out of the ens of Adam, the encorporate voice of grace said in him: Rule over sin, and let it not prevail! It was not God's purpose in

the wrath that could say this in him, but only the encorporate voice of grace.

30. But how was it that Cain did not rule over sin? Could he not? Answer: No, he could not. Why could he not? Had God hardened him, so that he could not? Answer: God had not hardened him, but the Adamic self-will springing from the attraction of the unground had in Adam brought itself by imagination or desire into animal vanity, that is, into self-formation, into evil and good; and thereinto the devil had introduced the serpent's poisonous ens, which Eve had received.

31. This was the hardening in the self-will. For the purpose of God according to the fierce wrathful nature had compacted itself therein in Cain and made him deaf, so that he could not hear the encorporate voice of grace. Though he heard it outwardly, yet he heard it not in the ground of the soul; else the grace had moved itself, so that the soul would have prevailed against the serpent's poison. He supposed that he would and should rule over sin outwardly, and therefore he rose up against Abel.

32. Just as Reason at the present day supposes that it attains filiation or sonship in an adopted manner from without, namely, by outward works, or by a covering of grace under Christ's sufferings and death as an external satisfaction for sin, which a man should attach himself to and comfort himself with outwardly, though his self-will in the serpent's poison harbours there. But this is the same as with Cain, unless the inward ground be stirred, so that in the soul grace becomes moving, that is to say, the encorporate voice of God in the woman's seed, which is Christ in us, so that the soul hears God's voice in motion in its essence.

33. Reason here says: If the voice of grace in Cain lay under the covering of sin, did not God's in-speaking move it when He said: Rule over sin, and let it not prevail? For if He had moved the inward ground of the soul in the encorporate voice of grace, he would have heard Him inwardly in the soul, which is lord of the body, and thus the outward ground might not have elevated itself.

34. Answer: This voice which came unto Cain, saying: Rule over sin, and let it not prevail, was God's righteousness in his purpose, that is, in the speaking Word, the Divine voice willing that the self-will of the attraction of the unfathomable eternal will should bring itself into a Divine generation of the good. This Word requires God's righteousness, namely, that He wills not evil, and that is the true Ground of the law in the Old Testament. But it attains not grace, for it requires the power of the individual himself. Nor does it give itself up to grace, for God needs no grace. Grace must give itself up to it, *i.e.* to God's righteousness. And thus grace, which was revealed in Christ, or in the encorporate voice of grace, must give itself up to God's righteousness, viz. to the eternal one purpose for the manifestation of the glory of God in his speaking Word, that is, to the separability of the Father; and must introduce the will of man (which had turned aside from the purpose of righteousness) in it and with it into the wrath-fire of God, and bring the Father as the purpose of God into his righteousness as into the origin of the soul, and drown the soul's will (which had turned aside from righteousness) in his blood which sprang from the divine holy Ens of love, that the soul might be manifested in grace, in that blood of love, in the purpose of the righteousness.

35. Christ therefore had to suffer and die in the righteousness of God, in our humanity, in order that grace might be manifested in the righteousness. For in Cain grace was not manifest in the righteousness of God, as it had not yet taken a soul to itself.

36. Now the righteousness of God was in the soul, for the soul was God's image. Therefore God required his righteousness from the soul, namely, that it should rule over evil. As God ruled over the apostate will of the devils, and thrust them out from the good order of righteousness when they became apostate, so Cain was to thrust out from himself the source of sin. But it was not possible for him to do so, for sin possessed him, that is, was in possession of the free will; the human capability was lost. And it lay now in the second purpose of the righteousness as uttered in grace that the soul should give up its will to this grace and stand still to this inner Word; for in the speaking of the righteousness of God there was at present in the soul mere necessity and contra-will. For the righteousness required the temperament, which is to stand still to God as his instrument, whereby he would manifest his voice. But the instrument was broken, and gone out from the Divine harmony. Therefore it was now no longer a matter of Cain's willing or running, but of grace or mercy.

37. St. Paul says: He hath mercy on whom he will, and whom he will he hardeneth. Now we have here the whole cause of Reason's error. Reason understands not the willing of grace, how such willing can be effected. For that which wills grace is but one will with the grace.

38. For grace has no willing in the devil or in hell, but only in that which is born of God. The willing of grace is not to be found in the willing of flesh and

blood, nor in the willing of man's own seed, but only in the Divine ground. Not into Cain's introduced serpent's seed did grace will to inspeak itself, but willed rather to bruise its head. Not the head of the poor imprisoned soul in Cain did He will to bruise——for it also had sprung from Adam's soul—but the serpent's seed in the soul of Cain. But the serpent's poison had so hardened the soul in itself and taken possession of it, that the soul took a rash resolve and gave itself up to the wrath of the righteousness, so that the wrath received it and used it as an instrument, whereby the righteousness in the grace slew the man Christ in his type in Abel.

39. For by human works sin had come into the soul, and so also it had to be slain by human works in the grace in God's righteousness. As indeed took place in the humanity of Christ by the man-slaying of the Pharisees, who had and exercised the law of God in the righteousness.

40. And therefore Abel as the type of Christ, and also Christ himself, had to die by the works of man to their own Adamic will in God's righteousness; and those whom God's righteousness had laid hold of in the wrath of his purpose had to be an instrument in bringing it about, that the grace of God might be manifested in the righteousness of the purpose, in the wrath. For it is written (Matt. xviii. 7): Woe unto the world because of offences! yet it must needs be that offences come, in order that righteousness and truth may be manifested in the midst of untruth.

41. For otherwise grace would not be manifest, if falsehood were not an antithesis to truth. As the free will could not have been manifested in grace if the righteousness had not slain it, which, after it lost the self-elected will, grace made alive in itself, that it

might no longer live and will to itself, but live and will to grace, as was manifested in Christ.

42. Therefore we are all but one in Christ in the life of grace, for we have lost the natural life of the righteousness of God in his eternal purpose, and obtained the sonship in grace.

43. The Scripture says: God willeth that all men should be saved (1 Tim. ii. 4). That is, grace willeth this, for it can will nothing else but mercy; it is nothing else in its own nature.

44. But the natural righteousness in the purpose of God requires the soul to enter into the obedience of the divine order without grace; for it was not created unto grace, but unto the divine order. Now if the righteousness find not the soul therein, it takes it into its proprium of the separation of the word, of which the soul is a being. And if it be a false being, it takes on the same likeness as is to be understood in the case of Cain. The differing Adamic will has introduced itself into a creaturely selfhood, and the introduction of this soul's being into the serpent's poison gives a thistle, which is not capable of grace. For though the inspoken voice of grace lies therein in the inward ground, that being nevertheless grows into a thistle, crucifies Christ in itself, and is guilty of his death.

45. As the sun's power must necessarily become prickly in a thistle, though at the same time the sun withdraws from the thistle the good will or the holy life which he would reveal in a good plant, and lets the thistle make of its being what it will: so likewise is it with the godless thistle part of mankind, as the Scripture says (Prov. xx. 20): Their light shall be put out in the midst of darkness, that is, the holy life in the encorporate voice of grace.

46. But thou sayest: Why is it so? For, if he revealed the holy life in them, the soul would be holy. Answer: *No.* We have an example in the devil, in whom the holy life was manifested, but the ground of his will was a thistle. And so in like manner a thistle-child makes use of grace only for pride, as Lucifer did. For God knows the will (scientia) of the unground, how it has formed itself into a ground and manifested itself, whether it be a root out of the dark fire-life or a root out of the shining fire-life.

47. Thou askest: Is Cain a root out of the dark fire, and therefore cannot attain grace? Answer: No, that is not so; for he sprang from Adam's soul. But the dark fire from the wrath, or the property of the dark world, had forced itself into the true soul—not from without, but from the centre had it lifted up itself—and that at the fall of Adam; and from this root did Cain come. Therefore he was compelled to be a servant of the righteousness of God, wherewith the righteousness slew the free will in Abel in the grace.

48. In Adam's seed the properties separated themselves. The true soul's will, which in the beginning of God's image in the purpose of God was manifest in the one soul (and which was a free will, but was poisoned, so that it became blind as to God), separated itself in the death of its selfhood. It entered into dying, and God spoke his voice into the dying, that the first will might be resuscitated in grace. And therefrom came Abel.

49. The other will (new born in sin), which was not in the beginning, but had arisen at the fall, separated itself into the natural life. This was Cain. This will was therefore a thistle-child which God had not created, but it had arisen from the centre of the soul.

50. After the one soul went out from the temperament, so that the dark ground manifested itself in Cain, the darkness came to a willing in the soul, which was not in the beginning. In respect of the being of the soul, both of them, Abel and Cain, proceeded from one essence; but in respect of will they separated. We are not to imagine that Abel was born pure and without sin, for sin adhered to him by the will of death; but the voice of the righteousness in the grace slew him, that it might make him alive in it. In the flesh was manifested the will of sin, and therefore the righteousness of God slew him by Cain; for according to the flesh he too was subject to the law of sin. But the voice of grace within him had slain the will of the soul, and made it alive in itself; therefore he was a type of Christ and was Christ's image.

51. Therefore the true ground of Cain's hardening is not that God of His divine will hardened him, for this God cannot do, seeing that He is good only. But the newly arisen will from the centre of the soul hardened itself in its own desire. For when the desire in the wrath of nature entered into its likeness, it found in the purpose of nature, viz. in the separation of darkness and light, the said likeness. This likeness occupied the will and possessed it, that is, the newly arisen false will, which was a murderer and a servant of the wrath of God. But the true soul that was formed and created from Adam's essence, wherein lay the encorporate voice of God, was not yet judged, or destined to damnation. Such judgment is not in the province of any man, but belongs to the righteousness of God.

52. Cain was not, as some suppose, born from the devil's will or the seed of the serpent, but from Adam's soul and body. But Adam's assumed natural will ruled him. He was an image of the fallen unregener-

ated Adam, in whom the promise and the inspoken Divine voice existed without an actual life, yet as a true possibility of a new birth. Now, this possibility was not in Cain's power in consequence of the false will, but it lay in the ground of the soul and waited for the voice of Christ, who in this possibility moved himself in the precious name Jesus, and received poor sinners into grace; and with his voice called inwardly to the shut-up sinners, and awakened that stationary ground of the first Inspeaking, as was the case with the thief on the cross and has happened to many besides.

53. For if God in his purposed will had hardened Cain, no judgment could be passed upon him by the righteousness of God, nor could any curse have entered into him. What God's purpose does, that is not cursed by the righteousness of God as befell Cain.

54. For the righteousness is the order of the original expressed Word, and in this order all things should remain, according as the Speaking has brought them into life. And nothing falls into judgment that remains in its order unto which it was created.

55. If a will springing from God's purpose had hardened Adam and Cain, then the righteousness would have no opposition, for this will of hardening would stand in the Divine order.

56. Therefore the will to hardening in Adam and Cain originated in the downfall, in the inequality of the divided properties, all the properties having comprehended themselves in being, and darkened and slain the image of God in the light.

57. God's purpose is the centre of the human ground, which is the spoken and re-speaking Word of God. And that comprehended human will has truly been hardened in the purpose of God, but the ground of the purpose lies in man himself, and not in God.

58. If God had had a purpose to make a devil, that purpose would have been a will of the devil. But in the separation of the Speaking the purpose to badness entered into a Principle, and became manifest in itself in the comprehended separation. And in accordance therewith God calls himself an angry God, and yet is not God, but the centre of nature, as the cause of the Divine manifestation of the kingdom of joy. For in God no anger is manifest, but only a burning love.

59. For if in God there were a will to hardening, those passages would not be true which say: Thou art not a God that hath pleasure in wickedness (Ps. v. 5); As truly as I live, I have no pleasure in the death of the wicked (Ezek. xxxiii. 11). Further, the Ten Commandments, which forbid evil.

60. If God had willed that Cain should kill Abel, then the sixth commandment would thus not be right. Moreover, God instituted a heavy penalty in connection with Cain, saying: Whoso sheddeth man's blood, by man shall his blood be shed (Gen. ix. 6). If He willed to have evil, no one could keep His commandments: where then would be His righteousness and the judgment in the truth? The Scripture says (Hos. xiii. 9): O Israel, thy destruction cometh from thyself.

61. Now, we should not condemn any one, but only the vices and sins which appear manifestly in the godless. For these proceed from the self-will of Adam and Cain, from the centre of the dark world, and this will God did not manifest or produce in man in the beginning; but the devil is to blame for that.

62. It is this false will in a man's ways and doings that we ought to condemn, and not the poor soul which lies hidden in this hard prison in the inspoken

voice of grace. This voice of grace of the first incorporation in Paradise after the fall may indeed be roused by Christ's voice, through His children, in whom His spirit dwells, as took place in the thief on the cross, in the publican, in Mary Magdalen, and has been the case with many hundred thousand poor imprisoned souls. For the Scripture says (1 Tim. i. 15): This is a true saying, and by all means worthy to be received, that Christ Jesus came into the world to save sinners. In Rev. iii. 20 it is said: I stand at the door and knock; that is, at the door of the poor imprisoned soul. And Matt. xi. 28 runs thus: Come unto me, all ye that labour and are heavy laden, and I will refresh you.

63. He stands in the inward ground of grace that was inspoken into Adam, in the centre of the soul, and calls it, so long as the soul bears the body on earth, to see whether the poor soul will turn towards him. And then, if it turn to him, he says: Knock, and it shall be opened unto you; knock at the encorporate first voice of grace, and it will begin to stir. Further: Ask, and ye shall receive. And again: My Father will give the Holy Spirit to them that ask him (Luke xi. 9-13).

64. Therefore it depends now not on our own ability and taking, but on asking and knocking. For the promise of grace has been inspoken in Christ Jesus, and in such a way that it will give itself up to the asking. For it is written: Christ is come to save that which was lost (Matt. xviii. 11).

65. Who are the lost? Answer: Cain, Ishmael, Esau, and all men who are hardened and imprisoned in sin. These Christ is come to seek and to save, and willeth that they should not be lost. But the self-generated false murderer in Cain he will not have,

nor the mocker in Ishmael, nor the hunter in Esau; but he will have the true ground of the firstborn soul, wherein lies the voice of grace.

66. Because he would not have the mocker Ishmael, he thrust him and his mother out of the house, that is, he thrust out the mocker in Ishmael, viz. the self-formed and evil will that had arisen in Adam, together with Hagar as the separable nature, understand the separated properties of nature.

67. Hagar fled from Sarah, and would not suffer herself to be corrected, for she wished to bear rule with the mocker in Abraham's goods. But when she came into the wilderness, the angel of the Lord said unto her: Hagar, Sarah's maid, whence comest thou? And she said, I flee from my mistress Sarah. And he bade her return to her mistress, and submit herself under her hand. And the angel of the Lord said unto her: I will so increase thy seed, that it shall not be numbered for multitude. Thou art with child, and shalt bring forth a son, and shalt call his name Ishmael, because the Lord hath heard thy trouble. He shall be a wild man. His hand against every man, and every man's hand against him: and he shall dwell over against all his brethren (Gen. xvi. 6-12).

68. This figure sets before us the true ground, showing how Adam with the kingdom of nature has gone out from God into the wilderness of the animal properties, as it were from the freewoman, which is the temperament, and has in his own desire, viz. in the self-originated will, become pregnant with the mocker. The kingdom of nature had separated itself into properties, so that one went against the other, as was said with regard to Ishmael: His hand against every man, and every man's hand against him. But the properties of nature were not on this account separated

from God, as is to be seen here in Hagar. For the angel said unto her, he would so increase her seed, that it should not be numbered for multitude ; but she was to return to the freewoman and submit herself under her hand. This signifies the repentance and conversion of the poor sinner, that Christ by His voice within him meets him and comforts him in his wilderness of the world, and speaks in his heart, saying : I have heard thy trouble, thou poor imprisoned soul, in this desert. Turn round. Thou art indeed pregnant with the mocker by the kingdom of nature belonging to thy constellation, and thou wilt give birth to him. But I will bless thee, and thou shalt beget from the kingdom of nature twelve princes, which shall come in my blessing. This signifies the twelve apostles of Christ, who came in His blessing, and whose seed cannot be numbered for multitude. Also the poor sinner, if he turn round at this call of the angel, enters into the same apostolic grace ; but he must return to the freewoman with the will of the soul. But the mocker is born in his constellation with a will of his own, and this will shall not inherit the kingdom of God.

69. For Abraham had to cast out the mocker from the heirship of his goods, though not without a gift. For the freewoman, viz. the temperament in the kingdom of Christ, would have it that the mocking self-will should be cast off, which God commanded Abraham in the figure of Christ to consent to. But the gift which Abraham gave to Hagar and Ishmael denotes the true gift in Paradise.

70. Before Adam was cast out, God gave to him the gift, viz. the inspoken Word of grace, and in that gift lay the blessing. But the kingdom of nature had to give the twelve princes, which signifies that the soul is from the Eternal Nature, and that the same

order must remain; that there can arise in man no new creature, and though men produce a mocker in the divided forms of life, yet the inward ground is God's Word.

71. Therefore nature shall not pass away, but only the false self-originated will that has arisen from disequality,—that shall be cast out and die. And of this we have here a figure. For when Hagar had run forth with Ishmael (she being pregnant with Ishmael) and the angel had comforted her, she called the name of the Lord that spake unto her, *Thou God seest me.* That is, thou seest my inward ground of the soul, in which lies the Adamic gift, for she said: Surely, I have here seen him who hath directed his look after me. That is, the poor soul said: I had gone out from the freewoman, viz. the temperament or God's kingdom, and had become blind as to God, but now I have seen him who hath looked upon me in my misery with his seeing of grace. That is, he hath directed his look after me when I was already blind as to God's seeing, when the kingdom of nature had already become a mocker with the new will. Therefore she called that place or fountain the fountain of the living one who hath looked upon me.

72. This fountain is Christ, in the inspoken Word of grace. And in that same Word of grace of the serpent-bruiser is the fountain of the sweet love of God, in the name Jesus from out of Jehovah. This is the fountain of the living one who looked upon the poor soul after the fall, as well as upon Hagar and upon Ishmael in the womb. And it was intimated to her that the mocker or mocking will would spring from the kingdom of nature, which will the poor soul in its prison and blindness would have to bear; but that God had looked upon her affliction and the child's

from the fountain of the living one in the centre of the soul, in its inward ground; for the outward ground should be a mocker. But God willed to bring forth to him from the inward ground (wherein grace had become encorporate) twelve princes, whose seed should be innumerable; though outwardly Nature would remain in dominion by twelve princes of the corrupt nature; and indeed outwardly twelve princes did come from him. Thus the Spirit of God in Moses points at the inward ground, as is plainly to be seen.

73. For when Ishmael was born the outward ground, conformably with the corrupt kingdom of nature, was a mocker, which God commanded to be cast out. But when he was cast out, and Hagar had laid aside the child from her, that she might not see him die in the wilderness, the child Ishmael lay and wept. And God heard the voice of the child, and the angel of God called unto Hagar out of heaven and said unto her, What aileth thee, Hagar? Fear not, for God hath heard the voice of the child, where he lieth. Arise and take the child, and hold him by the hand, for I will make a great people of him. And God opened her eyes, that she saw a well of water. Then went she and filled the bottle with water, and gave the child drink. And God was with the child (Gen. xxi. 17-20).

74. The mocker Ishmael in the external kingdom of nature was evil, and was rejected from the sonship. But when he lay and wept, which denotes repentance, God opened the eyes of Hagar (or the kingdom of the inner nature in respect of the soul) in the encorporate fountain of grace, so that she saw the fountain of Christ and gave to drink to the child, that is, to the poor soul in the divided properties of life.

75. This giving to drink signifies baptism along with

circumcision, whereby Christ from his fountain would give to drink to the divided forms of life in their thirst. But Ishmael, the mocker according to the external nature, must first be cut off by circumcision, which is accomplished through repentance and repudiation of the mocking will. Then Christ baptizes with the Holy Spirit from the fountain of the living and seeing one; and thus then the soul dwells by that fountain, and God is with it as he was with Ishmael.

76. For the seed which God blessed is not the mocking will, but the inward ground in the gift of grace. For God said unto Abraham: In Isaac shall thy seed be blessed; that is, in Christ shall Ishmael obtain the blessing. It is not the corrupt natural will that shall be heir in God's kingdom; on the contrary, it shall always be rejected. But nature in its ground and origin is God's word, that is, the expressed word in its separation; and therein has sprung forth the fountain of life from Jehovah, viz. the fountain of love in the name Jesus, and this it is that shall inherit God's kingdom.

77. This inner nature also indicates Japhet, concerning whom the Spirit says in Noah: He shall dwell in the tents of Shem; that is, in Isaac's, which is Christ's fountain. The tents of Shem signify the new birth from Christ, into which Japhet and Ishmael were to enter. For the text says: And God was with the child; yet not with the mocker, but in the inward ground, which was to be revealed in Christ. Seeing then God was with him, and that he and his mother dwelt by the fountain of the living one, that is, by Christ in his gift of grace, who then shall condemn him, as the erring world doth? The outer Ishmael, or the will of mockery, is rightly condemned; not indeed Abraham's inherited true nature which sprang

from the blessing, but Abraham's earthly will which sprang from the serpent's seed.

78. For Ishmael is a figure of the kingdom of nature according to the poor corrupt Adam who must die and pass away in us, and yet must rise again according to the first created image in Christ, and leave the mocker Ishmael in the earth. And Isaac is a figure of the new man in the humanity of Christ, where Adam's nature and Christ are in one another, and where the false will is dead in Christ. Although Adam's nature is there, yet it lives in the Spirit of Christ (Gal. ii. 20).

79. Jesus therefore took Adam's nature upon him, yet not Adam's self-generated false will, but the poor separated form of life in nature, in the purpose and righteousness of God, in order that the first Adam might exist in his righteousness in Christ.

80. Thus Ishmael came from the image of the righteousness of God which he created in Adam. And Isaac is seen in the image of grace which gave itself up in Christ to God's righteousness, and filled it with love, and appeased the wrath. For Christ was, with his love-tincture of his blood, to transform the mocker in Ishmael (which had become manifest in God's righteousness) so that he might in Christ attain again to the sonship from which the righteousness had cast him out as from Abraham's goods, that is, from the inheritance of nature in respect of the formed and expressed word of God.

81. The figure of Jacob and Esau is the counterpart of the figure of Isaac and Ishmael. Jacob, that is, Christ, was cast out from the kingdom of nature and its generated false will. For when he had assumed and taken upon himself our sins in the Adamic nature (*i.e.* the source from which sin flows, or the divided

forms of life in the human nature), he then said: My kingdom is not of this world; that is, not in the divided four elements, but in the temperament.

82. But Christ having assumed humanity in the divided qualities, the righteousness of the outer order would not suffer him in itself, for he had sprung from another righteousness which is the heavenly, and came into our poor humanity in this world's property in order to help us.

83. Therefore he said: The Son of Man hath not where to lay his head (Matt. viii. 20); and yet he also said that all power was given unto him in heaven and on earth by his Father (Matt. xxviii. 18). Here he refers to the inner ground of all beings, viz. eternity, which lies hidden in this world and had become manifest in Christ. Such manifestation was not at home in this world, and possessed nothing of this world as a possession or property.

84. The figure, representing how Christ was destined to be expelled and thrust out from this world, was given in Jacob, whom Esau as the kingdom of the outward natural righteousness continually wished to kill, so that Jacob had to flee from Esau, as Christ did from the pharisaical righteousness in the kingdom of nature, until Jacob came from Laban with his present, and went to Esau and gave himself up to him, for him to slay him or let him live. But Jacob was not the right one whom the righteousness of nature in God's purpose was destined to seize and to slay. That right one was Christ.

85. Thus we see here again the figure of Christ and of Adam. For when Jacob went to Esau, and sent a present before to meet him, Esau's anger was dissolved and turned into great compassion, so that he fell on Jacob's neck and wept (Gen. xxxiii. 4), and

did not do anything to him, but received him in love. In this way the figure of Christ is contained in our humanity.

86. In our humanity lay the wrath of the Father, as it were the angry Esau in the righteousness awakened in the wrath, like Esau in opposition to Jacob. But Christ sent his gift of grace, viz. the love in his blood, of the essence of the heavenly world, to meet the wrath of the Father in our nature, in God's righteousness, as in the first Adamic birth of nature. And when the first birth saw and felt this love in itself, the wrath of God in his righteousness of nature was turned into great compassion, whereby the wrath lost its right and was broken to pieces, and the sun was darkened in God's righteousness, and the earth in this dissolution quaked, the rocks were rent, and the dead (whom God's righteousness had swallowed up in death) rose again in this compassion.

87. Esau was set upon the righteousness of the first birth, which he had sold to Jacob, and knew not that God had so brought it about as to represent thus the figure of Christ and of Adam. And therefore he hated Jacob, because Jacob had the blessing of Abraham, which the righteousness of the individual natural will in Esau, *i.e.* in Adam's corrupt nature, wished to possess. But this natural disposition of the self-will had lost the inheritance of God, which inheritance the second new Adam in Christ brought back into nature. Therefore the first right, viz. the first natural life, must die, and become alive again in Christ. Esau in his hunter's craft could not inherit God's kingdom in the righteousness, but he was thrust out even in the womb, when the children had not done either anything bad or good, in order that God's righteousness in his purpose of the creation might be satisfied.

88. But in Christ God received Esau again according to the gift of grace, according to the inward ground of the true Adamic man. But not according to the right of his life's nature, wherein he was named or called Esau. The E is the inward ground, in which lay the paradisaic gift. But the SAU was the rejected beast of the kingdom of self-will in accordance with earthliness, concerning which the Scripture says: Esau have I hated, when he was even yet in the womb (Rom. ix. 13). That the Election of God might stand, and that not Esau in his false individual natural life, but Christ in the true Adamic nature in Esau, should be the child of God.

89. The Adamic nature in SAU was to lose its right entirely in regard to its will and life; but the essence of the Adamic nature, which was the formed expressed word of God, was to remain in Christ, and be appeased with the free gift of Christ in the wrath. The figure of this was set forth by Jacob sending the present to meet Esau and calling him his lord. Then the anger in Esau on account of the natural right was appeased, and began to show itself in great compassion, and fell about Jacob's neck and kissed him, and gave up its will to the birthright or first birth in Jacob (Gen. xxxiii. 4).

90. For Christ had to give himself up wholly to death, and submit the human natural right to his Father as the righteousness. Then Esau died, and God awakened in him the first Adam, viz. the right man who was created in God's purpose, in the grace of the love which filled the righteousness before God. Then there was no longer Esau, but a member of Christ.

91. But that the Scriptures thus relate to predestination is correct. For Esau is the image of the wrath

of God which arose in Adam, and that is damned, in order that the righteousness of God might be satisfied and the riches of his grace in Jacob, *i.e.* in Christ, might be manifested in God's righteousness. The life in the natural will (which was called Esau) was Adam's new life according to the properties of the dark world that had been awakened in him, as it was also with Cain and Ishmael. This life the righteousness of God had laid hold of in the wrath and revealed itself therein; and this life was damned. Not that the soulish ground, *i.e.* the formed word in respect of the soul, was rejected by God. No; they had sprung from the children of the Saints, and not from the SAU, as in many is now the case, whereby the inward ground is full of devils.

92. The present of grace as given in the encorporate voice lay in the inward ground, but not in the essential constituent of the life as in Jacob, Isaac and Abel. This constituent was Christ, who with his voice would inspeak himself into this inspoken word, into the inward ground of the poor soul. As it is written: I am come to seek and to save that which was lost; such as Ishmael, Esau and their like, who in God's hate were laid hold of, and lost. Thus Christ said he had come to seek the poor sinner that was lost, and not the righteous (Matt. ix. 13).

93. Jacob, Isaac and Abel were the righteous, for grace had manifested itself in them, and killed the self-will of sin in the life, and given itself as a new life to the true primitive ground of life. Accordingly they were righteous in this new life, and had peace with God's righteousness, that is, as to the soul; but as to the outer life they were still under the curse, and therefore their external body had to die. For they themselves were not by nature the righteous, but grace

made them righteous. This grace gave itself to their life's ground wherein the life burned, and as a new Divine fire transformed the hate and anger of God into love.

94. But thou sayest: Why not then also in Cain, Ishmael and Esau? Answer: *No.* The purpose of God must stand, namely, the order of His expressed word. That word He will not reverse. His wrath must not be slain and broken, for it is a cause of grace being manifested. Moreover, it is the cause of grace being transformed into a kingdom of joy, and also of its becoming a fiery love. But Christ is the second purpose. This purpose He manifested in Abel, Isaac and Jacob, and presented the figure showing how it was to be.

95. For Christ had to be manifested in the righteousness of the wrath of God, that it might be known what grace is. Adam had his subsistence in God's grace and in His wrath; but in the temperament neither of these was manifest in his life, for they were in equipoise. Now if grace is to be manifested, wrath must first be manifested, that grace may be occasioned to put itself in motion in the wrath, and give itself up to the wrath and extinguish it. This giving up and extinguishing is the cause of the divine kingdom of joy and of the fiery love in the life of man; and therefrom God's mercy, as well as faith, love and hope, that is, confidence in God, has had its origin in man; and this in the temperament could not be.

96. For a thing that is in equipoise has no movement or desire towards anything; it is one, and belongs to itself. But if it go out from the temperament, it becomes many and also fragile, and loses the ipseity. Now this thing has need of help, that is, of grace and mercy. If, however, it be not soon helped,

it enters into hope; and if to hope a promise of help is made, it enters into faith; and faith gives rise to desire in the hope, and the desire takes the promise into itself, and comprehends it in itself, so that it becomes essential; and in this essentiality is grace and mercy. This essentiality is laid hold of in the promise and embodied in a being; and this being must give itself up to the first right, which has made the thing in itself. When that is done, the primary factive principle finds within it a new life, which has arisen from hope, faith and desire by the process of embracing these in itself; and it finds that this life is more spiritual than the first life from which the thing arose. Therefore it cannot offer resistance to it, but must suffer the spiritual life to dwell in it.

97. Here there takes place the restoration of the first existence, which had been broken up. And the last body is better than the first, for it is wholly spiritual, born of faith, hope and love. And the first fire kindles it with its desire, whereby the fiery love arises.

98. Understand us correctly thus: Adam was the entire image of God in love and wrath, but he had his subsistence in the equality of the properties, and no one of these was manifest before another. When, however, by the devil's deceit he permitted himself to be led away into lust, this image perished, and the properties in the temperament became separated. Now he was in need of help, and so God inspoke the Word into him. The Word received the hungry desire for help, grasped it and put its will thereinto, as into a hope that it would be assisted; and the desire formed the hope into an ens of a being. And now the inspoken Word was become essential, and was called faith or taking. And this did the attraction

of the eternal will receive into itself and give itself up to; for this being was more noble than the first being from out of the purpose of the spoken word. Thus the fiery love began to burn from the wrath-fire in the purpose of the eternal nature. For this ens of faith was indestructible, and subsisted in the wrath-fire. And in that receiving by the wrath-fire, the fire of wrath was transmuted into joyous love.

99. And this is the ground of Christ as springing from the inspoken Word. It separated itself in Adam into a figure in the being of nature, and therefrom came Abel; and from the broken-up figure came Cain. Now Abel also had Cain's nature in the ens of faith, wherein the soul stood; but the disrupt will was transformed into an entire will, for the disruption was at rest in the ens of faith; and that was the figure of Christ. Now a promise was made to Adam's soul, viz. to the disrupt nature of the soul's and body's property, that the woman's seed should bruise the head of the introduced serpent's proprium, and help Adam. This serpent-bruiser must therefore be another person than Adam, namely, one in whom God were revealed, one who could do this, and who should awaken in Adam the inspoken Word, that is, one who should possess the might and power of the inner Word.

100. For though in Adam the inner Word was made living and manifest, yet it was a question of his children (whose inspoken ground was covered with sin, and not yet separated as in Cain and Abel), and also involved this point, that the human essence in the sinner, which God's righteousness had laid hold of in the wrath, should have a voice of grace to speak into it and awaken the inner primal inspoken ground of the Word of divine power.

101. God Jehovah spoke the name Jesus into Adam

after the fall for a working life, that is, he manifested it in the heavenly nature, which was deadened. By this inspeaking a divine desire was again awakened in Adam's soul, and this desire was the beginning of faith. It separated itself from the false desire into a figure, and therefrom came Abel; and from the selfhood of the Adamic soul by earthly lust came Cain.

102. Now there lay at the basis of the soul's selfhood in the being of Cain the sound of the Word that God spoke. But this being was not capable of the divine life in the inspeaking of the Word, for the awakened wrath of God in his purpose of the speaking forth to Nature in the separability had been manifested therein. Accordingly the same soulish being now needed another and further inspeaking into the spoken forth word, that it might also become alive in the soul's being.

103. Now this could not be effected unless the inspeaking came from a Divine sound or speaking, in which the speaking should proceed both from the divine life and also from the soulish ground of life, in which there were a Divine holy soul that should inspeak itself in soulish and divine power into the corrupt soul which was blind as to God, in such a way that the soulish element should enter into what is soulish and the divine element into what is divine, and awaken themselves one in the other.

104. For this was the purpose of God, that he would not abandon the poor corrupt right Adamic soul. He presented that soul in the figure of Cain, and put over against that figure the name Jesus in the other line, wherein also was the soulish ground, that the name Jesus with the new life of the soulish ground might inspeak itself into Cain's soul. The figure thus indicated was Abel, and from this line came Christ in our

humanity. He came to call to repentance the poor sinner, who was imprisoned in God's hate. He had a human soul new-born in God, and could inspeak into the soul and also into the inspoken Word of God (as took place in Paradise), and awaken the soul by a new Divine hunger in itself, so that it received in itself this inspoken inherited Word, whereby a new life originated for it.

105. Therefore understand us aright. We speak dear and precious things, as we well know in the grace of God. The figure of Cain, Ishmael, Esau and their like represent all unregenerated men; they are the true Adam after the fall. These God calls with his inspeaking word which he has conveyed to us by Christ, and which he still to-day in the new-born children inspeaks into this corrupt Adamic nature, and calls them therewith, saying: Come ye all to me; not only some, but all.

106. But the figure of Abel, Isaac and Jacob represent all men who suffer themselves to be awakened by the inner Word, and in whom the Divine inspeaking takes hold. These obtain in the soul a new life and will, that is, a Divine hunger, which takes the first paradisaic encorporate Word into itself in the name Jesus, comprises it and makes it essential. Then Christ is born in them, and by that new-born ground they are no longer in this world, but in heaven. For He himself is the holy heaven or the true temple of God, wherein God is man and God, where the Word becomes flesh (heavenly, spiritual flesh), of which the fire of the holy soul eats and has its life therefrom.

107. And we thus set before you the understanding with regard to Esau. The Scripture says that God hated Esau and loved Jacob, when the children had not as yet done either anything bad or good, that the

purpose of God might stand (Rom. ix. 11-13). Esau was Adam's corrupt image, and Jacob was the image of Christ. God shows here in figure how hate in the purpose of the word which speaks forth was manifested in Adam, wherein he lay in death and the wrath of God, and was a mere hate of God's. For the holy life was dead, and of this the image was Esau; he was conceived in God's hate in the womb. For the image of Christ had separated itself in Jacob from Esau, and now confronted Esau with its holy soul, and was to inspeak into him and move the poor sick imprisoned soul with its indwelling Divine sound, that the corrupt Adamic soul might be awakened by the inspeaking of the name Jesus.

108. But the inspeaking was not to pass over, but was to give itself up to God's righteousness, to the hate and wrath, as Christ had to give himself up to God's hate, to the righteousness, and awaken the mercy with his love in the name Jesus, and with his giving up transform the wrath-fire into a love-fire, as into the great yearning compassion of the dear sonship. Just as Jacob transformed his brother's anger into great compassion when he despatched his present before him, and sent word to him that he gave himself up to his grace, that is, to his righteous anger, because he had taken away from him the birthright. And that he might obtain grace with him by this present, he wished to surrender himself with all that he had into Esau's possession. This was fulfilled in Christ, who had taken our soul into himself. But he had taken also into himself from Adam the holy jewel of God that lay concealed in Adam. And therefore God's hate had arisen in connection with the birthright (first birth) or the righteousness of God. For the jewel belonged of right to the first Adamic image in

God's likeness; and this jewel God took from Adam into a new figure by means of Abel.

109. And now there was hate in the image on account of God's righteousness in relation to the jewel. Hence Esau was angry with his brother Jacob in the image of Christ. Therefore Jacob had to give himself up to Esau together with the jewel and all that he possessed. So likewise Christ had to give himself up wholly with the same jewel of the name Jesus to the righteousness of the purpose of God, and again deliver up the jewel to the hate of the purpose.

110. But thou askest: Why did God carry on such a process? Could he not leave the jewel to Adam, who had it by a natural right (as the firstborn in the Word of the purpose of God), by a Divine formation? Answer: No. Question: Why? Answer: Because the jewel would have remained concealed in the highest love of God in man, *i.e.* in the image of God. It had to be manifested in regeneration by such a process, in order that the love and grace of God might be known and revealed in man, and that man might have reason to love God and uplift his praise to the grace. And this uplifting is a pure Divine forming and generating in the wisdom of God, whereby the Word of God is born also in man, and man also brings forth God, that he may thus be an essential God and a harmony of the Divine kingdom of joy.

111. For when Christ gave up the jewel to the righteousness of God, to the hate, the wrath was transformed into a highly triumphant joyfulness, and praise to God was manifested; and this could not be in Adam when he was in the temperament. Further, the wrath rejoiced that it had been transformed from enmity into a fire of love.

112. Now this is the resurrection of Christ and of

his children, whom he thus transforms into a fire of love by his process; so that if the soul suffer itself to be drawn when Christ calls it within it, it must give itself up to him. Then Christ arises in the fire of wrath, and transforms it into the Divine joyfulness, into praise to God.

113. Understand, then, brethren, that God hated Esau, though it was not God, but God's purpose or the righteousness in the separable attraction that hated this image, because it was not the primal true image which had been created in the righteousness. For the jewel as the ens of Divine love was extinct therein, and Jacob possessed it. Hence the purpose of God hated this image of Esau, because it was not God's first image in love, but was the image in wrath.

114. Esau was the image of hate itself. Nevertheless, God could not hate him, but it was the purpose which hated him, that is, the fiery nature in the separation of His speaking, where fire becomes enkindled and comprehends itself in a Principle for the manifestation of God, in which the creaturely life stands.

115. For the creaturely life without the manifestation of the light is mere fire, hate, anger and envy. Such was Adam after the fall (without the new inspeaking of grace), and this holds also of Cain, Ishmael, Esau and all men outside of the grace-ens of love from which the light springs.

116. The question now arises as to whether God's righteousness in the purpose hated Esau even to eternal perdition. Answer: *Yes.* In His own Might nothing else could possibly be. Further, it may be asked: Was it the will of the pure true God that Esau, Cain and many thousands should perish eternally?

Answer: *No.* Christ was God's purpose in so far as God is called God.

117. In Christ God willeth that all men should be saved; but his wrath is desirous of swallowing up all in whom it is manifested. For God sent not his Son into the world, into humanity, to judge, harden and destroy it; but that the world through him might be saved (John iii. 17). Thou wilt say: Yes, those whom he pleases to save. Answer: He calls them all to him, they ought all to come. Why do they not all come? Thou sayest: He draws them not in themselves to him. Answer: That is not true; he draws them all, he teaches all men in themselves. For they know by the light of nature that he meets the godless in their understanding and shows them the right; which they themselves also teach and confess that it is right, but do it not. Question: Why is that? Answer: Christ says: Father, I will that they whom thou hast given me, be with me where I am (John xvii. 24). Further, No man can come to me except the Father draw him (John vi. 44). Question: How is it that he does not draw them all? Answer: Here is the reason, thou dear besoiled piece of wood: Smell in thy bosom. Of what dost thou smell? If thou art laid hold of only in the purpose of the wrath, in its constellation, like Esau, Ishmael and such persons, then assuredly there is remedy. But if thou art a thistle that has sprung from inherited and actual sins, in which God's purpose in the wrath has fashioned itself into a figure of life, and of which God in his righteousness of the purpose said, He would visit the sins of the parents upon the children unto the third and fourth generation, then the position is full of danger. For this living purpose in the wrath of God already possesses a figure in the attraction of the speaking Word,

and has separated anew from the encorporate ground of grace; not as the result of God's purpose, but in consequence of the fountain of sin, which has wholly united itself with the wrath in the purpose, and introduced itself into a life of darkness. In such case the encorporate grace is far off, and Christ is dead and rests in the grave; and before he rises again, this evil spirit must have gone into the abyss. Such ones the purpose of God holds, and gives them not to the grace of Christ, for they are thistle-children. Their will is a living devil in angel's shape among other men.

118. The purpose of God knows every being while it is yet a seed in the man and woman, and knows what this wood is fit for when it shall become a tree. The thistle not only comes from the womb out of the first ground, but also arises through the external influences of time, whereby most beings are corrupted.

119. Christ calls all these. Many of them have still a spark of the Divine drawing in themselves, by which the purpose gives them to Christ, so that at times they hear Christ teaching in themselves. Now these are called. But external influences destroy this again, and crucify Christ's voice and inward calling before He becomes man in them, and introduce the element of the serpent in Christ's stead. And when it comes to the Election at the time of harvest, when the grain is threshed out and winnowed, these are but the chaff of the grain, and have not Divine weight or gravity in themselves. Thus it is that they remain behind in the centre of darkness, in God's righteousness in the wrath. Hence it is said: Few are chosen. For the Father chooses only the good fruit for his food; anything else he gives to the beasts. So likewise here: That which does not grow up in the Divine element and is born of God, cannot see God.

120. Thou askest: Has Esau, who sprang from God's hate, finally been born anew and saved? Answer: This we are not to judge; for God says: Vengeance is mine, I will in my righteousness repay (Rom. xii. 19). We say with reason that Esau was born in Adam's sin as a true image of Adam after the fall, and was laid hold of in the womb by the purpose of God's wrath, as all poor sinners are. But Jacob is seen in the image of Christ, in the new-born love, as a type of him who came to call and to save poor sinners; so far as the righteousness of God in the wrath suffers them to follow Christ, both on account of the inherited abominations comprehended in the eternal attraction, and on account of actual abominations, which are the confining power.

121. Esau came from and was born of holy parents, and only stood in separation as an image of the corrupt nature. God also had separated the image of Christ, viz. Jacob, from the same seed of his parents, and set it over against Esau. And at last Jacob by his present and humility brought Esau to great compassion. This signifies the present or gift of Christ in Esau, which was to turn him, and to draw him out of the angry formed purpose of the righteousness of God, so that in contrition for his evil will he should weep and repent. As he did when he embraced Jacob and wept on his neck and dropped the spirit of murder against Jacob. And hence we ought certainly not to condemn him. We condemn him only according to Scripture, which condemns him in Adam's iniquity, when he was not yet new-born. Therewith God's righteousness is satisfied; but grace is manifested in repentance.

122. We know not but that God converted him. This certainly is intimated by the figure of Jacob

coming to him from Laban. In Adam he was dead, but in Christ he was able to be made alive. For the gate of grace stood open before him as well as before his parents, who were in the line of Christ. But that they also had Adam's poison and death in the flesh, and the fountain of sin proceeding from Adam, is exhibited in Esau, Ishmael and Cain.

123. But we must not here believe Reason, which says, God hardened Esau and condemned him to eternal damnation. It cannot be shown in the sacred Scriptures that the Divine will hardened Esau; but the purpose in God's righteousness did this. Not by an encroachment of some formed Divine will, but through the corrupt nature springing from Adam's property in Esau's own being; and not by way of an external accident or interference, as Reason judges, which knows nothing of God, and always pictures man as far from God, whereas God is manifested in all men, though in every one according to his life's property. This ground we have expounded in such detail to the reader, that he may understand our meaning in the following short conclusions.

CHAPTER X

A BRIEF COMPILATION OF OBJECTIONS FROM SCRIPTURE THAT KEEP REASON A PRISONER, AND HOW THEY ARE TO BE UNDERSTOOD.

1. THE Epistle to the Romans, particularly the ninth and eleventh chapters, confound Reason, and are a stone of stumbling and a rock of offence to the godless, but to the holy they are a light of life. There it is said: They are not all Israelites, which are of Israel: neither are they all children, because they are the seed of Abraham: but in Isaac shall thy seed be called. That is, they which are children after the flesh, are not the children of God, but the children of the promise are counted for the seed. For this is a word of promise, About this time will I come, and Sarah shall have a son (Rom. ix. 7, 8, 9).

2. Explanation: Reason understands that the promise is to be regarded as beginning in this seed of Abraham, but we see that the promise began in Paradise. And in the case of Abraham it was formed into a figure of the kingdom of nature in Ishmael, and into a figure of the kingdom of grace in Isaac, that is, into an image of what was to come, as it was also in Cain and Abel.

3. The kingdom of nature had in man been laid hold of in the wrath in the original purpose relating to the image of man, and was no longer able to bring forth children of God and the right seed of God, but only children of wrath and of the corrupt flesh. Therefore Paul said that not all the children and seed

of Abraham become children of God, but only they who are new-born of the promise, that is, of the encorporate Word in Paradise which God renewed with Abraham when He would exhibit his image out of the promise.

4. In every man who is to be saved the word of promise from grace must become an ens or being, and this is accomplished in repentance and conversion. God says in Isaiah (i. 18): Though your sins be as red as scarlet, if ye turn, they shall be as white as snow. This takes place when the kingdom of grace is manifested in the kingdom of nature. This is really the same as was said to Abraham (Gen. xviii. 10): This is the covenant, About this time will I come, and Sarah shall have a son (Rom. ix. 9).

5. That is, when the poor sinner repents, God comes in Christ's spirit and brings forth a new son out of Christ's flesh and blood in him. That is to say, the soul lays hold of Christ in itself in faith and in hope, and brings the hope into an ens or being wherein lies the living promised Word. And thus commences the gestation of the new man out of Christ; and that is then a right seed of faith, from which children of God are born as dew from the dawn. And then the old Adam is only attached to them as to Abraham, Isaac and Jacob, who by the external man were also mortal and sinful; but the temple of God, or the inner man in them, was holy. And so in like manner in us.

6. Again, Rom. ix. 10-13: And not only this; but when Rebecca also had conceived by one, even by our father Isaac; (for the children being not yet born, neither having done anything good or bad, that the purpose of God according to election might stand, not of works, but of him that calleth;) it was said unto her, The elder shall serve the younger. As it is

written, Jacob have I loved, but Esau have I hated. Explanation: Here Reason lies blind, and what we have here has already been explained at length; for this was the purpose of God which He bestowed on Adam after the fall. The first purpose is the natural first Adam. He was the elder, viz. the first image of God in the purpose of the divine scientia as springing from the speaking Word of the separation of powers; but in him grace was not manifested, much less the great love and humility seen in Jesus.

7. And therefore God came with the second purpose which lay hidden in grace, and gave it to the first image, and manifested the grace through the first image, and slew the first life in the grace, and exalted the life of grace in the first purpose above the purpose of the elder image, that is, the first natural image.

8. Therefore the text in Moses says to Rebecca: The elder shall serve the younger (Gen. xxv. 23); in order that the purpose in the manifestation of grace might stand. For Esau in the elder first image of Adam have I hated, because he would be an individual lord and live in evil and good, and would not recognize grace. But Jacob in my right Divine purpose which I have produced out of my Divine will of grace from eternity, I have loved, and set him as a lord over nature. Therefore Christ said that all power had been given unto him (Matt. xxviii. 18). For he was the lesser or younger, as springing from God's humility and love, and these God set over the kingdom of his wrath, that the kingdom of his wrath in the younger, that is, in God's grace, might be subservient to God and make him manifest.

9. And therefore outwardly the inheritance was withdrawn from Ishmael, to signify that God had

given it to the man who was born of grace. Now in regard to this hate Reason errs, and understands not the ground, as has been mentioned above.

10. Further, Rom. ix. 14-18: What shall we say then? Is God then unrighteous? God forbid. For he saith unto Moses: I show mercy to whom I show mercy, and have compassion on whom I have compassion. So it lieth not then in any man's will or running, but in the mercy of God. For the Scripture saith unto Pharaoh: For this cause have I stirred thee up, that I might show in thee my power, and that my name might be declared in all lands. Thus hath he mercy on whom he will, and whom he will he hardeneth. Explanation: Here Reason lies dead and without Divine light, as it is written: The natural man perceiveth nothing of the spirit of God. It is foolishness unto him (1 Cor. ii. 14).

11. St. Paul accordingly vindicates God, and says that He does or judges rightly in showing mercy to whom He will. And this indeed is the ultimate ground. For He will have none in his mercy save such as are born out of his purpose of grace from Christ: on such poor imprisoned souls He hath compassion. That is, if the soul lays hold of the word of promise and embraces it as Abraham did, this embracing of the new entity of grace is reckoned unto it, as it was to Abraham, for righteousness, as it is written: Abraham believed God, and it was counted unto him for righteousness (Rom. iv. 3).

12. For to believe means taking and embracing in oneself, that is to say, embracing in oneself the word of promise so that it becomes essential. In this process mercy springs up. The lesser or minor, which originally is but a word of power, becomes so considerable that it overcomes the major one, viz. the

fiery soul of the eternal nature in God's first eternal purpose.

13. But that it is said, He hath mercy on whom he will, and whom he will he hardeneth : this is understood in the two purposes. In Christ is the Divine purpose, where God hath mercy. For Christ is His will to mercy, and in God there is no other will to mercy but the one will which He has made manifest in Christ.

14. The first Divine willing in Adam's first image, when he lived in innocence, has disappeared in man, as the light of a candle goes out. That good willing is lost; not in God, but in man. And out of the same good willing (which willing is the name Jehovah) the willing of love and grace in the name Jesus revealed itself in Adam after the fall by the inspeaking of the serpent-bruiser. For with this new good willing in the name Jesus, God gave the good willing in man to his Son Jesus, as Christ said (John xvii. 6): Father (that is, thou great God or Jehovah in fire and light), the men were thine, and thou gavest them me, and I give them eternal life.

15. The other willing is in the purpose of the primal ground of God Jehovah. When the constituent of light disappeared in Adam, the fiery quality in this willing (*i.e.* the angry God) became manifest. Now this angry God desires, in accordance with his property, to consume everything and to put all into darkness.

16. Thus the Spirit in Moses speaks of the will of God according to love and wrath as proceeding from the two purposes, namely (1) from the first righteousness wherein God created Adam, and (2) from the purpose of Christ by grace. Whom I have compassion on in love (and whom I lay hold of in love), to him I show mercy; and whom I find in my wrath

defiled with deadly sin, and living in the sinful source of a false life, which is a thistle and the devil's will, him do I harden in my jealous purpose. God knows them well, whereunto each serves.

17. It is not to be imagined that in God's purpose, so far as he is called God, a will to hardening passes into man from without. On the contrary, the source and origin of the hardening is in the individual's own ground, in the purpose of the righteousness of God; for it is the wrath's willing, in which the wrath hardeneth whom it will. The whole creaturely being of man in God's wrath represents this will to hardening; for it wills only vanity, and that hardens it also.

18. Therefore it depends not on the will nor on the work of his hands that the wicked man be saved; but it depends on God's mercy that he turn round and become with the false will as a child, and be new-born out of the mercy of grace. Else, if it depended on the will of his own nature, then the Adamic corrupt nature might attain to the sonship. But no! The Adamic nature must die to the self-will and be born out of the will of grace, that the grace of Christ may be manifested in God's will: in this process alone is mercy and goodwill. It may thus be said that He willeth the wicked man in the wrath and the holy man in the grace, each of them from and in his own ground or principle.

19. Understand it aright. To Pharaoh it was said: Even for this same purpose have I raised thee up, that I might show my power in thee, and that my name might be declared throughout all the earth (Rom. ix. 17). Pharaoh was not born out of grace or the grace-will, but out of the wrath-will. And when God would make his name known, how that He

is Lord and that his grace rules over the wrath, then He stirred up the wrath in the hardened Pharaoh and laid hold of him in the purpose of His wrath within him, and held him, so that he could not see the works of God; for he was blind as to God, until God exhibited the forms of his wrath in the great judgment.

20. But that in the meantime the iniquity of the Egyptians was full is intimated by the Scripture, in that it says, that Israel would have to serve the Egyptians etc. (Gen. xv. 13-16). In the case of Pharaoh the iniquity was full, and hardening existed in him; therefore the purpose of God in the wrath used him as an instrument. For the Egyptians had roused the plagues; and so they had to be subservient to the glorious manifestation of the Divine grace in God's children, that thus God might cause his anger to be seen in the wicked, and grace to be seen in his children.

21. For the time of Pharaoh was a time of limit, in which all things stand in limit, measure, number and weight (Sap. xi. 20).

22. The supposed purpose from without is in this single text of St. Paul emphatically overthrown, Reason supposing that God chooses some special people of a particular name: as the sects in their contention rage, and desire in their own name to be blessed, and to be the called children above other peoples.

23. And again, St. Paul says (Rom. ix. 24-26): Even us, whom he hath called, not of the Jews only, but also of the Gentiles. As he saith also in Hosea, I will call them my people, which were not my people; and them my love, which were not my love. And it shall come to pass, that in the place where it was said unto them, Ye are not my people; there shall they

be called the children of the living God. Explanation: Here we see the first calling in Paradise, potent by virtue of the inspoken Word of grace, which presses from one upon all.

24. For the Gentiles were not of the seed of Abraham, with whom God made a covenant; yet the first covenant of the Word that was inspoken in grace lay in them as a fundamental ground. Therefore St. Paul says that God has called and chosen not only the Jews in their covenant, but also the Gentiles or heathen in the covenant of Christ; and has called that people his love, which knew him not and outwardly in their ignorance were not his people. The purpose of grace, which in Paradise after the fall had embodied itself through the inner Word, lay in them; and after this God calls them his love. This encorporate Word he awakened in them by the spirit of Christ, when this voice of grace had assumed a soul, so that their soul, which lay shut up in darkness, heard the encorporate voice of grace in the voice of Christ, as by an awakening of a new inner speaking, and love was enkindled in the soul. God has not regard to man's knowing, and chooses not by means of his purpose a people for sonship that know how to speak of his name above other peoples; but he has regard to his purpose that was established in Paradise (which purpose he had from eternity in the uncreaturely figure of man), that is, he has regard to the primal ground of humanity, as man was seen in the name Jesus, in the Divine wisdom, without creaturely being in a magical figuration. This figuration existed also in the heathen by the inward ground, since it passed upon all; excepting only the children of wrath, in whom it fashioned itself in the wrath. Such figuration of the wrath, however, passes not

upon whole peoples, but only upon the thistle-children as apprehended in the purpose of the wrath, in their inherited and actual sins.

25. As it was said to Elijah: Yet I have left me seven thousand who have not bowed the knee unto Baal. These are they who, though outwardly they ran with the heathen and dwelt among the false Jews, by their heart were directed to the true God, albeit they showed their zeal in blindness and want of understanding: like Saul, until grace awakened within him, so that he became seeing.

26. For Saul supposed he did the true God service when he extirpated those that wished to walk in the divine Law under another form, which he recognized not. He was zealous in the law of God from the bottom of his heart, in order thereby to please God. He did not do this under guidance of the purpose of God's wrath in such a sense that the latter had laid hold of him and transported him into the life of darkness, and that God looked upon him as one wholly hardened in death in consequence of a special purpose of a particular election. *No.* He was one of the seven thousand, in whom lay the covenant of grace from the true seed of Abraham and the promise made in Paradise. But the way to this grace was not yet revealed to him. He was zealous in the law of righteousness, and desiderated what he himself was unable to do; but the hidden grace within him, which manifested itself in his zeal and used it as an instrument for the evidence of grace, was able to do it.

27. Therefore it is blindness and ignorance when a people says: We have Christ's doctrine; God causes Christ to be preached among us, and not among that other people; and hence God through his purpose has chosen us to be children of grace.

And though in our life we are no better than they, yet he has chosen us in his purpose, and in Christ has expiated our actual and inherited sins, so that we need only comfort ourselves therewith, and accept the position as a free gift of grace. For our works are of no account before God, but the choice of his purpose is valid and authoritative; because in his purpose he justifies the ungodly, and by the purpose of his will draws the wicked man out of hell and saves him.

28. Hearken, thou blind Babylon, concealed under the purple mantle of Christ like a harlot under a chaplet of flowers, who is full of the lust of fornication and yet calls herself a virgin. What is the election and the grace with which thou comfortest thyself, and spreadest this mantle of grace over thyself, over thy whoredoms and vices of all malice and wickedness. Where does it stand in the Scriptures that a harlot can become a virgin by a royal warrant or a gift of favour? What emperor can make a deflowered woman a virgin through his favour and good-will? Can that indeed be? Where, then, would be the virgin in heart and in chastity? God requires the abyss of the heart, and says (Matt. v. 18), that one jot or one tittle shall in no wise pass from his law of righteousness, till all be fulfilled. Wherewith wilt thou fulfil the righteousness, if thou art in thyself without Divine essence?

29. But thou wilt say: Christ has once for all fulfilled it for me, and satisfied the law. Answer: That is true; but what is that to thee, who art and livest out of Christ? If thou art not in Christ, in the sphere of actually operative grace, thou hast no part in him, for he said: He that is not with me is against me, and he that gathereth not with me scattereth (Luke xi. 23).

30. No grace imputed from without avails. On

the contrary, it is an inborn filial grace springing from Christ's flesh and blood which draws the merit of Christ to itself. It is not the individual born of man and woman from the corrupt nature that attains to the grace of filiation, so that he can comfort himself and say: Christ hath done it; He frees me from sin; I need only believe that it is done. *No.* The devil likewise knows this, as well as the damned; but what does that avail them, when in fact they are damned? For, Not all they that say unto me, Lord, Lord, shall enter into the kingdom of heaven; but he that doeth the will of my Father which is in heaven (Matt. vii. 21).

31. Now, what is this will which they must do, so as to attain to the filiation? Christ says: They that turn and become as children (Matt. xviii. 3), and are born of God, of water and of the spirit (John iii. 5), these are they that attain to the filiation or childship. For Christ is the will of God, and they who would do this will must be new-born from Christ's flesh and blood, from the Word which became man, which cancelled death and sin in humanity and transformed them into love, and must put on the merit of Christ in the soul, and by the inward encorporate ground of grace become the living Christ, as a true branch in his vine.

32. Not by comfortings from an adopted external shine or lustre, but in an essential way, as self-subsisting essential children of Christ, in whom the inspoken covenant of grace is fulfilled substantially, in whom the soul eats of Christ's flesh and blood and has life, and that not from without but in itself, in whom Christ continually saith to the fiery soul in God's righteousness: Take, eat my flesh and drink my blood, so abidest thou in me and I in thee (John vi. 56).

33. The fiery essence of the soul, according to the inner eternal ground of the true righteousness of God in his purpose relating to the creaturely being of the soul, must introduce itself into Christ's flesh and blood in reality; not through an alien outside shine or lustre, but through the lustre which God revealed in Adam after the fall, and fulfilled in Christ with the humanity, whereby God became man and man became God. And this holds also of his members, who spring from the same root, and in whom Christ becomes alive in the encorporate covenant of grace, and takes to himself soul and humanity.

34. Therefore it is not now a question only of external knowledge, as that I know I have in Christ a gracious God who has cancelled sin in humanity; but rather the matter lies in this, (1) That such take place likewise in me; namely, that Christ, who has risen from death, rise up also in me, and rule over sin in me. (2) That he kill sin, viz. nature in its evil will, in me; that this same will in Christ also be crucified and slain in me. (3) That a new will proceeding from nature in Christ's spirit, life and will arise in me, which has God for its object, and lives in him and is obedient to him. This will fulfils the law, that is, it gives itself up in obedience to the law and fulfils it with the Divine love-will, so that the law in its righteousness becomes subject to the love-desire, and moreover rejoices in the love.

35. Then the wrath of God sinks down from the soul, and the soul is released in the love-spirit from pain, and lives in God. Now, this implies earnest repentance, in which the poor soul opens wide its jaws or fiery mouth in God's purpose of wrath, and in the encorporate grace lays hold of the promise of Christ, that he will give the Holy Spirit unto them

that ask him (Luke xi. 13). This offered grace must be comprehended through the soul (through the centre of nature and the divine scientia of the unground) as a living speaking Word in the inward ground of the first voice of grace that was inspoken into Adam, so that it become a purpose to repent, and to turn round from the will of abomination. In this purpose the spirit of Christ in the primal ground of the encorporate grace (which presses from one upon all) generates a new life; and in this new life the will to sin dies and perishes, and a true branch grows forth from Christ's tree, sin thereafter ruling only in the mortal flesh. This new branch has in Christ passed through the wrath of God, in the purpose of the wrath, through eternal death unto the life of grace, as Christ says: Whosoever believeth on me shall never die, but is passed through from death unto life (John v. 24).

36. Accordingly faith is not an outward thing, that any should say: With us is the election of grace, for Christ is taught and acknowledged; he has chosen us before other peoples, that we may hear his voice. And though we are wicked, yet he has forgiven us our sins in his purpose, and slain them in the merit of Christ. We need only appropriate this and comfort ourselves therewith; it is imputed to us from without, and bestowed on us as a grace.

37. *No, No*; this is of no effect. Christ himself is the imputed grace, the gift along with the merit. He who hath Christ in him, and in whose inward ground Christ himself is, he is a Christian, and is crucified and dead with Christ, and lives in his resurrection. To him is imputed the grace in Christ's spirit and life; for he need not suffer himself to be hanged on a cross, but he puts on Christ with his entire merit; he puts on the crucified and risen Christ in himself,

and takes his yoke upon him. But it is not a question merely of knowing and taking comfort, for Christ dwells not in the body of iniquity.

38. If Christ is to arise in thee, then must the will of death and of the devil die in thee. For Christ has broken death to pieces and destroyed hell, and become Lord over death and hell. Where he makes his entry in a man, there must death and hell in the inward ground of the soul break and give way. He destroys the devil's kingdom in the soul, and makes the soul into God's child and into his temple, and gives it his will, and slays the will of the corrupt nature, that is, he transmutes it into the true image of God, for it is written: Christ is made unto us righteousness through his blood (1 Cor. i. 30). Now if a man will have this righteousness, he must drink His blood, that it may justify him; for justification takes place in the blood of Christ in man, in the soul itself, and not through an external, imputed, alien shine or lustre.

39. God gives us this free gift of grace in ourselves for a new life, which slays sin and death, and sets us before God as children of grace. For Christ with his blood of love in us fulfils God's righteousness in the wrath, and transforms it into Divine joy.

40. Now if a man find not himself in the Divine will, or even in a heartfelt desire to will, in such a way that he would fain repent, be obedient to God and put on Christ, then let him not say that he is a true Christian. Lip-babble, in which men with the tongue confess Christ to be the Son of God, and comfort themselves with his grace, yet retain in the heart the serpent with its poisonous will to pride, covetousness, envy and malice, desiring only to do evil,—this is of no avail. Such an individual does but crucify Christ and mock at His merit; for with his tongue he

confesses Him, and with the serpent's poison in his heart he casts dirt and stones at Him. He does no more than the devils did, who confessed Christ to be the power of God, when He drove them out of the possessed.

41. For they that confess Christ only with the mouth are not therefore children, but those are children that do the will of his Father which is in heaven, namely, in Christ himself. For Christ is the Father's good will, which no one can do unless he be in Christ and do it in Christ's spirit and life.

42. For not all they that proceed from Abraham are God's children; but the children of the promised seed, new-born of that seed, are the children. These are new-born from the blood of Christ, and die to the first principle in the blood of Christ, in the grace and love of God; and rise again a new man, who lives before God in righteousness and purity. Sin only adheres to them in the animal mortal flesh by a desire, and over this sin the new man in Christ rules, brings it into subjection, and repudiates the will of the flesh. But he who lives and acts according to the will of the flesh is dead, even yet alive; his lip-confession availeth him nothing.

43. For lip-confession without the inward essential ground of Christ is the real Antichrist, which confesses Christ and with vigour denies him, and has put itself in Christ's place. It says one thing, and wills and does another. Therefore the prophet Hosea says, that the Lord calls them his love which were not his love; meaning thereby those that have not knowledge of Christ in name and being, and know nothing of his revelation in humanity, yet enter with the soul into its inward ground, where grace became encorporate in Paradise through the inner Word, and lay

hold of grace in God's mercy. These are they that hear not nor have the gospel, but believe in the one God and give themselves up in all their powers to him, and would fain acknowledge and love God, if they but knew what they ought to do. Moreover, they are zealous with their whole heart in righteousness and truth. Because these neither hear nor know Christ in his manifested voice, they are outwardly not God's love; but by the inward ground they are rooted in the love of the grace, viz. in the paradisaic ground or encorporate Word. These, God says, he will bring to his Supper. For they were his love. And because they testify in power that the work of the law and the love of the grace of God is written in their hearts, they are a law unto themselves (Rom. ii. 14). This law hath Christ in his grace once fulfilled by his blood, which passed from one upon all: upon all that are born of the encorporate grace in the Will-spirit.

44. For though the text (John iii. 18) says: He that believeth not on the name of the only begotten Son of God is condemned already; yet it cannot be said that those above referred to do not believe on him. It is true their outward man does not believe him and confess him, for they know not that the Son of God became man. But their inward encorporate ground of the inspoken Word of grace, in which they have embodied themselves with the soul, that believeth in them against the day of the revelation of Jesus Christ, when he shall make his kingdom manifest.

45. For even the fathers of the Jews knew not Christ in the flesh, but only in prefigure, that is, in the encorporate grace which manifested itself by figure in the covenant in their law. They did not put on Christ in the flesh until his manifestation in the flesh; but in the first encorporate covenant and

Word they put him on in power. But when Christ had fulfilled that covenant with the humanity, and had fulfilled the law of the wrath in sin with his blood, and slain sin in them (which had kept back the humanity), then they put on Christ in the flesh, even all who had believed on him in his covenant. That is, they who had put on the covenant in power or in spirit, in them the covenant was fulfilled with heavenly essence. Further, they who in their external bodies had long rotted and corrupted, but whose souls lived in the covenant of power, did put on Christ in his resurrection in them; and many of them arose with him after his resurrection from death, and showed themselves at Jerusalem: for a testimony that they had risen again in Christ and had put on Christ in the flesh, who in his humanity had fulfilled their faith.

46. Therefore it is declared to thee, thou blind Christendom with thy lip-babble, that thou art without Christ in the flesh, and as far and much farther from Christ than the pious heathens, Turks and nations which know not Christ, and yet tend to the inward primal Ground.

47. For besides Christ man has no God; for God Jehovah has given men to Christ, *i.e.* to the name and power of Jesus, which is revealed out of Jehovah. Now if an alien draw near to God Jehovah and give himself up to him, God Jehovah giveth such an alien to Christ. For Christ says: Father (*i.e.* Jehovah), I have lost none of those which thou gavest me. That is, God Jehovah is revealed in the soul in the converted sinner. The encorporate covenant of grace gives itself to this Revelation as a possession; which covenant of grace with its occupancy of the soul shall be made manifest when God shall reveal what is

hidden in man, on the day of the second coming in the flesh and of the resurrection of the dead.

48. Therefore, thou titular and false Christendom, it is declared to thee in the zeal of God that thou art in thy lip-babble (without Christ's spirit, flesh and blood in thee) just as pagan, turkish and alien in the presence of God as such peoples themselves are. Thy supposed election, or the peculiar assumption of sonship apart from the new birth, is thy snare and fall. The anger of God maketh thy false way which thou goest a snare to entrap thee, and leadest thee in thy outward adornment into the pit of death and hell, so that thy children are at heart nothing but murderers, whoremongers, thieves, covetous, envious, malicious, perjurers and perfidious, unruly and opposers of the truth, proud arrogants, seekers in accordance with the devil after power, honour and authority, to oppress and trample upon the wretched. Outwardly they make a specious show with hypocrisy, and cover this knavery with the grace of Christ. Thy election and purpose, O God! must be the cover of their wickedness. And yet thou hast chosen for thyself nought but Christ in his members, which are born of him; and Christ is himself the election of grace. But thy righteousness in thy zeal (not God) findeth them in thy wrath: therefore it shall be ill with them.

The author's sighs, wish and prophecy.

49. O deep grace of God! rouse thyself once again in us poor, confused, blind children, and pull down the throne of Antichrist and of the devil, which he hath built up in hypocrisy, and let us once again see thy countenance. O God! the time of thy visitation has come; but who recognizes thy Arm before the great vanity of Antichrist in his kingdom that he hath

built up ? Destroy thou him, Lord, and break down his power, that thy child Jesus may be revealed to all languages and peoples, and that we be delivered from the might, pride and greed of Antichrist. Hallelujah ! From the east and north the Lord roars with his power and might ; who shall prevent it ? Hallelujah ! His eye of love sees into all lands, and his truth remains eternally. Hallelujah ! We are delivered from the yoke of the oppressor, no one shall build it up any more ; for the Lord hath shut it up in his wonders. Hallelujah !

CHAPTER XI

A FURTHER COMPARISON AND EXPLANATION OF THE PASSAGES CONCERNING ELECTION.

1. ST. PAUL says (Rom. x. 6-8): The righteousness which cometh of faith speaketh on this wise: Say not in thine heart: Who will go up into heaven? (that is nothing else than to fetch Christ down) Or, who will go down into the deep? (that is nothing else than to fetch up Christ from the dead). But what sayeth the Scripture? The word is nigh thee, even in thy mouth and in thine heart. This is the word of faith that we preach. Explanation: Who will preach to us of an external adopted grace, if it is the word of faith alone which moves in our mouth and heart in power?

2. How is the wicked man to be converted by the external shine or lustre of an assumed sonship, unless he receive the word which he carries in his mouth, and with which he confesses Christ, into his heart, so that the soul in its inmost ground apprehend it? Where is this sonship that is taken on to be found, save where the Word takes root and dwells in the heart of the soul? Where does God take men who are dead in sin, and in whom his wrath alone has life, and constrain them by a special election into the purpose of his grace? He suffers the Word to move in the mouth and in the ears of the wicked man, but if his heart apprehend it not in the soul, then He lets the light in the Word go out in the ears and hearts of the wicked; and that because the wicked are laid hold

of in the purpose of his wrath, and the soul has awakened and kindled the life of darkness by its inherited and introduced vanity, so that there is a thistle-life and serpent-life, with which the Word of God in the expression of love does not unite itself.

3. Now if the Word, which moves in our mouth and heart, makes us children of faith, then can no external form of adoption be applicable, by virtue of a peculiar outwardly elected shine or lustre; but it is the inwardly born Word that speaks forth again from such inward birth, Christ speaking from his own ground with the soul and through the soul, this it is that constitutes the sonship of adoption. For, if thou shalt confess with thy mouth Jesus as Lord, and shalt believe in thine heart that God hath raised him from the dead, thou shalt be saved (Rom. x. 9). Not by the aid of a peculiar conceit; but the Spirit of Christ must confess in thee, that Jesus Christ has risen in thee from the dead. Thy lip-confession without the resurrection of Christ in thee availeth thee nothing, for Christ said: Without me ye can do nothing. Further: No man can call God Lord without Christ in him; for without Christ he apprehends not the word LORD in power, and therefore his pronouncing the appellation of Lord is without life. For there is no distinction between Jew and Greek; for the same Lord is Lord of all, and is rich unto all that call upon him (Rom. x. 12).

4. Whosoever shall call upon the name of the Lord shall be saved (Rom. x. 13). Explanation: Here St. Paul makes no distinction between the nations; but whosoever desires God in his heart, to him He gives the salvation which He offers in Christ.

5. Where is then the chosen people who boast that God has chosen them in preference to other peoples,

that they may speak of the humanity of Christ; when in fact He has His kingdom among Jews and Greeks, and he alone is a Jew and a Christian who is so in the heart of his soul? Where is the outward imputed grace apart from the childship of the soul? When did God choose a devil and make him a child of God? *Never.*

6. Therefore mark this: Grace comes not from the merit of works, but solely from the fountain of life which is Christ. But works attest that the grace in Christ is alive in the soul. For if works follow not, Christ in thee has not yet risen from death. For he who is born of God, doeth Divine works; but he who is born of sin, ministers to sin with his works.

7. Let no one vaunt himself a Christian unless he desire to do Divine works in the love of Christ. Otherwise there is but an external semblance without the life of Christ.

8. Election to sonship passes only upon those who are alive in grace, and in grace do good works. The others, however, who comfort themselves with sonship through an assumption of grace, and work only abominations in their hearts, these the purpose of the wrath of God hardeneth. Of those, again, who are not born of grace, and yet would attain it by their works and merit, who outwardly make a specious appearance, but inwardly are dead, and thus shine only in semblance, of such St. Paul speaks:

9. Rom. xi. 7-10: What then? That which Israel seeketh for, that he obtained not; but the election obtained it, and the rest were hardened. As it is written (Isa. vi. 10): God gave them a spirit of stupor, eyes that they should not see, and ears that they should not hear, even unto this day. And David saith: Let their table be made a snare to take them withal, an

occasion to fall, a recompence unto them. Let their eyes be blinded that they see not, and ever bow down their backs (Ps. lxix. 23, 24).

10. Explanation: Which of the people of Israel do the Spirit (Isa. vi. 10) and St. Paul refer to here as not being under the election, so that God in his anger wills to harden them? Answer: Those are meant who, when they hear the word, receive it into their ears and apprehend it in a process of study in reason, but receive it not into the soul, that it may take root in the abyss. It attains not the first encorporate grace, for pride and self-will stand before it, as well as care for the belly. Covetousness is a bar before it; and the pride of selfhood or inherent love of the flesh has put itself in God's place.

11. These outwardly make a show with grace, and include it in the work of their hands, and claim to merit grace by works, as the false Jews did, who clung only to works, and possessed not the essence of faith in the ground of the soul. Of these St. Paul says, That which Israel seeketh in works, that he obtained not; but the election obtained it (Rom. xi. 7). For the election was set upon those Jews only who were Jews in the abyss of the soul, and were born from the seed of faith; who were born from the promised seed, as from the inspoken Word in the covenant of Abraham and Adam, and who were circumcised by the Word in their hearts.

12. For it was not circumcision of the foreskin that availed before God, but circumcision in the heart. The circumcision in the flesh was the seal and sign of the inward ground, intimating how grace cut off sin from the soul. In the case of those, however, who were occupied only with external works, it was not so; for they were among the people of Israel as weeds

among the wheat, which extend above the wheat, lustily wave in the wind, and would be seen to be big plants. But they bear not any good fruit, and are of no use but to be burned at harvest-time; for they only sting and prick on all sides, and take up room.

13. So likewise the false man enters into the temple of God and calls himself a Christian; and also does many seeming works, by which he would obtain respect and authority as if he were the best Christian. He learns arts, he studies, and knows how to speak much about God. He teaches others, but for the sake of profit and honour, as the Pharisees did, who professed great holiness and enlarged the borders of their priestly garments, and made long prayers as a pretence of outward religiousness.

14. But Christ said they devoured widows' houses, and compassed sea and land to make one proselyte; and when he was become one, they made of him a child of hell, twofold more than they themselves were (Matt. xxiii. 15). Now these are they that put forward such a great show, and say they sit in Christ's place, and that their words are God's word. These spread and raise themselves aloft, and strive in their hearts only after honour, covetousness and pride. What they say, that people have to observe, as if it were the voice of God from heaven. And though the voice from a false heart has established itself in the written word, and waves among the letter of the word like weeds among the wheat, still such is to be regarded as being God's word. If any one speak against it and indicate the bastard child, self-pride cries out: He is a visionary and despises the Office; be on your guard against him, he will mislead you. Come only to me, for here is the right Office as instituted by God. And though they are

not appointed by God, but by the favour of men; and moreover serve not God, but their belly, pride and self-love; still in their own minds they are the fair child of grace. These suppose they have such a superfluity of grace that they may sell it dearly to others for money on the ground of the authority of a supposititious great holiness; but he who buys, buys a thistle instead of good seed.

15. The other part of the false Israelites from Abraham's natural seed are those who, by the power of nature, are set over Israel as princes and rulers in all offices from the greatest to the least, to be the protectors of righteousness and justice. All these put forward a great show under the disguise of truth, and under colour of their offices raise themselves so highly in their self-conceit that they think they are absolute gods. Let them do what they please, and it is right. They hold that their office has authority, so that whatever they do must be called right. Yet they seek not the righteousness of God in his purpose of the order of nature, and much less the righteousness in love which he has manifested through the grace of Christ; but they put their own fictitious righteousness, with a view to their own honour of carnal sensual pride, in the place of the Divine righteousness and truth, and move along with the law of God in their mouth only. But their heart has comprehended itself in the right of a thistle, which waves above the good plants, stings and pricks on all sides, and spreads abroad, yet itself bears not any good seed.

16. These two parts (with the exception of the children of God, who still live among them) are represented as the whore and the beast in the Revelation of John, and through them the devil is a prince of

this world among men; and the beast is cast by the angel into a lake of fire burning with brimstone. These are not true Israelites born from the seed of the promise, and they attain not sonship; but the Election, which seeks and receives only the children of faith in the righteousness of grace, does attain this. But the whore together with the beast are hardened in their lusts of malice, pride, covetousness, envy, anger and unrighteousness, and are Antichrist or the titular and false Christian, a devil in angel's form, as Lucifer in heaven was, who was expelled as a false seed.

17. For the election maintained by the House-father of all beings seeks only good seed; it chooses not thistle-seed and makes wheat-grain of it, as Reason supposes, which imagines that God takes the false seed as a whole and makes of it a child of God, that thus he might exhibit his riches in the grace of a peculiar purpose. No; that does not happen. The godless man, who has sprung from a right seed, but through his inherited constellation has introduced into himself the inclination for abominations, let him repent and enter into his inward Ground, and be born of grace, and in this way it may happen.

18. For God said to Moses: I will show mercy unto a thousand generations of them that love me and keep my commandments (Ex. xx. 6). This beneficence is nothing but a planting of the covenant of grace in their seed, as was promised to Abraham, Isaac and Jacob, namely, that he would so exceedingly bless and multiply their seed according to the promised encorporate grace, that it might not be numbered.

19. But the kingdom of nature in God's purpose of righteousness also existed in this seed according to

the soulish property, and was to be operative as well. But in many the soul's will turned away from the kingdom of the purpose of grace. Now if many souls were laid hold of in the kingdom of nature, in the wrath, and grew into thistles, this was no fault of God's, but the fault of the attraction of the soulish ground, which springs from the eternal ground of nature,—it was the fault of the free-will of the unground directed towards the natural ground of the soul.

20. Here we have the primary cause of the thistle-children, who with the feet of their false desire tread upon the encorporate grace of the inspoken Word, and will not be the children of grace; concerning whom Christ, that door of grace, says (Micah vii. 1): I am become as one that goeth a gleaning in the harvest; and again: How often would I have gathered thy children together, even as a hen gathereth her chickens under her wings, and ye would not (Matt. xxiii. 37).

21. Here Reason says: They could not, and indeed they cannot. Answer: Why? Reason: They are thistle-children. Answer: Why? Reason: It belongs to God's purpose. Answer: Yes, it comes from the purpose of the divine righteousness according to the order of the creation of nature, that is, from the separation of the speaking in the Word, where the attraction or the selfhood of the unground comprehends itself in its primal ground. For there God's wrath compacts itself in the centre of nature, in the seed of men, as the result of their inherited sins, including also future actual abominations. There God's wrath often forms a root in the sin of the parents, and imprints itself in the attraction of the unground, from which afterwards in the seed a thistle-root arises.

There God visits the iniquity of the fathers upon the children unto the third and fourth generation, in conformity with the Scripture.

22. Thus these thistle-children come also from Israel, but not from grace. That is, the grace which was embodied in them in Paradise, grows in them unto judgment. Just as the hot ens of the sun gives itself indeed to the thistle, though not according to the love-tincture, but in accordance with the nature of the thistle. For the thistle can receive the sun no otherwise than in the likeness of its essence, as a toad sucks only poison from a good ens.

23. And as the sun's heat finally dries up the thistle, and cuts it off in its life; so Christ with his encorporate grace sits upon his judgment-seat in the godless man. He lets him for a while misuse the holy name of God in his mouth as an asseveration of his falseness, and under the merits of Christ lets him boast himself of being a true Christian in his supposed office. He suffers him to play the hypocrite and put on a false show as he pleases; and also suffers him to prophesy in Christ's name, as Caiaphas did, who gave counsel unto the Jews that it were better that one man should die for the people, than that all the people should perish. He lets him, moreover, fatten and grow big in his pharisaical office. He gives him in His sacraments the grace which calleth, as the sun with its good power gives itself to the thistle and lets the thistle flourish and grow tall therein up to harvest-time; then dries it up and brings it to destruction. For the thistle has generated false seed in itself, and therefore the master of the house weeds it out and casts it into the fire.

24. St. Paul speaks here in reference to this, and quotes the prophet Isaiah (vi. 10) and the royal

prophet David (Ps. lxix. 23). Let their table be made a snare; that is, they eat of God's word in their mouth, but it is withdrawn from their inner life of the soul, that the holy element may not enter into the thistle. Christ says, Satan taketh away the word from their hearts, lest they believe and be saved. For Satan sits in the thistle of the ground of the soul, and in this connection Christ calls him a prince of this world.

25. And the wrath of God has given them a spirit of stupor, eyes that they should not see the Ground of grace, and ears that they should not hear Christ's living voice. Therefore Christ said to the Pharisees: Ye are from beneath, from the father of this world; and again, Ye are of your father the devil (John viii. 44) and hear not my words, for ye are not of God. He that is born of God heareth God's word: ye therefore hear them not, because ye are not of God.

26. So also the present disputers, wranglers and despisers of God's children are not of God, but only belong to lip-labour, to the pharisaical root, and hear not Christ teaching in them. Neither do they wish to hear him, but thrust him purposely from them, and put themselves in his place. They are not the apostles of Christ, nor their successors; but they serve their idol-god Maozim [Dan. xi. 38, 39], which in their mouth soars as a thistle above the wheat. They run, and no one has sent them, save the fictions of their own hearts, for the lust for human honour. They do the service of Maozim or Antichrist, which they have set up as Christ's substitute. Christ calls them ravening wolves (John x. 12), which with their blaspheming devour the simple flock, and kill with the poison of their scorning of Christ. They soar aloft like thistles among the wheat, and establish themselves in human

honour, and confuse the world. They cause the thistle-children to make war and to ravage countries and people, to which they faithfully contribute and conduce with their poisonous envenomed spirit.

27. They are therefore those of whom St. Paul speaks (Rom. xi. 8-10), and he quotes the prophet David (Ps. lxix. 23). Let their table be made a snare to take them withal, an occasion to fall, a recompence unto them. Let their eyes be blinded that they see not, and ever bow down their backs. That is, let them recompense one another in their blindness, in that they in Christ's office do but strive after power and pleasure, that they may persecute, revile and despise each other, and ascribe the name of Christ within them to the devil. Upon their beds they seek a way how they may meet each other with guile and colour their business with the Scripture, as if they did it out of divine zeal for the truth, in order to please God and serve their brethren thereby.

28. These run like rabid dogs, wolves and evil mad beasts, in the fierceness of the enkindled wrath of God, and devour the name of Christ out of the layman's mouth. They pour forth their heart and mouth as full of the blasphemies of their heart's false devisings, so that, on account of Christ's name and their own imaginary opinions, one individual despises, reviles and hereticates another, and regards him as reprobate and good for nothing. And yet they only devour themselves, so that one party extirpates the other; and they render unto one another their wickedness and falseness, as David says.

29. These are they of whom Christ said: They love to have the chief seats in the synagogues, and love to be saluted in the market (Matt. xxiii. 6, 7); who put

forward a show of reason, but their hearts are full of bitter gall. Their ways are pernicious, the poison of asps is under their lips, and in vain do they worship me, saith the prophet. None of these fall under the election of the children of God, but only those of whom Christ says: Love one another; by this shall all men know that ye are my disciples (John xiii. 35). Again: If ye know these things, blessed are ye if ye do them (John xiii. 17). And again: He that leaveth not houses, money, goods, wife, children, and denieth himself and followeth me, is not my servant (Luke xiv. 26, 33). The heart must give up everything and hold nothing to be its own, but consider that in its station it is only a servant of God and of its brethren; and with regard to its sphere of administration, that it has therefore to do as God requires of it and will have it do, and not cover itself with the mantle of Christ and his merits, and remain thereunder a covetous, proud, envious, wrathful individual.

30. All these, so long as they are such, are those of whom St. Paul and David speak. They are indeed called; but they are not under the election of grace, unless they turn round in the time of grace, abandon everything in their hearts and follow Christ.

31. No grace imputed from without receives them, unless they become children of grace; and then the imputed grace (which is Christ) receives them into itself. Out of Christ are mere Pharisees and hypocrites; let them shine with the imputed grace as they please, they are wolves, and against such Christ bids us be on our guard. Though they say: Here is the church of Christ! 'tis all nought. By their fruits ye shall know them, says Christ (Matt. vii. 16). If they follow not Christ, they are thieves and murderers, says Christ. And though they raise the objection that

the law maketh men high priests which have infirmity, and seek to cover themselves with their office, it all avails nothing; the heart must be and live in Christ. And though St. Paul said that lust clings to the flesh, and that sin dwells in the outer flesh (Rom. vii. 17, 18); yet it is evident who they are that desire to kill lust and to follow Christ. For where covetousness and pride are within, there a Pharisee is lodged; excuse thyself how thou wilt, thou hast him about thy neck.

32. Further (Rom. xi. 15, 16): For if the loss of the Jews be the reconciling of the world, what would that be but receiving life from the dead? And if the firstfruit be holy, the lump is also holy; and if the root be holy, so are the branches. Explanation: This single text overthrows all opinions which hold that God imputes grace to the godless man, and it establishes the position on the basis of the root, indicating that God does not by his will harden some, in order through them to show what his grace is. For St. Paul says: What would that be but receiving life from the dead? He puts the hardening upon the root, and declares that an evil tree bears evil fruit and a holy tree holy branches, and the wrath of God brings forth children of wrath, and this in consequence of man's sin and vanity, which however must serve as a light to the heathen, as he (Rom. viii. 28) says: To them that love God all things work together for good, even to them that are called and born according to the purpose of grace.

33. The forgiveness of sins, regarding which the Scripture says, God forgives them their sins and imputes grace unto them for justification, passes only upon those in whose inward ground Christ lives. And if sin cleaves to these in the flesh, as it did to

David and others, so that they often fall, then grace within them helps them up again, and cancels the sin or transgression.

34. To those who are hardened this does not relate, without repentance and complete turning round. They are not to sin on the view that God will take occasion by their damnation to exhibit his grace in them, and to convert them with a peculiar call and compulsion, as if he should make an angel out of a devil in accordance with a special purpose; otherwise, Lucifer and his followers would have the right to hope for this. But he lets his sun shine the whole day of their life in their mouth and ears, and calls them and says: Harden not your hearts with actual sin, that the word may sound in your hearts and take root.

35. For it is possible that a poor dead sinner may be converted if he will stand still from his images and imaginations, and for a moment hear what the Lord speaketh in him. But the hardened, embittered spirit refuses to hear the Lord's voice speaking within itself, but says only: The letter! the letter! the written word is alone to be regarded. He pulls the written word this way and that, and makes a boast thereof; but the living Word, which has uttered the letter, he will neither tolerate in himself nor hear. But if he is to attain to understanding, he must first suffer himself to be slain as to the letter, and then the spirit in the letter maketh him truly alive. That is, he must die to all the letter, and account himself so unworthy that he is not worthy of the literal word, like the poor publican in the temple; and hold that he has no longer any righteousness by reference to the literal word, as one that hath lost all and is not worthy to lift up his eyes to heaven, or that the earth

should bear him, or that he should be reckoned among the number of the children of God. Thus he hath lost all and the letter hath slain him, for in this way he gives himself up to God's judgment. At the same time, he must hope in the pure mercy of God apart from any worthiness of his own, and sink down into this mercy, whatever it may do with him, like one dead, who has no life in himself. He must despair of all his works, and sink only with hope into the inmost purest grace of God.

36. This the soul must do. And if it does this, and can continue therein for a moment, then the first encorporate covenant or the bestowed grace lays hold of it, and gives itself to the soul. When that happens, the spirit of Christ, as the inspeaking living Word, arises in the soul and begins to speak God's word; and the holy Spirit then proceeds from the Father and the Son, and maketh intercession for the soul in God's righteousness with unutterable sighs in prayer (Rom. viii. 26).

37. We, that is to say, the poor soul, knows not how to pray as it ought; but the Spirit itself maketh intercession for it with groanings which cannot be uttered, as it pleaseth God. And then the letter, which has slain the soul in the law of God's righteousness, resuscitates it and institutes it as a teacher of its word, both in the power of the living Word and in the literal word; for such accordingly enter at the door into the sheepfold of Christ, and the sheep hear their voice, as Christ says.

38. But all the others together, of what name soever they are, who enter not in by the door of the living Word through the literal word, climb up some other way and are thieves and murderers (John x. 1-3), and the sheep hear not their voice.

39. For Christ alone is the door, understand, the living Christ in his life and speech in and through the soul. By the literal word he goes to the hearts of men, as by the preaching of Peter on the day of Pentecost. Whoever otherwise sets up as a teacher of the literal word is not sent by God, and comes only with intent to steal, that is, he would rob Christ of his honour and take it from him.

40. And thus the poor man that is slain in God's wrath may become alive again, even though he is already dead. For Christ came not to call the righteous, but sinners to repentance. And if such a poor sinner shut up in the wrath of God cometh, there is joy in heaven before the angels of God more than over ninety and nine just persons (Luke xv. 7), who have been laid hold of [from the beginning] and are twigs of the saints, and need not this ground, for it is already present in them. But in the above mentioned sinners the ground contained in God's wrath becomes manifest; and thus God shows how life has sprung from death, and how Christ destroys the devil's kingdom and breaks hell to pieces.

41. This is therefore our true conclusion, that no deliberate decree of damnation has been made with regard to any individual, in such a sense that it is impossible for him to be converted. For though man is not able to convert himself, yet his soul has from its origin out of the eternal scientia of the unground the power to plunge into the abyss, that is, into the ground in which God brings forth and speaks his Word. And in this abyss of the creature there lies in all men the free gift of grace, and inclines itself towards the soul to a greater degree than the soul does towards this deep grace. Here then the soul may well be laid

hold of in God's grace, so that it thus falls into the arms of Christ, who much rather gives it ability and power than itself desires them.

42. But if any should say that the soul cannot plunge into the abyss, he speaks like one that is far from understanding anything of the mysteries of God, as to what the soul or what an angel is. He would break off the twig from the tree, in which indeed it lives.

43. The soul has been spoken forth from the abyss into a creaturely being. Who then shall break the right of eternity, that the eternal will of the soul, which has gone out of the eternal one will into a creaturely being, should not by the same will in the creature plunge again into its mother out of which it has proceeded ?

44. Into the light which is extinguished for the will it cannot by its own power plunge. But into the cause of the light, wherein there is neither evil nor good, it can plunge; for itself is this ground. If it but sink down from its images into itself, into the abyss, then it is already there. And in this abyss lies its pearl, and there Christ arises from death, and sits there on the right hand of God in power, in heaven in man. Oh, if we would but once see where it is that Christ sitteth on the right hand of God.

45. O ye men, be not so blind ! see how God opens wide to you his door of grace. Take note of it ! Look upon the time, your visitation is born. Trample not with the feet of your deaf reason upon the free gift of the divine revelation of grace.

46. As long as a man lives he has a gate of grace open before him. There is no decree unto death from the Divine will in regard to him. For the Father

has given the determination of his justice to the grace of Christ, as his Son. Your hardening comes from yourselves; God's wrath hardens you in your inherited and actual sins, and not a strange will coming from without.

CHAPTER XII

A BRIEF ACCOUNT OF SOME QUESTIONS THAT CONFOUND REASON, IN CONNECTION WITH WHICH IT SUPPOSES THAT GOD HARDENS MAN BY A SPECIAL PURPOSED WILL; AND HOW THEY ARE TO BE UNDERSTOOD.

1. In Acts xiii. 48 it is said: And as many as were ordained to eternal life believed. This is a stumbling block to Reason, and Reason understands it not.

2. When did the ordaining begin? Thou sayest: From eternity, prior to the creature. I say so too; but not from eternity in the creature, for as yet the creature was not.

3. God saw in love and wrath what would be if he embodied the eternal nature in a creaturely existence. For he saw from eternity in himself that if the temperament [unity] should be brought out into a divisibility, and the divisibility should comprehend itself in creaturely will, there would be contrariety; and this is the very foundation of the divine manifestation. But the Scripture does not say that God has from eternity ordained the wills in the divisibility to an eternal evil willing and to an eternal good willing, so that each of them is compelled to will that for which God has inevitably disposed it. For Lucifer's and Adam's act of changing their will shows that they were free in will. But at the fall Adam lost the good willing.

4. In the above text it was said: They who by the eternal will were ordained hereunto at this time. That is, they who were seen in the light of grace from

and in the inward ground, and to whom the Divine Eye was open. As is more clearly expressed in Acts ii. 47: And the Lord added daily such as should be saved. Not such as were saved from eternity, but such as should be saved through the eternal election in Christ Jesus; these He added daily to the congregation.

5. Question: Why not at one time? Answer: They were not yet saved. They were indeed in the foreknowledge or seeing of God, and in such a way that they should be saved; but the ordaining first came with the adding to the congregation, when they were saved.

6. Why were only three thousand souls converted on the day of Pentecost, and afterwards more and more? They were not yet elected in themselves, that is, chosen in this place. When grace rises and breaks through the wrath, then the creaturely election from out of the eternal grace-seeing or insight begins. For how can a thing be ordained from eternity that has not been from eternity?

7. How can the soul from eternity, when it was as yet an ens and sport in the Divine wisdom, have been ordained to become a devil? It were horrible to think or to speak of; and yet no other meaning can be admitted if one would go upon an ordaining from eternity; and hence all teaching would be in vain. What needs to preach grace to those that cannot err or fall, and who live in an irrefragable predestination?

8. This ordaining from eternity is understood in Christ, that such as believed were foreseen from eternity in wisdom; namely, that when God should once put himself in motion and bring nature into separation for a creaturely manifestation, the name Jesus (as the highest love of God) should give itself

up to the attraction of the fiery will in the separation, and in the fiery attraction introduce itself into the kingdom of joy, and transform the wrath into a love-fire in the soul of man; whereby grace in the name Jesus was to join itself for a banner to the soulish ground, as indeed took place in Paradise after the fall. This banner was fixed in the seed of the one woman, wherein lay the foreordination from which all men have proceeded. But the separation in the fiery attraction continues as long as souls are born.

9. There is no certain ordaining from eternity with regard to any individual soul that may be born, but only a general predestination by grace. The ordaining begins with the time assigned to the tree. The seeing is even in the seed: before it becomes a creature, God knows the ground and what will be produced. But judgment belongs to the time of harvest, according as Christ speaks in all the parables.

Of Lydia, the seller of purple.

10. When it is written (Acts xvi. 14): The Lord opened the heart of Lydia that she gave heed unto the things that Paul spake, and believed in the name of Jesus; it was with her as with all alien peoples who know not the name of Jesus, and yet tend to the inward Ground beyond all images, and desire to know the one God and to give themselves up to him. These are laid hold of by the encorporate grace of the inspoken Word, and without the knowledge of reason are elected and born children of grace; and thus we are to conceive concerning this Lydia. Though at first she may have regarded Paul as a strange teacher, yet when she heard that he preached the law of righteousness, and that the law of sin, which keeps man

a prisoner, was fulfilled in such a measure of grace, then in her hunger for justification the inward Ground contained in the encorporate grace moved, and Christ became alive in her, so that she heard Christ's voice in the words of Paul, what Christ was teaching in her: Christ was become the hearer in her.

11. But with the other heathen this was not so, for they lived wholly in images. Their heart was not directed towards the one God, in order to know him; for they had their own pagan idol-gods whom they served, and only wished to hear from Paul some new thing. Nevertheless the word entered into their ears, and penetrated into those who were of a good will, who afterwards even were converted when they heard more preached about Christ; as indeed afterwards in the same place many thousands were converted, when the Word laid hold of them still more strongly. So also many of those were afterwards converted who heard Peter on the day of Pentecost, and yet mocked him on that day. But when the word sounded in them to a greater degree, the hour of their inward hearing arrived. As it was with the soldier who pierced Christ's side: the hour of his conversion only arrived when he heard many say that Christ was the Son of God. And he became a martyr for Christ's sake, as the histories tell.

12. It must not here be said that Lydia above others was from eternity ordained to this, that she alone should hear Paul. She was at this time in a Divine way of preparation, and would fain understand the true ground relating to God: her heart longed after it, and therefore God opened her heart. The others, however, at this time were not yet prepared; but when the holy Spirit began to knock at their heart, they apprehended it only with their ears, until they

opened to him, and meditated on it, and searched the Scriptures to see whether those things were so, as Paul says (Acts xvii. 11). As is said likewise concerning the Ephesians: When they heard the word further, they had a hungry door open in their hearts, where Christ with his word had place.

13. Thus it fared with all the Gentiles or heathen, and also with the Jews who at first mocked Christ when he was hanging upon the cross. But when they beheld the things which were done, many of them smote their breasts and turned round (Luke xxiii. 47).

14. This happened to those Jews whose inward Ground at this time was open: to them God opened the encorporate grace in the spirit of Christ. And indeed in the histories much is found to show that many a man in his introduced pagan imaginations has for a long time mocked Christ, and yet at last, when he has entered into the earnest depths of himself, and wished to understand exactly what fables (as they call them) were told regarding Christ, has been converted.

15. For as soon as the heart stands still from images, and plunges into the ground of itself, the voice of Christ in the word presses in, and in the essence of the soul knocks.

16. The imagination of the earthly nature prevents the heart from standing still to God and entering into its inward Ground, where God teaches and hears. For God himself is present in all places through all things, as it is written: Do not I fill heaven and earth? (Jer. xxiii. 24). What needs the soul then to plunge elsewhere to hear God, than into its own abyss? There God is and dwells from eternity to eternity; he needs only to become manifest in the

creature. For this end he stands in the spirit of Christ in the same inward Ground, and knocks at the soul. Now if the soul turn towards him, then Christ himself opens to it the door of grace, and comes in unto it, and sups with it, and it with him (Rev. iii. 20).

Explanation of Matthew xiii. 11 and Luke viii. 10.

17. In these passages it is said: Unto you it is given to know the mysteries of the kingdom of God, but unto others in parables; that seeing they might not see, and hearing they might not understand. To the disciples Christ expounded the parables, but not to others.

18. Here Reason lies dead in the sense that it sees nothing without the Divine light, and supposes only that Christ would not impart the explanation to others, that they were not worthy of it. The people, however, followed him with a hungry desire to hear him. But there is here another alphabet or meaning. Christ said to his disciples: My Father will send you another Comforter, the Spirit of truth, which proceeds from the Father. When he is come, he will put you in remembrance of all that I have said unto you; for he shall take of mine, and shall declare it unto you (John xvi. 13, 14).

19. The voice of the Father in Christ, in God's righteousness, was not therefore to enter into the hearts and ears of the laymen and hearers, with the exception of some through whom the Father would work miracles; but the voice was to enter into them whom the holy Spirit should bring with him out of Christ's sufferings, death and resurrection, as the voice of the open door of grace.

20. For before Christ's passion the voice of the holy Spirit in Christ was as yet in God's righteousness, *i.e.* in the law; but in Christ's death the law of the righteousness of God was fulfilled. Accordingly after this the holy Spirit, in consequence of the fulfilment, in consequence of Christ's wounds, blood and death, went forth in the greatest compassion, in the spirit of Christ; and it was this voice that the poor sinners, who followed him with desire, were to hear. But to the disciples was given the Father's voice in God's righteousness, that they should hear it from Christ. For they were first to be clothed with the same fiery righteousness in which lay the Father's omnipotence, that is to say, the soulish principle. Afterwards there was given to them on the day of Pentecost the holy Spirit proceeding from the grace-love, from Christ's fulfilment of the righteousness.

21. And thereupon among them tongues, as the Father's righteousness, became divided; and the spirit of Christ, by the dividing of God's righteousness, went forth with the flame of love. This, therefore, happened to them, that they might be grounded in the spirit of the law and the gospel by grace; for they were to do miracles. But the power of miracles comes from the Father's omnipotence and property, and not through the property of love and humility, which has to suffer and give itself up to God's law and righteousness in the wrath, and fulfil the wrath with love and suffering, and also transform it into a love of mercy, as is seen clearly in the person of Christ.

22. When Christ would perform miracles, he first prayed to his Father, that is, to the fiery omnipotence and righteousness. But when he had fulfilled the Father's righteousness with his love and humility,

in his blood of the love-tincture called by the name Jesus, then the Father's righteousness in the wrath became subject to the love. And by that subjection others (besides the disciples) after Christ's ascension were to hear the holy Spirit speak, and to understand the parables of Christ; as indeed took place in such a way that afterwards they came to understand all mysteries. For the spirit of Christ by his fulfilment and by his resurrection opened their understanding, as was likewise the case with the two disciples on the way to Emmaus, as well as with the considerable number of people who, after his resurrection, heard the spirit of Christ speak parables without any proverb out of the mouth of the apostles, through the true Sender, as the result of Christ's passion and death.

23. And therefore Christ, when he walked upon earth before his passion, taught in parables, lest they should apprehend this same spirit of Christ other than in the Father's righteousness; for such was not the ground which he wished of his grace to give to them. But the ground was this, namely, that which arose on the day of Pentecost from his merit, when he had cancelled sin and sealed it up in God's righteousness (Matt. xiii. 34).

24. They were not all to go about doing miracles and deeds like the apostles, who were appointed to this by the Father's gifts, for Christ said: Father, I have lost none of those that thou gavest me out of thy righteousness, but the son of perdition (who was lost before); that the Scripture might be fulfilled (John xvii. 12). By this Christ meant those whom his Father had given him with a view to the ordinance and office of invitation into his kingdom. But the others were to be born through the spirit of humility

from Christ's love, from the process of the passion and death of Christ, and were to follow him in his process under the banner of the cross in patience, and, passing out of God's righteousness with their humility, surrender and sacrifice themselves in the spirit of Christ, in consequence of which the murdering by Jews and heathens began.

25. For by the blood of the Christians God's righteousness in the wrath was brought into the great compassion of love, so that in God's righteousness such miracles and deeds were done among Christians in the humility of Christ. This now for a period has been awanting, namely, from the time of seeking to place the spirit of Christ in man upon soft cushions, and to set up fat bellies in power, pomp and glory. But the spirit of Christ has only been revealed and manifested because he was willing to suffer, and to fulfil God's wrath in his righteousness with the act of surrender in his suffering.

26. Therefore look closely at thyself, thou so-called Christendom, to see whether thy righteousness is rooted at present in the patience of the sufferings of Christ, and whether thou seekest in thy appellation of Christian anything more than that Christ with his love may be manifested in thee in his passion and death, so that thou only desirest to become like unto his image, with which he has fulfilled God's righteousness.

27. Do but look closely at thyself. Seekest thou not vain subterfuges, and coverest thou not thy heathenish idolish image with the sufferings of Christ? What doest thou, thou would-be Christendom? By means of disputation and investigation thou wilt be a Christian; foreign languages shall make thee an apostle. Contending, quarrelling and wrangling constitute thy apostolic heart, under which lies nothing

but thine own honour, full of the infection of the black devil. What hast thou done with the sufferings and the patience of Christ in his condition of obedience? Thou evil one! Lo! there cometh a messenger out of God's righteousness and demandeth this with fire and sword of thy appended name of Christian, in order to extirpate thee as false and faithless, and to manifest his true children of obedience in his love. This thou shalt experience intimately, if we speak as we ought. Amen.

Of the words of Christ: Father, forgive them.

28. The words of Christ on the cross are likewise raised in objection, when he said: Father, forgive them, for they know not what they do (Luke xxiii. 34). Explanation: As has been already mentioned, the mysteries of the kingdom of Christ and of the true justification of the poor sinner before God were not revealed to the Jews until justification had been accomplished in the blood of Christ. Accordingly those whom the Father had chosen for an instrument and for the process of Christ were not destined to know beforehand what they should do. But after they had done it, God opened their understanding for their conversion. Therefore Christ supplicated the Father's righteousness, which would have swallowed up these murderers and executioners in the wrath, that his righteousness would forgive them in Christ's blood.

29. No one rightly knew the Saviour of the world, not even the Apostles themselves, till the revelation that resulted from his death. And it must not be said that God hardened these men specially for this purpose, so that they might not know Christ. *No.*

No one rightly knew him and what his office was, till after his fulfilment of that for which he had come.

30. The men who judged Christ and put Christ to death, sat in the office of the law of the righteousness of God. The law, viz. God's righteousness, put Christ to death. But they thought they did service unto God, and were zealous in the law of God's righteousness; which law had chosen them to be instruments for the fulfilment of the law in Christ, as being officers of the law.

31. And so likewise Saul, who was zealous in the law of the righteousness of God with true divine zeal, as the law required. This he carried on till the fulfilment of the law laid hold of him in the zeal of his purpose, and indicated to him that such zeal in the law had been fulfilled with blood. Henceforth he was no longer to be zealous in the law of the righteousness of the Father, in fire, but in the law of the fulfilment in the love of Christ.

32. Those are not the greatest sinners who crucified Christ, for they were obliged to do it by reason of the office in the law which they held. But those rather are the greatest sinners, who, after the fulfilment of the law, mock Christ and slay him in his members, and themselves remain dead in sin after grace has been offered to them in the fulfilment of the law in the power of the spirit with miracles and deeds; who have stopped their ears and blasphemed against it. These have blasphemed against the holy Spirit in the merit of Christ in his glorious revelation and offered grace.

33. We should therefore view the Scripture aright, and not speak of a special hardening because Christ said: They know not what they do. No one knew

who Christ was till after his death: then it was that they first knew him.

34. Now if any one in the words of Christ should say: I do this and that, and know not what I do; God has hardened me thus, I must do it; also, I must steal, lie, be greedy of gain and be angry, and along with this cherish pride: let him carefully consider himself, as to what he is, and whether he be not a child of the devil, who has hardened him with this conceit. If God has hardened him so that he cannot but do it, then the law of His righteousness is lacking in him, and also the teaching of the gospel; for he does what he must and of necessity has to do, and necessarily he cannot be otherwise. All which is contrary to the law of the righteousness of the Father, and also to the law of the Son in the gospel. And he has no proof of it, with which to excuse himself, when God's truth shall cast him as a liar into hell, whose child he is in the apprehended wrath of God, and is born of the father of lies, as Christ said of Satan (John viii. 44).

35. Further, Reason raises the following objection: Christ made supplication for Peter, that his faith should not fail (Luke xxii. 32); why did he not also make supplication for others, that their faith should not fail? There must therefore be some purpose, says Reason.

36. Explanation: As already mentioned, Peter and the other apostles received the ground of faith from Christ's voice before the fulfilment of the law. Their faith still rested upon the law of the Father, *i.e.* upon the spirit of the righteousness of God. Therefore Christ said unto them that he would send them another Comforter, even the Spirit of truth, who should draw faith out of Christ's fulfilment and death, out of his

resurrection and restoration ; the same should remain with them and guide them into all truth, and should take of his and declare it unto them.

37. The first faith was given them from the Father, when he gave them to Christ to be his disciples. In it still lay God's righteousness in the wrath. This faith Satan desired to sift and to penetrate, to see whether it were the one that should and would take away from him his kingdom in man, and destroy hell. For this faith in relation to the wrath of God was not yet able to resist the true test or fire. And therefore the name Jesus made supplication for them, that this ground, in which afterwards they were to do miracles in the faith of love and humility, should not fail in them. Otherwise the miracles would not have taken place in so fiery a way over life and death, that is, over God's righteousness, which love overcame in the blood of Christ.

38. To others, however, this faith was not yet given, for they were not apostles, but had to wait for the promise : in it was given unto them the faith of grace. And in this faith of grace Christ makes supplication for them as well as for Peter, that their faith may not fail. As it is written : He sitteth at the right hand of God and maketh intercession for us, and without ceasing supplicates the righteousness of God for us, in ourselves, with groanings which cannot be uttered. If we would but once learn to see and understand the Scriptures, and go out from unprofitable babble into the ground of truth.

39. Let no one, therefore, say that Christ maketh not supplication for all men, as he did for Peter, that their faith may not fail. For he is the active supplication or prayer in ourselves. Why then are we juggling a long time with such objections ? It is upon request

that we have explained these objections, and with sincere intent. When Christ said: Father, forgive them, they know not what they do, he made supplication for all who did not yet know him, and yet would learn to know him.

40. But the following objection is raised: He suffered Judas to despair. Here consider the Scripture, what it says regarding Judas. Christ says (John xvii. 12): I have lost none of those that thou gavest me, but the son of perdition; that the Scripture might be fulfilled which says: He that did eat of my bread, hath lifted up his heel against me (Ps. xli. 9). Seest thou not that Christ calls him a child of perdition, as one who was already a thistle, which the wrath in God's righteousness had generated in itself as its life.

41. Therefore this Judas, as a figure and as the betrayer of Christ, had to be called an apostle, in order to indicate what kind of people there would be among teachers of Christ in the future: that, in fact, they would eat the bread of Christ's cup under a show of great holiness, and yet would only betray Christ in his members and help to condemn him to death. As the ministers of the antichristian church among the sects have done for a long time, and still do to this day, betraying and traducing the true Christians, and helping to crucify and slay Christ.

42. Hence Christ said that thus the Scripture must be fulfilled which points out regarding Christ that he should continually be betrayed and slain in his members, in order that God's righteousness might continually be fulfilled in Christ's members to the end of the world. Therefore these brethren of Judas must be an instrument of God's righteousness in the wrath for this purpose, and must be reckoned also

among the apostles, that men may believe them to be apostles.

43. They must get apostolic calling from men, and sit in Christ's place, and eat the bread of Christ, in order that Christ in his process may be betrayed continually in his members, and that the process of Christ may not cease till he come again and fetch home his bride. For these brethren of Judas also serve God in his severe righteousness, that this righteousness may continually be fulfilled in the blood of Christ, in his members. For the wicked are to God a good savour unto death, and the holy a savour unto life.

44. Seeing then God is a wrathful God and also a lovable God, the figure and Christ's office had and still always have to stand side by side with each other, in order that one may urge the other, and that one in another be manifested, to the praise of the glory of God at the day of his appearance.

45. No one can with reason say that God hardened Judas by a special will and purpose, so that he could not have turned; but the righteousness of God in the wrath had laid hold of him, and formed and generated him into a thistle before he was an apostle, even in the seed, before the soul was born, in consequence of inherited sin, for God punishes unto the third and fourth generation.

46. Thus God's righteousness presented in Judas a figure, showing how man has been laid hold of in God's righteousness for condemnation to death, and how this righteousness should manifest Christ in his death, in that he was destined to die to sin in the righteousness for the sake of the people, and satisfy the righteousness. Thus the wrath installed its own figure in Judas alongside of Christ in his office, that

it might be known it was God's will that his wrath in man should be extinguished. And yet the wrath's own will remained, dwelling in itself in God's righteousness, as a centre for the manifestation of God.

47. But should any one say: How can a child in the womb help becoming a thistle? To him it is declared that it is the fault of the root, from which the thistle itself springs, as Christ said (Matt. vii. 18): A corrupt tree cannot bring forth good fruit. The wrath of God wills to be creaturely, and yet that is not due to God's purpose, but to the purpose of the fierce wrath which is proper to the eternal Nature itself. This purpose, however, is not God, but fierceness; and is a cause of fire, by which the light is manifested. If thou seest nothing here, then God assist thee.

48. But if it should be said that Judas was sorry for his crime, that is certainly true. The devil also is sorry that he cannot be a good angel, but must remain a devil. And because he cannot attain to the former, he despairs of the grace of God, and that constitutes his eternal hell.

49. And this holds also of Judas. He was sorry that he was expelled from God's grace; yet he desired not grace, for the fountain of the desire of grace was not in him. He was not begotten of faith, *i.e.* of the promised seed. And though he came from the same nature wherein faith also lay, and also possessed the encorporate Word in the abyss of the soul, yet his soul already had a figure of the darkness, which was wholly dead as to grace and quite incapable of life. For though a thistle were planted in honey, only a rank thistle would shoot forth. To such, grace does not belong; for Christ said to his disciples: Take and drink; this is my blood, which is shed for you and for many. In the blood was the tincture. The sun gives not its

holy tincture to the thistle, which has a false life contrary to the tincture; it gives it indeed being, but the thistle is not capable of the jewel; it only receives from the sun a property in conformity with itself, in so far as such property serves it. And so likewise it is to be understood here. St. Paul says: Because they discern not the Lord's body, the godless receive it unto judgment, as the thistle receives the sun (1 Cor. xi. 29).

50. Further, an objection is raised by Reason regarding the blind man (John ix. 2), when the disciples asked: Who did sin, this man, or his parents? Christ gave them this answer: Neither did this man sin, nor his parents: but that the works of God should be made manifest in him.

51. Explanation: God has enclosed the kingdom of this world in time, limit, measure and weight (Sap. xi. 22): and the works of God stand in a moving figure. When the figure is to be made manifest, the same thing also will stand there, in and by which the position shall be manifested.

52. Since Christ, before his passion and fulfilment of the law of nature, was destined to be manifested in this believing man that was born blind; the law with the eyes of nature had first to kill him, in order that Christ might open for him the eyes of faith, which eyes of faith afterwards should open by grace the eyes of nature. And it was a figure, showing how in Adam we have become blind as to God, and how in Christ we should again become seeing. For the blindness of this blind man was not due to a special inherited sin, for he was a seed of faith in whom Christ with his assumption of humanity had become active, and in this condition he believed on him. But this inward seeing of faith that sprang from

Christ was not yet applicable; he was first to become seeing through the human voice.

53. For when Jesus became man, human seeing was born into God's seeing. But the law of God still kept this seeing imprisoned in poor sinners, till our eyes came to see by means of his death, by the fulfilment of the law. Therefore, although this man in the seed of faith in the womb had become seeing through Christ's entrance into and revelation in humanity, nature killed his seeing, so that he could not see with faith by the light of nature; for God's righteousness in the law of nature was not yet satisfied.

54. This man, then, had to be born blind, in order that the divine Eye might make him seeing in faith, through the inspeaking of the holy name Jesus, that the glory of God might be manifested. And it must not be said that this blind man was born blind in consequence of a special purpose; but he was one who sprang from the root of the seed of faith, and this faith the name Jesus (*i.e.* God's light in love) was to make seeing. He was one in the clockwork of Christ, given to Christ for his process by God the Father; as the Pharisees in the clockwork of the law of God's righteousness came also to the process of Christ.

55. Further, the following passage (Matt. xxiv. 24) is raised in objection by Reason, whereby it seeks to maintain that God wills that men should be led astray and damned, for Christ says: There shall arise false Christs, and false prophets; insomuch that, if it were possible, the very chosen should be brought into error.

56. Explanation: This text says, they shall arise; but it does not say that they are sent from God, much less from Christ, unto whom all power was given in heaven and on earth.

57. These false prophets arise out of the purpose of the wrath of God, out of the zeal of the righteousness, and shall sift the heart of the false lip-Christians, who call themselves Christians. Such lip-Christians were to be sifted from the process of Christ by this exacerbated spirit of the wrath of God, that they should believe the spirits of falsehood, seeing they call themselves Christians and yet Christ is not in them, but they are children of the wrath. Accordingly those false prophets were to exhibit their images of abomination and erroneous interpretation, that the children of the false name of Christ, covered with Christ's purple mantle, might cleave unto them, and the true Christians separate themselves from them, in order that it should be known who Christ is. Moreover, through false prophets the process of Christ was to be manifested by betrayal, suffering and putting to death ; and Christ was destined continually to be slain by the Pharisees and heathen for the sake of their false worship.

58. For God's righteousness requires the Church of Christ in blood, and always presents an occasion by means of false prophets and false Christians, who with the heathen or tyrants do without intermission slay Christ in his members, and sacrifice to the righteousness of God, whereby God's anger is killed in the true Christians.

59. If we would know these false prophets at the present time, who they are, let us consider those who have compounded their opinions from the letter, and composed fine postils full of revilings and railings of the wrath of God, by which one sect grievously wounds another and proclaims it to be false. And yet these criers live one like another, and write only for their own honour, that they may be regarded as

very learned persons, upon whom all the world ought to look, that they may be said to be Christ. But they are only the titular or false Christ, without grace. They live also entirely out of Christ's process in vain lusts of the flesh, and daily devise further how they may invent new orders and new forms of worship, from which they get a specious lustre and are honoured the more, and furnished with riches so as to fill the belly of their belly-god Maozim.

60. These have not Christ's spirit in them, neither are they apostles of Christ, but all of them together only false prophets, who interpret by the letter without knowledge. For what they say, they themselves know not nor believe. These are the ravening wolves, of whom Christ said, They have not the knowledge of Christ in them, and yet they prophesy.

61. But of those who are in Christ he said, that it was not possible they could be led away. These are they in whom Christ has become man. They are by the inward Ground in Christ in heaven, in God, and hear Christ speaking in them; for they hear only God's word, and not the false prophets. If at the present time these false prophets were to be weeded out in all the sects, the apostolic band of those who call themselves apostles would be insignificant.

62. We must therefore by no means say that God decrees that such false prophets should come because he will not grant salvation to individuals who otherwise might attain it, Reason erroneously supposing that God has ordained one aggregate of persons to salvation, and the other aggregate to eternal damnation, and that he will have it so, and therefore sends them strong delusion, so that they should fall, that he may show his anger against them.

63. Ye dear brethren, who are perplexed with this

conceit, we give you the following advice: Teach not opinion and conjecture. Be first radically assured in Christ's spirit within you, else you will be laid hold of in God's righteousness among the number of the false prophets. If you have not the door of Christ open in your soul, so that you may go in and out in the spirit of Christ, and find true certain pasture for the sheep, and feed them in Christ's herbage, then let it alone.

64. Your academic arts, in which you vanquish and defeat one another with terms of reason, and afterwards write and teach such victory of reason as the truth of Christ, avails you nothing in the sight of God. For Christ calls those thieves and murderers who, apart from his spirit and the knowledge of him, climb in at another door (as by conclusions of reason), without the knowledge and will of Christ. If ye be not armed with Christ's spirit, take not the field against such a powerful foe, viz. the devil, and against God's righteousness in the wrath. Ye shall with your conclusions of reason, without the blood of Christ in you, obtain nothing there; but ye shall be taken prisoner in God's severe righteousness in your rationalistic inferences, and chosen to be false prophets in the wrath of God.

65. For no one is a prophet unless he be born out of God's righteousness in the great clockwork of the divine order, in the expressed word in the limit of that time, as the holy Spirit of God speaks in the divine order through that limit. He must be a limit in the clockwork in the great mystery, through which the Spirit of God points to another limit of manifestation. Such were the prophets and such they still are in the present day, who stand in the limit of the great clockwork, in the grace-predestination in Christ Jesus, in

whom God has chosen us before the foundation of the world. He must with his prophetic spirit stand in God's righteousness, and in the very limit where God has foreseen the name of his love in the righteousness, in such a way that he is born out of the ground of the law of the righteousness according to God's purpose, and also out of the ground of the purposed grace; so that he may teach the law or God's righteousness, and likewise the gospel or God's love and the fulfilment of the law.

66. Such a one is a genuine prophet, and no other; for he is the limit of a kingdom in the great mystery, by and through which arises the order of the kingdoms upon earth. He is the mouth of that kingdom. But seeing he has to teach, both that God's righteousness in the wrath must be slain by grace, and that grace must first give itself up wholly to the wrath, to mortification in the righteousness, he is in the process of Christ sacrificed to the same righteousness of God by the false prophets and Pharisees. For this must and has to be, in order that his limit may be brought in the blood of Christ through the wrath, and the limit of the righteousness be turned into grace. Therefore the prophets of Christ must be martyrs.

67. Observe this well, all ye that will teach, and think ye are called to it. Consider your calling within you, as to whether ye be called of God in his clockwork in Christ, and whether Christ has called you with his voice within you. If not, then ye are nothing else but false prophets, who run unsent, and enter not into the sheepfold by the door of Christ.

68. That you are intent upon a human calling is of importance in the eyes of men, and God is content with what men do when it is done in his order; particularly when you give yourselves up to God's call

from a human call, and consider how you are to become capable of the divine calling in your human calling. Where this is not found, and you remain in your human calling in self-will, you sit upon the seat of pestilence and are Pharisees and false prophets. And though there were many hundred thousand of you, yet the office makes you not prophets and shepherds of Christ, unless you enter in through Christ's living door. And though the Pharisee will not relish this, yet the time is born and the limit at hand in which it shall be revealed, and human subtlety will no longer be of any help. Woe unto the people that despise this; they shall be devoured in the zeal in God's righteousness.

69. Further, the prophet Jonah is raised in objection by Reason, as its proof that God constrains men to evil and good, *i.e.* to his purpose, as he constrained Jonah so that he was compelled to go to Nineveh.

70. Explanation: Hearken, Reason, be not deceived, God's Spirit is not to be judged by reason. Jonah was a prophet, born out of the goal of the covenant, and stood in the figure of Christ, intimating how Christ should be cast into the wrath of God, into the jaws of the great whale of the divine righteousness, in order to fulfil this righteousness; and how he should enter into the sea of death, and how the wrath of God (which he overcame in that same whale of death) should let him go forth from it again alive and freed, as Jonah did from the whale's belly.

71. He was a figure of Christ, and was born out of the limit of the great clockwork, out of the great mystery, out of both the purposes of God, viz. out of his grace and out of his righteousness, and was exhibited as a figure or play of the Spirit of God. Thus the Spirit in this figure had regard to and

pointed at Christ, intimating how the humanity of Christ, that is, our assumed humanity, would be terrified at Nineveh, at the danger to life. As Christ, when the time was come that he should enter into Nineveh, viz. into God's wrath, said : Father, if it be possible, let this cup pass from me (Luke xxii. 42). Moreover, he hid himself several times from the Pharisees or Ninevites, as Jonah did to avoid going to Nineveh.

72. This figure also indicates that when we poor Jonahs should declare to the people the punishments and judgments of God, and have to venture our life among them for the truth's sake, that excuses are sought, and there is a setting out upon the sea of the world in search of days of ease and fatness, and a flight from God's command, and a silence from fear of the Ninevites. Then cometh the whale of God's wrath, and swallows up the prophets.

73. But the fact that Jonah was driven thereto by force, signifies that the purpose of God the Father in Christ was and had to endure. That though Adam had turned away from the obedience of God to the images and imaginations of this world (whereby man was given over to the great whale death), yet God's purpose was to stand, and Adam was to rise again in Christ out of the belly of death.

74. Such is the figure in connection with Jonah, dear friends, and not your determination or compulsion to evil and good. It is the figure of Christ. Therefore desist from these inferences, and blaspheme not against the holy Spirit in his wonders in the figure of Christ by hints and suggestions conveying erroneous opinion, or you will with your reasonings be cast into the sea of God's wrath. We ought to and we will warn you in love in a brotherly way.

CHAPTER XIII

A SUMMARY CONCLUSION TO ALL THESE QUESTIONS

1. FINALLY, Reason brings in also the saying of Christ, John xvii. 6, where he says: Father, I have manifested thy name unto the men which thou gavest me out of the world. With this text Reason seeks to show that Christ manifests his name to none, unless the Father by his purpose first give them to him, whether they will or not.

2. Explanation: O thou miserably deluded Reason, how blind thou art! Knowest thou what the Father's giving is? It is the centre of the soul, viz. the Father's will in the attraction of the eternal righteousness, the attraction being laden either with the desire of abominations or with the Divine love of grace: to them the attraction gives up the speaking Word in God's righteousness, either to a root of a thistle or to a root of the seed of faith. To the root in the seed of faith Christ becomes manifest; for it is Christ's root, from which a Christian is born in Christ. To such Christian souls Christ has always manifested himself from the beginning of the world, and given them God's name; for he himself is God's name.

3. This text is not to be understood as if God before the beginning of the world had made a decree, and established it in a certain order and compulsoriness, as to how many and whom he would give to Christ, and that this number could not be exceeded, as imprisoned Reason thus understands it. *No.* The tree of Christ is immeasurable. God's grace and also his

righteousness in fire are both immeasurable. For had God set a limit in love and wrath, it would rest upon a measurableness or a beginning, and hence one would necessarily have to think that it would come to an end. *No.* The tree of the knowledge of good and evil stands in the eternal ground, in which there is no time nor limit. God's grace in Christ is immeasurable and exists from eternity, and the same holds true of the kingdom of nature in the great mystery, by which the fiery attraction springing from the will of the unground has revealed itself. As Christ has manifested God's name to men, *i.e.* to the root of the seed of faith, from the beginning of the world, thus it is also to the end of the world. For he said to his disciples when they asked him regarding the end of the world: As the lightning goeth out from the east, and shineth unto the west, so shall the coming of the Son of man be (Matt. xxiv. 27). As the sun gives itself to all things the whole day long, and shines upon them, and penetrates into everything, whether it be good or bad; so likewise does the Divine sun Christ, as the true light of the world.

4. Christ withdraws himself from no one with his light of grace. He calls them all and shines with his voice in them, none at all excepted. But they do not all hear and see him, because they are not of God. The attraction of the unfathomable will of the Father in the soulish creature has introduced itself into an alien image so as to become a thistle of the serpent, and such a thistle sees and hears nothing when God's righteousness says in it: Do right, or I will slay thee; this and that is sin, do it not, else thou wilt be cast out from God.

5. When the soul hears this within it, the devil comes in his form of a serpent and says: Tarry yet

in the flesh, in this and that lust,—in covetousness, pride, envy, anger, whoredom, gluttony, mockery; there is still time to repent at thine end. Lay up for thyself first considerable treasure, so that thou no longer needest the world; then enter into a godly mode of life, and thou mayest live in retirement without the reproach of the world, and needest not the world.

6. Thus one day and year is added to another until the hour of death. Then one has a mind to be a child of grace and be saved, though he has remained in the serpent the whole time. Thereupon the priest must come with God's body, and bring with him the angelic new birth; whereas many a priest has it not himself, and is also but a stranger there.

7. Those referred to, while they remain in the serpent, are not given to Christ, but to the wrath of God. The wrath will not let them go, unless the will of the soul turn itself to the source of grace. And when this takes place, the giving results. For the Divine sun shines forthwith into the stationary will and kindles it; and the kindling now is the name of God, which Christ gives to the soul, whereby it begins to be active in Christ and to carry out repentance to forgiveness, that is, when it begins to stand still from false imagination.

8. It is said: No longer to be doing is the greatest or best repentance. This is the case when the ground of the soul begins to be still from imagining, and enters into its abyss. This the soul has power to do, unless it be already a thistle; then it runs and grows till the end of its time. Yet there is no judgment from without upon it, but only its own judgment, as long as it remains in the life of this world, until the time of harvest. But it is difficult if the inner and also the

outer ground of the external constellation be false: such commonly run on so to the end. Then comes the repentance of Judas; and tickling and flattering with the sufferings of Christ avails little, when no root of faith is there.

9. The pomp of the splendid funeral of the dead animal is merely the scorn and derision of the devil, by which he mocks the soul. For imputed grace from without is of no effect, that we should be absolved with outward words of grace, as a lord or prince grants a murderer his life out of clemency. *No.* The imputed grace of Christ must be manifested in us, in the inward Ground of the soul, and be our life.

10. Repentance should not be put off to the end, for an old tree takes root badly. If Christ is not in the soul, there is no grace or forgiveness of sin. For Christ himself is the forgiveness of sin, who with his blood transmutes in our soul the introduced abominations in God's wrath. Thus, in the presence of the Pharisees, he said to the man sick of the palsy: Thy sins are forgiven thee. This was accomplished when he seized the voice of Christ in his soul; then the living Word within him forgave him his sins. That is, it overpowered the sins, and trampled upon the head of the will of the serpent's introduced abominations with the fire of love.

11. No one can forgive sins but Christ in man. Where Christ lives in man, there is absolution. For when Christ said: Receive the Holy Ghost. Whose sins soever ye remit, they are remitted unto them; and whose sins soever ye retain, they are retained,—this relates to the true apostles and their genuine successors, who have received the Holy Spirit from Christ, and who themselves are and live in Christ, and have Christ's voice in them. These have power to

inspeak into the hungry soul the living word of Christ that dwells in them; but others have not this power. Let them be called what they will and make what show they please, they must be apostles of Christ if they are to exercise his office; otherwise they are but Pharisees and wolves.

12. The soul must also open its hungry mouth to the inspeaking, else the word entereth not into it. And indeed it entered not into all when Christ himself preached and taught, but only into the hungry and thirsty souls of whom he said: Blessed are they which hunger and thirst after righteousness, for they shall be filled; that is to say, with the fulness of his word.

13. For the forgiveness of sins is not in man's power, but in the power of the word of Christ that dwells in man. Man's speaking forgives not sin, but God's speaking in man's word. Now this speaking enters not into the false thistle, but only into that soul where the seed of faith lies in the sound of motion, and where the soul stands still from formation of the serpent's desire.

14. Therefore rely not upon men. They cannot forgive you your sins and give you grace, unless you yourselves hunger and thirst after righteousness. To put off repentance to the end amounts to a repentance of Judas. It is not merely a matter of taking comfort, but it is necessary to be new-born.

15. Thus, dear brethren, I have striven to reply briefly and fundamentally to the points in question. And this is my belief, that the Scripture-passages are all true, but our reason errs, and understands them not out of Christ. The Apostle says: We have not received the spirit of bondage again unto fear; but we have received the spirit of adoption, whereby we

cry, Abba, Father (Rom. viii. 15). We have not received the mind of the world or the flesh in the promised grace, but we have received the filial mind of Christ, who hath made us free from the law of sin. Therefore let the same mind be in everyone, that was in Christ Jesus, the one man in grace (Phil. ii. 5). And whoever hath not this mind, understandeth not the things of the Spirit of God; for they are foolishness unto him, and he cannot know them (1 Cor. ii. 14).

16. Now, though in this deep exposition we may to many a one be dumb, and a stumbling block or offence, for he will say we use strange unusual speech in our argument; yet we declare with truth in the sight of God that we have it to give no otherwise than it was given to us in the mind of Christ. He who is of Christ will well understand it. For others, as mockers and sophisters who have Reason for their master, we have written nothing.

17. But we exhort our dear brethren in Christ to read and peruse this treatise with patience, for its name is *The longer the better liked*: the more sought, the more found. Seeing that Christ himself bids us to seek, knock and pray, and has promised us that we shall receive and find, we ought not to stand still in sin and wait till the grace of God fall upon us and compel us; nor ought we to think that God's Spirit will make good out of evil. Certainly it often falls upon the poor sinner (who is not yet a thistle) in his sin, and draws him away therefrom. Then, if he suffer himself to be drawn, it is well. If, however, he will not, but enters again into the serpent and crucifies Christ, he blasphemes against the Holy Spirit; and regarding him the Scripture says, he hath no forgiveness ever (Heb. vi. 6, 7; x. 26).

18. There is no man who is entitled to say that he

has not sometimes been drawn, especially in his thoughts; even the godless man is so drawn. Christ shines for all peoples, for one as well as for another: for one people in his revealed name, and for another in a name of the one God. He draws them all. And because of his drawing and the knowledge which is written in their hearts that there is a God whom they ought to honour, and they do it not; in accordance with this they shall be judged.

19. But how much more rigorously shall we be judged who call ourselves Christians and have the true knowledge, yet keep back the truth and change it into a lie for the sake of a formed opinion which we have imagined, and by which we have made ourselves known to the world. And though we be afterwards brought to the light, we give to ourselves more honour than to God, and seek to conceal, defile and cover up the light with false interpretation, in order that human conjecture may sit as an idol in Christ's place. And in fact it often fares so, and Babel lives entirely in this element, so that many a one ceases not to maintain his once acknowledged opinion, even though he has to drag in the whole of Scripture.

20. Dear Sirs and brethren, let us give the honour to Christ, and conduct ourselves one with another in a kindly way, with sober speech accompanied with instruction. Let one show forth his gifts to another in a brotherly will. For there are various kinds of knowledge and exposition; and if only they proceed from the mind of Christ, they are all rooted in one ground.

21. We should not on account of dissimilar gifts persecute one another, but rather rejoice with each other in love that God's wisdom is so inexhaustible; and think of the future, how it will be well with us

when all this knowledge shall be manifested from one and in one soul, so that we shall all recognize God's gifts and have our joy in one another, every one rejoicing in the gift of another, as the fair flowers in their various colours and virtues rejoice in one mother side by side upon the earth. So likewise will be our resurrection and reappearance.

22. Why then will we wrangle here about a knowledge of the gifts? In Christ are all the treasures of wisdom. If we have Him, then we have all; but if we lose Him, then we have lost all, and ourselves too.

23. The one ground of our religion is, that we love Christ in us, and love one another as Christ has loved us, in that he gave his life for us. But this love is not manifested in us, unless Christ become man and be manifested in us. He giveth us his love, so that we love one another in him, as he loveth us. For he continually gives to our soul his flesh and his blood to eat and to drink; and the soul which does not eat and drink thereof has no Divine life in it (John vi. 54).

24. Therefore I exhort the loving reader, that if to his mind there be something too profoundly penetrating in this treatise, that he would give God the honour, and pray and read it aright. All that the sun shines upon and heaven contains lies in man, as well as hell and all deeps. He is an inexhaustible fountain. He may in time fully comprehend and grasp this high ground which God has given to us, that is, to a simple man.

25. But we would have him warned against aspersing and reviling, as he values his own soul and eternity; for he will not move us, but only the fierce wrath of God in himself. And yet I who have been induced to write this work, me he may indeed move, for I am

secure from his moving in the bonds of Christ. But I would have him exhorted in love to show himself a brother in Christ, and, if he can do so by Divine gifts, to set up a still clearer explanation. If then I shall see such an explanation, I will rejoice in his gift, and thank the Most High, who giveth us through one another so richly all manner of gifts. Amen.

QUÆSTIONES THEOSOPHICÆ

OR

A GENERAL VIEW OF DIVINE REVELATION

SHOWING WHAT GOD, NATURE AND CREATURE, AS WELL AS HEAVEN, HELL AND THE WORLD, TOGETHER WITH ALL CREATURES, ARE. FROM WHENCE ALL THINGS IN NATURE HAVE HAD THEIR ORIGIN, AND WHY GOD HAS CREATED THEM, AND WHAT THEY ARE USEFUL OR PROFITABLE FOR.

AND IN PARTICULAR REGARDING MAN, WHAT ADAM AND CHRIST IS.

FOLLOWED OUT THROUGH THE WHOLE PROGRESSION AND COURSE OF THE WORLD TO THE END AND INTO ETERNITY, AND SET DOWN IN 177 QUESTIONS BY A LOVER OF CHRIST AND HIS CHILDREN, TO PROMOTE FURTHER REFLECTION AS TO WHAT MAN IS.

Begun to be answered (but not completed) out of
a right true theosophic ground in the
year 1624

by

JACOB BÖHME
otherwise called *Teutonicus Philosophus*.

AUTHOR'S PREFACE TO THE READER

It is written: The natural man receiveth not the things of the Spirit of God; for they are foolishness unto him, and he cannot know them (1 Cor. ii. 14). And again, it is also written: The Spirit searcheth all things, yea, the deep things of God (1 Cor. ii. 10).

Now if Mr. Wiseling, without Divine light, should undertake to set to work on these questions and expound them, he would not be able to do it. Nay, perhaps he may account it a sin to ask such high questions, as he himself cannot understand them. To him we say, that he should leave them for those to whom the Spirit of God (which searcheth all things through man's spirit) shall give the understanding; seeing that to him it is yet something incomprehensible, and seems to be impossible.

But to those who love Jesus we say, that they may very well be investigated and understood, and that it is no impossible thing. For in a true Christian dwelleth Christ, in whom all the treasures of hidden wisdom are revealed: such a one knoweth them only in the Spirit of Christ, and not in his own nature and capacity. Thus we have clearly expounded and defined these questions in a special book; briefly and summarily it is true, though in our other writings they are treated at greater length and in a way that is sufficient. And we commend the reader of this book to the revelation of our Lord Jesus Christ.

THE FIRST QUESTION

What is God, apart from nature and creature, in himself?

ANSWER

1. GOD is the eternal Unity, the immeasurable one good, which has nothing after nor before him that can give him or bring him in anything, or that can move him ; and is devoid of all tendencies and properties. He is without origin in time and in himself one only, as a mere purity without attingence. He has nowhere a place or position, nor requires such for his dwelling ; but is at the same time out of the world and in the world, and deeper than any thought can plunge. If the numbers of his greatness and depth should be uttered for a hundred thousand years together, his depth would not have begun to be expressed ; for he is Infinitude. All that can be numbered and measured is natural and figurate ; but the Unity of God cannot be expressed, for it is through everything at the same time. And it is therefore called good, because the eternal gentleness and the supreme beneficence exists in the sentiency of nature and creature as perceptible sweet love.

2. For the Unity, viz. the good, does itself emanate from itself, and with the emanation brings itself into will and movement. There the Unity loves or pervades the willing or moving, and the moving or willing feels the gentleness of the Unity. That is the ground of the love in the Unity, whereof Moses says :

The Lord our God is one God, and there is none else (Ex. xx. 2, 3; Deut. vi. 4; iv. 39).

3. And it is not the case, as Reason supposes, that God dwells alone above the stars, outside of the place of this world. There is no place prepared for him where he dwells apart, but his manifestation only is distinguishable. He is in, with and through us; and where in a life he becomes mobile with his love, there God in his working is revealed. That is, his love or the Unity is there emanating, perceptible and endowed with will. There God has made for himself a place in the ground of the soul, in the eternal idea or object of the eternal willing in the love, wherein the love wills and finds itself, as is to be understood in angels and blessed souls.

THE SECOND QUESTION

What is the abyss of all things where no creature is, or the unfathomable nothing?

Answer

1. It is a dwelling of the unity of God. For the opening, or the something (*Ichts*) of the nothing (*Nichts*), is God himself. The opening is the unity, as an eternal life and willing; a mere will, which has nothing that it can will but itself.

2. Therefore the will is a mere love-longing that wills, as an outgoing of itself to its perceptibility. The will is the eternal Father of the ground; and the perceptibility of the love is the eternal Son, which the will begets in itself as a perceptible power of love; and the outgoing of the perceptible love that wills is the Spirit of the Divine life.

3. The eternal Unity is thus a threefold, immeasurable and unoriginated life, which consists in a mere willing, in a seizing and finding of itself, and in an eternal outgoing of itself.

4. And what has gone forth from the will, love and life is the wisdom of God, that is, the Divine intuition and joy of the unity of God, whereby the love eternally introduces itself into powers, colours, wonders and virtues.

5. In this opening life of the Divine unity five manifest *sensus* are understood in the perceptibility of the love of the life, viz. A, E, I, O, U; and therein lies the Divine willing and working. These bring

themselves into an outbreathing to separability and to understanding of the one Trinity, whereby the eternal life finds and understands itself.

6. The Trinity reveals itself out of the Unity with a threefold breathing, so that this threefold breathing in a threefold manner enters into itself to be something that is its own. And this threefold *sensus* is called by its sensual name JEHOVAH.

7. For the Unity or J goes within itself into a threefold being which is JE. And JE is the Father, which brings itself with its breathing will into HO, as into a comprehension of the love. And in HO the Word of all powers is understood, for it makes a circumference or encompassment of itself, as the eternal Something or *Ichts*, from which the love-longing goes out; and this outgoing is the Spirit, which forms itself into VA. For V is the Spirit or the outgoing, and A is the wisdom in which the Spirit grasps itself so as to become a working life.

8. Then this threefold breathing life in itself is virtually O, JAH. For the circumscribed longing is O, as an eye of the one sight, or a pure seeing. And JAH is the threefold entering in of itself, as for perceptibility of the will, which opens itself through the eternal breathing.

9. The opening, that is, the proprium in the *sensus* of the perceptible opening, is called ADONAI. And it includes six powers or forces, from which *Mysterium magnum* or the high name TETRAGRAMMATON arises, and from which all the entities of the visible and invisible have sprung, and come into shape and form.

10. In the word ADONAI, that is, in these six powers or forces, are contained the six properties of the eternal Nature or the natural life, from which

angels and souls have flowed in accordance with the inwardness of their idea; and likewise the six days of the creation of this world, which with the seeing life (which as O is formed into being) are shut up in a state of repose. There the six powers or forces lie and rest in the still love, *i.e.* the eternal Unity, and yet by their self-activity do without intermission will and go forth.

11. And that is O, the seventh day, in which God rested from all his works, and eternally does rest. That is, the six powers or forces [(1) desire, (2) motion, (3) feeling, (4) fire or life, (5) light or love, (6) sound, distinction, or understanding] rest in that from which they arose, namely, in O as the place of God. Thereby is signified the eternal love, that is, the Unity or the something of the Unity, which is the eternal sabbath of the whole of things as contained in the good existence.

12. Thus we understand that the eternal nothing out of or beyond all beginnings is a pure shine, as the eye of eternal sight. For all things are therein as a nothing. And as the something has arisen from this seeing, the nothing or the eternal Unity sees through all unhindered.

13. Further, we understand that God himself is the seeing and finding of the nothing. And it is therefore called a nothing (though it is God himself), because it is inconceivable and inexpressible.

THE THIRD QUESTION

What is God's love and anger? How is he an angry jealous God, seeing that he himself is unalterable love? How can love and anger be one thing?

Answer

1. Though we may here be difficult to be understood by the reader, yet in the Divine power and in calling upon God he may understand all, if real right earnestness be his.

2. The reader is to know that in Yes and No consist all things, be they divine, diabolic, terrestrial, or however they may be named. The One, as the Yes, is pure power and life, and is the truth of God or God himself. He would in himself be unknowable, and in him would be no joy or elevation, nor feeling, without the No. The No is a counterstroke of the Yes or the truth, in order that the truth may be manifest and a something, in which there may be a *contrarium*, in which the eternal love may be moving, feeling, willing, and such as can be loved.

3. And yet it cannot be said that the Yes is separated from the No, and that they are two things side by side with each other. They are only one thing, but they separate themselves into two beginnings or principles, and make two centres, each of which works and wills in itself. As day in relation to night, and night in relation to day, form two centres, and yet not separated, or separated only in will and desire. For they have two fires in themselves: (1)

the day, as opening out the heat, and (2) the night, as shutting in the cold; and yet there is together but one fire, and neither would be manifest or operative without the other. For the cold is the root of the heat, and the heat is the cause of the cold being perceptible. Without these two, which are in continual conflict, all things would be a nothing, and would stand still without movement.

4. The same is to be understood regarding the eternal unity of the Divine power. If the eternal will did not itself emanate from itself and introduce itself into receivability, there would be no form nor distinction, but all powers would be but one power. Neither could there thus be any understanding, for the understanding arises in the differentiation of the manifold, where one property sees, proves and wills the other.

5. It is likewise the same with joy. But if receivability is to arise, there must be a desire to feel itself, that is, there must be a special will to receivability, which is not identical with nor wills with the one will. For the one will wills only the one good, which itself is; it wills only itself in similarity. But the emanated will wills dissimilarity, in order that it may be distinguished from similarity and be its own something, in order that there may be something which the eternal seeing may see and feel. And from the special individual will arises the No, for it brings itself into ownness, that is, into receptivity of self. It desires to be a something, and does not make itself one with the unity. For the unity is an emanating Yes, which stands ever thus in the breathing forth of itself, being insentient; for it has nothing in which it can feel itself save in the receptivity of the differing will, as in the No which is a counterstroke

of the Yes, in which the Yes is revealed, and in which it has something that it can will.

6. For a one has nothing in itself that it can will, unless it double itself that it may be two; neither can it feel itself in oneness, but in twoness it feels itself.

7. Understand, then, the foundation aright. The separated will has proceeded from the identity of the eternal willing, and has nothing that it can will but itself. But because it is a something as distinguished from the unity (which is as a nothing, and yet is all), it brings itself into a desire for itself, and desires itself and likewise the unity from which it flowed.

8. It desires the unity in order to attain to the felt joy of love, that the unity may be perceptible in it. And it desires itself so as to attain to motion, knowledge and understanding, in order that there may be a diremption in the unity, that forces may take their rise. And though the power has no ground nor beginning, yet in the receivability distinctions arise, from which distinctions nature springs.

9. This emanated will brings itself into a desire; and the desire is magnetic or intrahent, and the unity is emanant. There is thus a *contrarium*, viz. Yes and No. For the flowing-out has no ground, but the drawing-in makes a ground. The nothing wishes to pass out of itself that it may become manifest, and the something wishes to be in itself that it may be sentient in the nothing, in order that the unity in it may become sentient. Accordingly the out and in would thus be an inequality.

10. And the No is therefore called a No, because it is a desire turned inwards, as shutting in to negativity. And the Yes is therefore called Yes, because

it is an eternal efflux or outgoing and the ground of all beings, that is, truth only. For it has no No before it; but the No first arises in the emanated will of receivability.

11. This emanated desiring will is intrahent, and comprehends itself in itself, and from it come forms and properties. The first property is Sharpness, from which comes hardness, coldness, dryness and darkness. For what is drawn in overshadows itself, and this is the true ground of eternal and temporal darkness. And the hardness and sharpness is the ground of sensibility. The second property is the Movement of attraction, and this is a cause of separation. The third property is true Feeling, as between the hardness and the motion, in which the will feels itself; for it finds itself in a great sharpness, as a great anxiety contrary to the unity, so to speak. The fourth property is Fire, as the flash of brightness. This arises in the conjunction of the great anxious sharpness and the unity. For unity is gentle and still; and the moving hard sharpness is terrible, and is a ground of painfulness.

12. Thus in the conjunction a terror appears; and in this terror (shock) unity is laid hold of, so that it becomes a flash or gleam, an exulting joy. For thus light arises in the midst of the darkness. For the unity becomes a light, and the receptivity of the desiring will in the properties becomes a spirit-fire, which has its source and origin from the sour cold sharpness, in the motion and sensibility in the darkness; and its very nature is a terrible consumingness.

13. And in accordance therewith God is called an angry, jealous God, and a consuming fire; not according to what he is in himself as independent of all receivability, but in accordance with the eternal

principle of fire. And in the darkness is understood the foundation of hell, as an oblivion of the good; which darkness is entirely concealed in the light, like night in the day, as may be read in John i. 5.

14. Thus in the above properties is seen God's anger. The first property of the indrawal is the No. It does not identify itself with the Yes or the unity, for it makes in itself a darkness, *i.e.* a losing of the good.

15. Secondly, it makes in itself a sharpness, which is the ground of the eternal dying of the gentleness or the gentle unity. Thirdly, it makes in itself a hardness, which is eternal death or a powerlessness. Fourthly, it makes in itself, in such hardness of death, a continual painful feeling. Fifthly, it makes in itself an anxious source of fire. In these properties God's anger and hell-fire is understood; and it is called hell or hollowness, because it is a hiddenness or shutting-in. It is likewise called an enmity against God because it is painful, whereas the unity of God is a pure gentleness. And they are opposed to each other, like fire and water; and therefrom fire and water have had their origin in the existence of this world.

16. The fifth property in this kindling of the emanated will is the perceptibility of the unity of God, that is, Love, which in fire becomes mobile and desireful, and makes in the fire (as in pain) another principle, as a great fire of love. For the love is the cause and origin of the light, so that in the fire's essence light arises. It is the power in the light. And thus the unity brings itself into movement and perceptibility, in order that the eternal power may be perceptible, and that there may be a will, desire and separation in it. Other-

wise the unity would be an eternal stillness, and imperceptible.

17. This love and light dwells in the fire, and permeates the fire, so that the fire's essence is transformed into the highest joyfulness, and fierce wrath is no more known, but only a pure love-taste of the Divine perceptibility.

18. For the eternal unity thus superincends itself that it may be a love, and that there may be something which may be loved. For if the love of the unity were not rooted in a fiery burning nature, it would not be operative, and there would be no joy or movement in the unity.

19. Thus in the fire's essence is understood God's wrath, and in the love-perceptibility or perceptible unity is understood the Divine love-fire. These form two centres in one Principle, as two kinds of fire.

20. (1) The wrath-fire in the emanated will of receivability is a principle of the eternal Nature, from which the angels and the souls of men have obtained their ground, and is called *Mysterium magnum.* From this eternal Nature the visible world also sprang and was created, as an objective representation of what is inward.

21. (2) And the centre of the love is the Yes as the fire-flaming breath. And it is called God's Word, or the breathing of the unity of God, the foundation of power. And in the efflux of the love-breathing is understood the true Holy Spirit, as the movement or the life of the love. The angelic spirit as well as the soul's spirit is also understood in this efflux, in which God is manifest and dwells.

22. But the ground of souls and angels, in respect of their own nature, is understood in the eternal Nature-fire. For the clear Godhood becomes not crea-

turely, for it is an eternal unity; but it permeates and pervades nature as a fire through-heats iron.

23. And here we understand the possibility of the damnation of angels and souls. If they lose the love-fire, so as to separate themselves from the Divine unity and enter into their own desire, then the wrath-fire burns in them, and is their proper life.

24. But if the Divine love-fire burns in their central fire, then their fire-life is a pure joy and gentle pleasing delight, and the fire of God and the fire of Nature subsist in them in a single principle.

25. In this fifth property the Glory and the Majesty of God is revealed as a light of love. Of which the Scripture says (1 Tim. vi. 16): God dwelleth in a light that no man can attain; signifying, that no creature was ever born from the central fire of love, for it is the most holy fire and God himself in his Triad.

26. And from this holy fire has emanated the Yes, as a ray of the perceptible unity. This ray is the precious name Jesus, which had to redeem the poor soul from the fire of wrath; and, in assuming humanity, introduced itself into the soul, into the dissident central wrath-fire of God's anger, and kindled the soul again with the fire of love and united it with God.

27. O ye men, observe this. Understand, then, the right foundation. In God there is no anger, there is pure love alone. But in the foundation, through which the love becomes mobile, is the fire of anger, though in God it is only a cause of joy and of power. On the other hand, in the centre of the wrath-fire it is the greatest and most terrible darkness, pain and torment.

28. These two are in one another like day and

night, where neither can take hold upon the other, but one dwells in the other. And they make two principles, as two eternal beginnings.

29. The first beginning is called the kingdom of God in love. And the other beginning is called the kingdom of God's wrath, or the foundation of hell, wherein dwell the expelled spirits.

30. The foundation of the kingdom of God is pure Yes, as powers of the separable Word. And the foundation of the wrath of God is pure No, whence lies have their origin. Therefore Christ said that the devil was a father of lies; for his foundation is pure No, and opposition to the truth as the Yes.

31. The sixth property in the emanated will is Sound, tone, understanding, speech, or distinction, that is, the true understanding; and it has its subsistence in the two central fires at once. In the centre of self-receptiveness of the natural fire, without co-operation of the holy fire (in so far as these two fires are separated, as is to be understood in the case of the devils and damned souls), there is no understanding, but only subtlety or acuteness, as a putting to the proof the foundation of nature; a vain abuse of the forces of nature, whence spring imposture, distrustfulness, folly and frivolousness.

32. In this sixth property stand the holy names, that is, the Divine powers in the opening of the Unity, in the working and willing. And they stand in the two fires at the same time, viz. in the fire of natural motion and in the fire of the flame of love.

33. And here we have the wonder-working Word in its operation. For the great name of God TETRAGRAMMATON (JeHoVaH) is here the centre of the wonders of God, and it works in both the central

fires. This name the evil spirits, in their transmutation according to the centre of the fire's nature, do misuse.

34. And the ground of all cabala and magic is contained in this principle, these being the active powers whereby the imperceptible co-works in the perceptible. And here the law of Moses forbids misusing this principle on pain of eternal punishment, as may be seen in the ten commandments. For our fellow-scholars enough has been said, and for the godless a strong bar lies before it.

35. The seventh property of the emanated desireful will is Essential being, where all the powers are contained and are operative in the being, as a basis of all the powers. From this the visible world has arisen, and by the motion of the wonder-working Name has flowed out, and gone into separation and form.

36. Hence in all the beings of this world there are the two central fires, according to God's love and wrath, as may be seen in the creatures.

37. But the holy fire lies hidden. The curse, or the motion of God's wrath, keeps it shut up in sin. As is to be understood by the tincture; and yet with God's permission there is a possible entrance.

38. This emanated holy fire, when it was yet operative throughout the earth, was Paradise. And it is Paradise still, but man has been expelled from it. And many a one meets his death with seeking in connection with this fire, and yet finds it not unless he have first found it in himself.

39. In this question regarding God's love and anger, two kinds of fire are to be understood. First, a love-fire, where there is light only; and this is called God's love or the perceptible unity. And

secondly, a wrath-fire derived from the receivability of the emanated will, through which the fire of love becomes manifest. This wrath-fire is a principle of the eternal Nature, and in the centre of its inwardness is called an eternal darkness and pain. And yet the two fires form but a single principle, and have been from eternity to eternity, and are unchanging. But they separate into two eternal beginnings, as may be considered of in fire and light.

THE FOURTH QUESTION

What was there before the angels and the world of creation were?

Answer

1. God was with the two central fires, with the great powers, as an eternal, infinite bringing forth of wonders, colours and virtues. There the angels and the souls of men, together with all the creatures of this world and of the inward angelic spiritual world, lay in an idea or spiritual model, in which God has from eternity seen all his works. Not in a creaturely formed mode and fashion, as in a separation, but in a formal existence of the powers, where the Spirit of God has sported with himself.

2. In these central fires was the [pure] Element. And the two central fires were a single being, yet distinct in two principles, as fire and light.

3. But when the central fire of the will moved itself, and brought itself into a more considerable desire with reference to its beholding and shaping, creation took place. This process did the eternal will of God put in motion according to both the fires, whereby the idea became figurate to the praise of the wonders of God.

4. And in the course of this motion the hellish foundation of God's wrath broke forth, which God expelled from his working and shut up in darkness. There it remains to this day, like a hungry maw full of craving after creation, and would also be creaturely and figurate.

5. And that is the cause and reason that Lucifer, the prince of a throne, turned himself away from God's love to the central fire of wrath, in which he opined that he was to rule over God's gentleness and love. But on this account he was thrust out from the central love-fire, and lost his throne in the light, and now possesses hell. So likewise it is the case with the damned soul.

6. This hellish foundation in the curse of God's wrath is a centre of the visible world, and is called Satan (of which Christ said, that he deceiveth the whole world), and is understood in the kingdom of darkness, where heat and cold are in conflict. Enough to those that are Ours.

THE FIFTH QUESTION

What was the ground and the essential principle from which the angels were created? What was that power in the Word of God which flowed out and became creaturely?

Answer

1. The Scripture says of God (Ps. civ. 4): Thou makest thy ministers winds, and thine angels flames of fire. In these words lies the whole understanding. For by the word *ministers* is understood the image or idea, that is, the spirit of the angels, which springs from the breathing of the Divine power, from the holy name of God.

2. And the term *flames of fire* denotes the central fire of the eternal Nature, in which the creature as to its essence stands, as the particular will of a being. This is understood as follows:

3. The idea or the image of God was a form of the Divine name in the opening name of God, in which God has from eternity known all things as an imaginary representation of the Divine will. There the will of the unground has shaped itself into a form; and yet was not a creature, but only an idea. As an image is formed in a mirror, so has the imagination of the Divine power shaped itself in the emanating name of God.

4. But when God would realize this idea into the form of a living creature, as into the form of self-will, he put in motion and separated the central fire of the eternal Nature. Thus the idea became manifest in

the fire, which was accomplished through the breathing forth or the Yes.

5. Thus the No, as the emanated will of self-receptiveness, took shape in the outbreathed Yes, in order that the creature might be established in its own will. And this its own will is understood in the central fire, that is, in the properties to fire, in which the creaturely life consists.

6. For if this had not been, then Lucifer could not in self-will have broken himself off from the good, and have fallen. If he had not possessed a volition of his own, then God's power must have fallen. But in this way the creature has broken itself off from the good, and willed to rule in the power and in the properties of the central fire of nature, *i.e.* in the sphere of transmutation and phantasy; to which the devil likewise came.

7. Christ therefore called him a murderer and a liar from the beginning, and this because the No has got the dominion in him. Accordingly he is a mere liar.

8. The essence and nature of the good angels is a power of the central fire and central light, and in these their image stands. But the idea in them is a figure of the holy name of God as the wonder-working Word.

9. Now as the Divine powers and names are many and without number, so likewise there is a difference in the ideas in them, just as one power has a different action from another. Although in God they are one, yet in the efflux, in wisdom, they are distinguished through the manifestation and the wonders. Thus then there is a difference in the angelic idea in the powers; and one such difference has a greater power and might than another, and also a different virtue.

10. As the stars in the firmament are differentiated, so likewise are the angels, in order that there may be a harmony, as a joy and knowledge of the Divine powers.

11. The true foundation of the angels is in the thrones of the powers of God, and they are all of them ministers in these thrones of the powers. For from the powers, as from the holy emanating names of God, or from the eternal Unity, the idea sprang. But there are distinctions and dominions among them.

12. Though they are all ministers of God, yet every throne has its offices and legions with special names, n accordance with the same thrones and powers. Hence there are among them prince-angels, according to the character of each throne. According to what kind of power the throne has, so is the prince-angel. The others are ministers, not servants. They are voices in the harmony of the throne, all conducive to the praise of the great God.

13. The whole deep of the world and out of the world is full of such thrones and dominions. Yet not in the four elements, but in the pure Element of the inner fire and light. They possess another principle or another world, which indeed is in this world, but in another quality, in another ground.

14. Understand then the foundation of the angels. They are of the essence of both the inner eternal central fires. Their powers are the great emanating names of God. All have sprung from the Yes and been led into the No, in order that the powers might become manifest. And thus there had to be an opposite, in which a difference could exist.

15. The name Jachiel (the Lord, the living one, my God) is the differentiating the idea of the virtues.

Therefrom flows Eliel (God, my God) and the holy names according to the Divine property, of which there are many. It is to be intimated to the reader that all these flow from the Divine *sensus.*

16. But the names of the prince-angels, which in the *sensus* carry R. T. or S., their power consists in the strength of the might of fire, from out of the high name TETRAGRAMMATON (JeHoVaH). They are princes over the stars and elements, for they have their dwelling in the inner Element, from which the four elements have emanated and still do emanate.

17. There are also external princes, which dwell in the four elements and are called astral spirits or ascendents, and which have their propria in the world, but are not like the inner princes. For they have another ground of an external nature, of which no further mention is to be made here, because of abuse and superstition.

18. If we would consider and rightly understand the powers and virtues of the angels, and not cleave to images, as foolish Reason always does, let us examine the spirits of the letters, in what *sensus* and power each of them stands. And then let us examine the conjunction of these spirits of the letters, from which the word or meaning arises. In this way we have the whole foundation with Yes and No.

19. Now, words are differentiated by means of the spirits of the letters (vowels), and their condition of differentiation exists in a creaturely image-like manner; as indeed the human kingdom exists so, and everything that is called creature. They are all of them Divine *sensus* derived from the two central fires, as composite expressions of the Divine powers.

20. For as the entire alphabet contains the entire meaning of all beings, so God's Word contains the one meaning of the whole of things, and the angels are its letters.

21. The prince-angels denote the letters, that is, the thrones. The ministering angels denote the combination of the *sensus*, and they are instrumental to the harmony of the Divine understanding, to the praise of God.

22. As force or power to distinguish the *sensus* lies in the letters, so the greatest power lies in the throne-angels ; the others are as the conjoining of the letters in the process of distinction, and are joint-powers. Like a tree with its branches, so is their government and order to be understood. For all the races living in the four elements, together with man, exist in such a fashion ; and every race has those in authority belonging to it, all which is a figure of the inner spiritual world.

23. If man were not so shut up in the No that he could understand what powers he carries in his mouth, and what sort of force resides in them, he would rejoice thereat. But he cannot understand this, because of the curse which lies before it ; for he would misuse the power.

24. He carries the power of all things moving in his mouth. If he had faith, so that he could develop these powers, he would possess the ground of all mysteries, and could do miracles like the angels. This the Scripture attests : If ye have faith as a grain of mustard seed (that is, if ye possess the word in an essential way as a grain of mustard seed), ye may say unto this mountain, Be thou cast into the sea (Matt. xxi. 21). Again : The word is nigh thee, even in thy mouth and in thine heart (Rom. x. 8).

25. This, as aforesaid, is understood by our fellow-scholars and no further, because of abuse and misuse. A strong seal is placed before it, that no unworthy person may understand it. Moreover, it is forbidden to write at length concerning it. Yet the time is born in which it shall stand revealed, but only to those that are worthy. Enough in this place.

THE SIXTH QUESTION

What is the office and the mode of activity of the angels? And why does the power of God bring itself into a formative modification?

Answer

1. As we men upon earth rule all things, that is, the whole sphere of intelligibility, through the distinction of words; so does God, as the eternal mind (*Gemüth*) of the one power, also work and rule through such image-like words in wisdom.

2. The angels are nothing but formed powers of the Word of God, as the mind (*Gemüth*) of man is a counter-form of the eternal power of God.

3. As all sense-faculty comes from the mind (*Gemüth*), and right thoughts come from the sense-faculty as a process of inferring or imagination, whence longing arises, which passes into an entity, whereby perceptible desire is produced, and from that a work:

4. So in like manner is God the eternal mind, and his emanations are the powers, as the senses are in man; and the powers bring themselves into an imagination in which lies the angelic idea, and the imagination brings itself into longing for perceptibility, which is the Yes. And the longing brings itself into desire, and that is the ground of self-receptiveness or the No; and the desire brings itself into properties till it becomes fire, from which the light arises. Thus these properties of the desire are the

Divine thoughts, and they are to be understood in two centres, viz. in Yes and No.

5. The Yes is divine, and the No is the selfness of nature, that is, the perceptibility of the desire. This desire of perceptibility has become a product or work, namely, angels. These are nothing else than God's thoughts according to love and anger, as a revelation of his mind or will.

6. Not that there are thoughts in God, but only in his emanated desireful will, which brings itself into fire and light so as to be perceptible.

7. Now as a man with his thoughts rules the world and all beings, so God or the eternal Unity rules all things through the functions of the angels. The power and the working alone is God's, but they are his instruments whereby he disports and moves himself, and by and through which he reveals the eternal powers and wonders, and brings them into a love-play.

8. They are one and all strings in the great harmony of the Divine kingdom of joy in the song and sound of the powers, and are one and all workers in the wonders of God, as fashioners of the powers, of the holy names of God.

9. As we men do fashion and figurize in our mouth the powers of sense, so as to produce sounding words; so in like manner is their work a mere fashioning of the Divine powers and forms.

10. For what the angels will and desire is by their imagination brought into shape and forms, which forms are pure ideas. In manner as the Divine powers have shaped themselves into such ideas before the creation of the angels, so is their after-modelling.

11. And herein lies the holy cabala of changes,

and the great kingdom of joy, in which the Divine wisdom and knowledge is fashioned and shaped by the spirits of the central fire and light. And there is such a joy of cognition therein, that for great joy and knowledge they bow and humble themselves eternally before such majesty, that the No may not get the dominion in them, and they be deprived of such glory.

12. Their alimentation consists in a drawing or an absorbent desiring of the unity of God. From thence their central fire obtains balsam, that the fierce wrath may not awake. And therefore they live eternally in resigned humility, lest the No should elevate itself in them, as was the case with the devils. And the fall of Lucifer is for them as a mirror.

13. Understand us aright. The whole creation of the inner and outer world, in the holy pure Element and in the four elements, is a mere fashioning and shaping of the Divine powers, but according to the two central fires, as in Yes and No. One emanation has advanced out of another down to the coarsest matter or compaction of earth and stones.

14. For the visible world is only the emanated word with the two central fires, which fires have made for themselves a basis with the external elemental fires wherein the outer creatures live.

15. The more inwardly anyone can enter into the power of a thing, the nearer he comes to the Deity. The four elements are what is outermost; next after them is the astral body; the third in order is the *quinta essentia*, as the principle of the emanated holy Element; the fourth is the tincture, viz. the highest power of the emanated word, in which the two inner central fires lie in one ground. After this, the pure clear Deity is understood.

16. If we would but awake out of the Adamic sleep and look about us, we should see wonders. If the earth were not so dear to us, we should see heaven. Sufficiently understood by our fellow-scholars.

17. This is then the conclusion regarding the activity of the angels, namely, that they are sociates of the Divine kingdom of joy, and are members and branches of the great trees of the Divine names, whereon the heavenly fruits grow. And they obtain their nourishment from the sap of their trees, that is, every angel from his throne. And as the throne is, or the name of God, so is the office of those angels. But the whole tree is God.

18. The wise heathen have honoured as gods the antitype of the angelic thrones, but have lacked the true principle of inwardness. And yet among the Christians this has become a dead letter, except in some few to whom God has revealed it, who have kept it secret in a parabolic way.

THE SEVENTH QUESTION

What moved Lucifer that he had a desire contrary to God, and turned himself away from the good?

Answer

1. His own receptivity, viz. the No, moved him. The emanated will in the central fire of the eternal Nature was the cause thereof. This soared aloft in him, and desired to fashion the Divine power in the might of fire.

2. He desired to put to the proof the property of the eternal Nature, and would not live in self-renunciation, but wished to rule in and with the Holy name of the throne.

3. The cause, however, that moved him to such a desire was the throne in which he was a prince, and indeed he remains eternally therein according to his proprium of fire-power. Yet he did not remain therein according to the Holy name of the light-power, but according to the darkness.

4. When the movement to the creation of the angels took place, the emanated will of self-receptiveness elevated itself; and the properties were in great activity, and desired to be creaturely.

5. In these properties did the creaturely will of Lucifer draw. When he recognized Omnipotence therein, and found in himself the wonder-working power, his creaturely will elevated itself according to the might of fire, and abused the Holy name in it. He would not continue in renunciation, but

willed to rule over the thrones, and broke himself off from the Unity.

6. He wished with the No to rule over the Yes, for the No had elevated itself in him and despised the Yes. Because power of separation and form lay in the No, the creaturely will desired to rule in the No, as in the source of transmutation, and broke itself off from the unity of God and went into the receptivity of the properties.

7. And forthwith properties were manifested in him, namely, cold fire; also sharpness, sourness, hardness, the bitterness, stingingness, hostility, anxiety and painfulness of fire. Hence he became an enemy of all love, humility and meekness; for the foundation of the wrath of God had taken captive the false will.

THE EIGHTH QUESTION

How can a devil have arisen from an angel? or, what is a devil? In what essence and being does he stand after the fall?

Answer

1. We are not to understand that the Holy name, in which Lucifer was a throne-angel, did in him become a devil. Much less did the central love-fire, viz. the power of the light, become one. *No,* that cannot possibly be.

2. For when Lucifer brought his desire into selfful might, and broke himself off from the will of God, the Holy name separated itself from him, and the light was extinguished for him in his fire-life. For he broke himself off from the Unity, which is a balsam of the fire, in which the fire receives its light-lustre.

3. Thus there remained in him only the No, as a formed creature, and the Yes departed from him. For the No separated itself from the Yes in self-will, and would not be under the Yes, that is, under the Divine breathing of the Unity, but would be its own breathing.

4. Accordingly he remained a mere cold, sharp, hard, piercing, bitter, stinging, poisonous, anxious, painful fire-root, in which the central fire is in mere conflict, hunger and thirst, and can attain no refreshment.

5. For if Lucifer were to become an angel again,

he would have to draw again from God's unity and love, and such a fire-life would have to be mortified with the love and be transformed into humility. This the hellish foundation in the devils will not do, nor can it any longer do it; for there is in them all no longer any longing or desire towards humility or repentance.

6. Their whole life is nothing else but the hellish foundation, a source of the wrath of God, a mere poison and stench, and a dying pang (*Qual*). When they hear love and humility spoken of, they flee therefrom, for love is the death of their false life.

7. They have indeed an eternal regret for their lost inheritance, viz. the good; yet they can have no belief that they could attain to grace, but eternal doubt constitutes their belief.

8. They have become separated from God, and therefore they curse or flee from God's power and will; such is for them an intolerable thing. For if they were touched by the holy power of God, it would divest them of strength; for it kills the self-will, and that the self-will does not will, as it would lose its power and might.

9. Thus Lucifer, who was the prince of a throne, abandoned the holy name in him. And there soared aloft the particular will, viz. the creature, that is to say, the central fire-life according to the properties of the eternal Nature.

10. Thus he forfeited the Divine image or the idea, so that it became inert and inoperative, like a withered tree without Divine power, or a figure without motion. And of this he is eternally ashamed, that an angelic character is in him, and no longer exists in an angelic nature and form. He has lost the image of God, and become like the venomous

worms and beasts, whose life has its subsistence in poison.

11. Such a monstrous misshape have the devils got, all according to the property of each of them. For their properties are distinct and various, according to the foundation of the hellish essence. They have among them also princely dominions, all according to the properties, such as devils of pride, devils of avarice, devils of envy, devils of anger, devils of lying, devils of sorcery, and very many others, as a *contrarium* in opposition to God's wisdom and truth.

12. Every Divine good power has in the hellish foundation, as in the No, a *contrarium* or opposite, in order that the Yes or the truth may be known. And thus the darkness, as the foundation of God's wrath, has also come into a state of form.

13. But it may be asked : How is it possible that a hideous fierce devil can arise from a fair angel ?

14. This is brought about through the two eternal central fires, in which the will moves in the properties. When one of these fires separates from the other, it is already effected. This takes place also among men, so that a good man perishes.

THE NINTH QUESTION

Seeing that God is almighty, why did he not resist Lucifer, and prevent this?

ANSWER

1. When fire and light separate, there is a great hostility between them. Water and fire are enemies, and neither any longer desires the other, for one is death to the other; but as long as they are in a growing life, and exist together in one ground, they love each other and live in great joy together. And so in like manner we are to conceive of the devil and God: God no longer desires the devil, nor does the devil any longer desire God.

2. If we now ask, why God did not check this in its movement, the answer is: God had given Lucifer his love and stayed him from doing this, as he likewise stayed Adam. But the central eternal fire-will, *i.e.* the anger of God, would not be stayed; it separated itself in its own way.

3. Here God's love and anger must be distinguished. They are indeed both called God; but God, in so far as he is the eternal good, is not anger; the anger or wrath has another principle. In the love-fire they are certainly one, but in the form of separation they are two. And as they are both eternal, without beginning, they have also an eternal will, neither being able to kill the other, but each remains in itself eternally. They are a twofold power,

and are two centres; yet they come originally from the unity, from one ground or principle.

4. Therefore, when I say of God's love, It is all-powerful, above all and in all, this is meant according to the will of the Yes or the Light. And if the No give it will, the Yes transforms the No into its power and love. And yet they remain two central wills in one another; but in one ground, in one love and desire. Otherwise, the angry God would not be almighty, if the love in its omnipotence alone had him. And yet there is only one God. But the love would not be manifest, and no love would be known, without the wrath.

5. The love therefore gives itself up to the wrath-fire, in order that it may be a love-fire. But if the wrath separate from the love into its own receptivity, that does not forcibly inhibit the love; else it would follow that God would be at variance in himself.

6. Thus the No, or God's wrath, has in the fallen angels gone into a separation from the love, as into a special kingdom of its own. This is a wonderful thing, and was done to the end that the other angels may have a mirror, and that the individual will may not elevate itself. And further, that there may be in them an eternal joy and praise of God that they live not in such fires' essence. Also that they may turn their desire the more towards the unity of God, and remain in renunciation and humility, that is, in the Divine harmony.

7. When we speak here of the will of God's wrath, and say that it broke itself off from the love and willed to be figurate, this must not be understood as outside of the creature. It was not a foreign external will,—such would not have been figurate in the

apostate angels,—but it was the angry God in the formed creature, which was figurate before. Otherwise their whole locus would have been a downfall. But that this was not the case is shown by their having been expelled from their throne.

8. The guilt of the fall must not be attributed to God, but only to the formed power in the creature according to the No. This power has thus been fooled away and has become a lie, not God, but the creature; not the unformed power of the wrath in which the love burns, but the throne in accordance with the receptivity and selfhood. And as their king and prince did, so did also his legions.

9. For when God's wrath hardens a creature, there enters not into it a foreign wrath which hardens it, but its own wrath does that. And on that account a judgment may pass upon it. If God constrained it to evil, no judgment could pass upon it, for it would do only what God willed to have. But in this way it does what God would not have from it, and therefore it falls into judgment.

10. Reason discourses much concerning God and his omnipotence; but it understands little of God and his nature, what and how he is. It separates the soul wholly from God, as if it were a peculiar distinct being, and knows not what an angel or soul is. And that is the great error of blindness, about which men wrangle and dispute, and never reach the true foundation.

THE TENTH QUESTION

What was it the devil desired, with a view to which he turned aside from God's love?

Answer

1. He desired to be an Artist. He saw the creation and understood the foundation of it. Whereupon he wished to be a God, and rule with the central fire-power in all things, and fashion himself in connection with all things. He desired to shape himself into all forms, so that he could be what he wished, and not what the creator wished. As indeed it is still to this day their greatest joy that they can transmute themselves, and bring themselves into manifold forms, and thus exercise phantasy.

2. He would be a fool, and such he became. But he knew not how it would be, when the light should be extinguished for him. Just as Adam knew not how it would be when he should feel heat and cold, and when the central fire with the properties should awaken in him, and that he should fall away from the harmony and lose the central light-fire. This did Adam not know.

3. The devil would be a lord in the No and possess another principle, that is to say, the power of separation at the basis of the formation of figure. Greatness, not subjection, pleased him. He despised humility and sweetness, viz. love and truth, and would not be in the unity, but only in the source of multiplication.

4. He wished to work with his own name, as with the central fire-power, and not with the Divine name of his throne. He put the No above the Yes. Thus he became an enemy of God, and a liar and murderer of the good fashioning of the good powers. He desired to destroy what God's working fashioned, in order that he might exhibit his own working and fashioning.

5. The magical foundation of Omnipotence pleased him. In the pursuit of this he elevated himself and opposed the Yes, because in its centre it was not a working of fire. And because he saw that the Yes, as the outflow of the unity in the fire-centre, brought itself into a light and into an active love, he supposed that the fire-nature would be stronger and greater than the gentleness of the Unity, than the formed names in the opening Unity, which he thought in his fire-power to rule as he pleased; but for such a will God had not created him.

6. Therefore, seeing he forsook God's order, the holy opening name of God separated from him and remained in the unity, and Lucifer remained in the properties of the central fire, dwelling in himself; and yet stood in his princely throne, where the holy name of God had fashioned itself into a throne; and was no longer an angel with his legions, but a false image and monstrous shape.

7. For when the light was extinguished for him, darkness and the cold sharpness of wrath was manifested in him, and he became forthwith an enemy of God and all the angelic hosts.

THE ELEVENTH QUESTION

What was the combat between Michael and the dragon? What is Michael and the dragon, and how was the victory and the expulsion effected?

Answer

1. Michael is the high name of the Divine figure of that throne in which Lucifer was a prince. It is that which separated itself from the No, as from lying; and in this name and power Lucifer was to work with God. It was the might and power of the strong love of God in this throne, and likewise remains so eternally. It is itself the throne according to the Divine figure in the Unity; not as a creature, but as a figure of the power of God in the opening or motion of the Unity.

2. This name afterwards, when the Unity once more put itself in motion, was with the emanation *Jesus* adjoined unto man. On this account the devil became an enemy of men, who are to possess his throne, and therefore he desires to get men into his kingdom.

3. But the Dragon is the hellish foundation in its manifestation, into which Lucifer had fashioned himself with his legions, who had elevated themselves with their throne-prince. That is to say, it is the central fire-kingdom in accordance with the receptivity of self,—not a creature, but the figure of God's anger according to the separation from the Unity and love.

4. It is the individual will, the anger's might, and cannot well be expressed in metaphorical terms. It is fierce wrath, a source and root of heat, cold, hardness, sharpness, stingingness, bitterness, anxiety and pain. It is the sensibility, the first Principle, a mere hunger and thirst, a desire of vanity and lying, a stench of poison and the agony of death.

5. This fire is like a brimstone fire, which burns in stench and poison; for it is the dying pangs of death, and is death and hell itself, which were revealed at the downfall of Lucifer.

6. But Satan, which deceiveth the whole world, as Christ says, is this false will of selfness, the first Principle, the will of hell, a cause of lying and opposition, a leading away from the good, a universal spirit of the hellish foundation. The same is not a creature, but is the false heart in the hellish foundation, and is the hellish science.

7. And though it also has devils of this property and name, which are likewise princes of their legions (for they have fashioned themselves into the hellish proprium), the principle above indicated is their life, and keeps them imprisoned in itself.

8. And as the properties of the hellish foundation are many, so are the princes as included among them many, which rule in these properties.

9. Thus Belial is the source of the false desire connected with impurity and disorder.

10. Beelzebub is the source of idolatry and false imagination.

11. Asmodeus is a spirit of fury or madness. All these are properties of the hellish foundation; and indeed such creaturely spirits exist in the hellish foundation.

12. But Lucifer is the source of pride or mounting upwards.

13. All these properties were awakened also in man after the fall, when he turned away from God; and they have developed with man.

14. Such is then the dragon, the old serpent, with whom Michael (as the figure of the Divine power) fought, and expelled him together with his legions from the holy name. And in man the name Jesus fights against this dragon.

15. This combat is not a creaturely thing. Certainly it went against the creaturely kingdom of false lying spirits, which desired to rule in the Divine name. It is a combat between Yes and No, between the typical wrath and the typical love, between the first and second Principles.

16. In this combat the Divine character of the idea must triumph, if it is to be an angel. In this combat Adam fell. And in this combat the name Jesus, in our humanity which He had assumed, gained the victory against this dragon in the wilderness, where He was tempted forty days; and at last in death He completely vanquished him.

17. This combat was with Moses on Mount Sinai, in the Father's property of fire, when he stayed there forty days. There Israel was tried, to see whether they would or could stand in the property of the Father.

18. But this not being possible, Israel fell away, and made for themselves an idol-god, viz. the golden calf. And the tables of the law were therefore broken, to intimate that the human will of selfness could not prevail against the foundation of the wrath: the human will must be broken and slain, and through death be introduced again into the holy name.

19. Christ accordingly had to die and bring the

human will through death, through hell and through this foundation, because the self-assumption of a will cannot subsist in God. If a will is to subsist in God, it must be impatible and non-suffering, so that it may be able to dwell in fire and yet not be laid hold of by the fire.

20. As the sun in the elements presses through everything, and kindles itself in the elements, and yet its light remains free; or as fire through-heats iron, and yet becomes not iron, but the iron is only an object in which the fire elevates and inflames itself: so pure also must the will be which is to possess God's unity; no assuming may be in it.

21. For as soon as it enters into assumption, this dragon, that is, the hellish foundation, arises in it. But it must penetrate purely the wrath-fire, and without assumption superincend itself in the fire. In this way, then, there are two purities in one ground, viz. fire and light. In fire we have nature or motion, and in light we have the Will-spirit as the true power of the unity of God.

22. Hence love and anger may remain unseparated in a single ground, and be wholly one thing; just as God is considered thus, and also the holy angels.

23. With regard to this Question, therefore, we are to understand that the power of the throne, viz. Yes and No, or God's love and the formed wrath of the eternal Nature of the central fire-will, have fought together. In this will Lucifer abode with his angels and would be a lord, and was also a cause that this central fire-will formed itself into a throat of the dragon, that is, into a hellish foundation. Which God permitted, that he might punish the apostate angel and keep him a prisoner in the gulf of hell, so that he should no longer disturb the creation.

THE TWELFTH QUESTION

How may the eternal counsel of God be contemplated in the Divine intuition, seeing the Spirit searcheth all things, yea even the depths of the Deity, as St. Paul says? And yet this is not in man's power (by reason of the creature), and nevertheless is possible. How may a man really understand this ground of the deep Unity?

Answer

1. Kindly reader, this Question is added here because unenlightened Reason regards it as impossible to know such mysteries, from its being unable to comprehend them; and therefore it blasphemes, ascribing such knowledge to the devil. Accordingly, for love of our neighbour we will explain the position a little, to see if some would become seeing and understand the deep meaning.

2. Reason runs in mere images in a creaturely manner, and supposes that God in his triad consulted as to what he should make, and how it was to fare with it; and therefore Reason concludes that the fall of Lucifer and of Adam was directed to a certain end, which God has decreed thus in his purpose. But a cogitation of Reason is not the originating cause. God needs not to take counsel about anything, for he himself is the counsel; the high emanating names of the powers are the counsel of God, that is, the wonder-working Word. There is in it no purpose in respect of anything; for the

origin of all things lies in the idea, in an eternal process of forming,—not as something formed, but in a perpetual process of forming, where God's love and wrath, viz. the two central fires of the powers, are in a continual love-wrestling. In this wrestling of the powers the wonder-working Word is fashioned into figures, which are mere counterparts of the holy names and powers, and are called ideas.

3. On the other hand, the powers of the eternal Nature likewise fashion themselves according to the mode of formation for fire, that is, in a dark, sharp, hard, fierce, stinging, bitter, anxious, fiery and cold manner. These, however, are not creatures, but only a fashioning of the powers in the No or God's wrath, yet are continually permeated and pervaded with the Yes and the central light, and transformed into a play of love; in such manner as from a bad thing something good is produced, or from a damned soul or angel a good holy angel arises.

4. Such fashioning of ideas has been from eternity, in connection with which the Spirit of God has foreseen everything that should or could arise when such fashioning should be brought into a creaturely form. Yet this comes not from a Divine decree of the holy name, but originates in the emanated free-will according to the two central fires of the powers, in which the powers form themselves. Thus the individual will takes form in the No, as in the fierce fire-nature; and the Yes, or breathing of the Unity, takes form in the light; and these two figures exist together in one ground. In the Yes is the holy name of the love of God, and in the No is the name of the wrath of God. And there the Yes in the holy name of the Divine love wrestles for victory with the No, as with the individual emanated will of self-

receptiveness, and yet it is only a love-play. For the light permeates and pervades the fashioning of the darkness, and hence the fashioning is turned into a triumph of joy. Thus there is an eternal overcoming of the dragon in God's wrath, and yet it is only a play of the two central fire-wills.

5. And here we have the purpose of God, of which the Scripture speaks; and yet it depends on the particular will. God, in so far as he is and is called God, enforces no figure, but the powers constrain themselves with a view to victory.

6. And here we have also the ground of the devil, in which it is seen how the self-will or the No has fought in a developed form against the Yes and turned aside from the Yes, and has through its own motion separated itself and become a devil, that is, an enemy to the Yes, and has entered into its own creaturely dominion.

7. Further, in this ground we see how Michael has fought against this dragon and the formed false wills, though originally the Yes or the holy name was in these false wills, when they were angels. But the individual will of the central fire of self-receptiveness separated itself from the Yes into its own self, and therefore it was cast out by the Yes in the name Michael.

8. This likewise may be shown in the Holy Scripture, both in the prophet Micaiah and in the case of king Saul, where an evil spirit from the Lord passed into Saul, and also into the prophet Zedekiah and his companions. And the Lord said: Who shall persuade Ahab, that he may go up and fall at Ramoth-gilead? And one said on this manner, and another said on that manner. And there came forth a spirit, and stood before the Lord, and said, I will

be a lying spirit in the mouth of all his prophets. And the Lord said: Go forth, thou shalt prevail (1 Kings xxii. 20-22). This Lord was the wrath of God which burned over Israel, as may be shown in many passages of Scripture, especially in Moses and the Prophets, that he threatened them in his fire-power that he would devour them.

9. Thus in this ground we understand rightly that such pouring out of the wrath of God comes from a corresponding foundation; for in the holy name of God or in the centre of the light there is no wrath-will, but pure love only, and this is God himself.

10. But in the No or the fire-power such rays of wrath arise. These are evil spirits, as in the case of Saul and in the false prophets, and also in the strife of Babel among the sects on account of opinions in religion, where men love not God purely and cleave to him alone, but will run on in art and reason. Hence such sources of error or such evil wrangling spirits appear, arising out of the fiery soul which has sprung from this ground of the eternal central fire and come into a creaturely being.

11. These sources are nothing but evil spirits from the Lord as belonging to the wrath of God, and have sprung from the individual will of self-receptiveness. They are true heretics, that is, spirits which have been spewed out, as they call each other among themselves. It is evident that they strive only for the victory of images, and always aim at overcoming in the letter the holy name, as the emanated word of God; for they fight only for the letter, in the way in which the inner combat takes place between Yes and No, between the two eternal Principles.

12. In this combat the holy name Jesus has implanted

itself in humanity, that it might overpower this source of the dragon and the wrath of God, and redeem poor men from the will of the No. And now it reigns in this combat over all its enemies, viz. over sin, death, the devil and hell, as the Scripture says: Till these his enemies (all which are foes of the royal and princely throne Michael, for they have been expelled therefrom) be made the footstool of his feet, and such domination and imagination in this throne cease.

13. Thus our thought and knowledge that we have got from God is sufficiently intimated to our condisciples, and we mean this in love. It is the highest gate, which God ultimately unlocks for us, for whoever is able to understand it. But for the mockers, so long as they are such, we have written nothing; and we seal this with the eternal Will, that no mocker may understand it. Amen.

14. But how a man may understand such depths of the Deity and search all things (as St. Paul says), and yet the rational natural man in his own power as the particular will cannot comprehend this, and nevertheless it may be made comprehensible in man, is understood as follows:

15. Man is an image of the Being of all beings, a right image of God according to love and wrath. Namely, (1) the soul is the eternal central fire of self-will, for out of it creatures have to come and not from the pure Deity.

16. And (2) the spirit of the soul is the central fire of light, sprung from the eternal idea, from the power of God, and is supernatural. Hence it is a temple of the Holy Spirit, wherein Christ dwells and feeds the soul with his flesh and blood, as with Divine and human balsam, and wherein death and

the wrath of God have been broken down. Then such Divine balsam continues to exist essentially in the spirit of the soul, as Christ says: He that eateth my flesh and drinketh my blood abideth in me, and I in him.

17. But (3) the outer body is from the outer world, from the four elements and the stars, and this external dominion rules the outward life. After this external dominion the Adamic soul lusted, and for the sake thereof broke off its will from the unity of God, and introduced it into the dominion of this world. There the will was taken prisoner in itself by the dragon of the wrath of God, and transformed into a monstrous shape. There the true spirit was eclipsed, so that the light of God was extinguished for it, and the idea became inert and inoperative.

18. To the aid of this spirit and the idea came Jesus, as an emanation of the Divine unity, and introduced the light of love again into the poor soul.

19. Now when this name Jesus, which, when he assumed humanity, is called Christ, makes its entry into the poor soul that has turned away, and penetrates it with this ray of the unity of God, the eternal idea as the right spirit becomes mobile again in such balsam of love, and thus the light shines again in the eternal darkness of the soul, and the No is united again with the Yes. There Michael in the combat stands against the dragon, and is the name of the throne in Christ Jesus.

20. In this light the soul sees again into its primal country, viz. into its origin from whence it sprang; for the name of God is in it, and works in the spirit. There it lives in the contemplation of God and may search all things; yet not in its own motion and will, but as the name of God moves in it. Then it

sees the fashioning of the wonder-working name, and it hears what God speaks in it,—not discourse in images, but active speech in the understanding, and yet incomprehensible to external Reason, regarding which St. Paul says : Our conversation is in heaven (Phil. iii. 20). But he also says, there was given to him a thorn in the flesh, even the messenger of Satan, a torment from the seducing spirit of lust, to buffet him (2 Cor. xii. 7).

21. Understand it aright. A man sees such mysteries in the spirit of Christ, in whom are all the treasures of wisdom, as is attested throughout by the Scriptures. Understand, then, correctly what the eternal counsel of God is, and also how man may attain to such beholding. The possibility only is here indicated ; but the process, showing how he may attain to it, we have described at length in other works.

THE THIRTEENTH QUESTION

How was the expulsion of the dragon and the legions of Lucifer brought about? Whither has he been thrust so as to be out of God, seeing God fills all things? Or, what is the foundation of hell, wherein he dwelleth?

Answer

1. The expulsion of the dragon implies the false, averse, image-like will of self-receptiveness, in which averse will Lucifer and his angels have formed themselves.

2. The dragon is the hellish foundation, and the expelled spirits are the natural formed properties of the hellish foundation. For when they broke themselves off from the holy name of God, from the being of the unity of God, and took form wholly in the No, as in falsehood or lying, they became such.

3. The expulsion was brought about through the holy Name of power of his former throne. He was with his legions cast out of his throne, and immediately shut in by the darkness and laid hold of by the fierce wrath of the hellish foundation.

4. Thus he is separated from God's holiness, and dwells under the firmament and upon the earth, between time and eternity, as a prince of darkness in the wrath of God.

5. His princely dominion is on high, but in several and distinct places, as well as everywhere in the elements, according to the nature and character of the four elements. For their propria are of many

kinds, and they have habitations in all the four elements, every race among them dwelling in the likeness of itself.

6. But this must be rightly understood. They possess not the elements according to their good qualities, but only the emanated wrath from out of the eternal fierceness of the hellish foundation.

7. For in the elements two kingdoms are always to be understood, namely, one in accordance with God's emanated love, and the other in accordance with his wrath. The devils dwell only in the part belonging to the wrath, and are shut up in eternal night, and cannot touch the good powers of the elements. But whatever flows from the wrath and is formed into being, in that they can dwell, and in connection with this sorcery is carried on.

8. There are indeed some powers, where the holy power of the central fire of light has emanated, which are wholly contrary to the hellish foundation. But in man there is good and evil together, and the good keeps the evil a prisoner, and permeates and pervades the evil, so that the devils can have no exercise therein. Unless man's will of its own power change this position, or it be changed by the *turba magna*, so that a movement of fierceness enters into an existence, by which the motion of the bad outstrips the good.

9. Their habitation is a gulf of lying, an abyss of eternal perdition, a formation of the phantasy with a false light, as this gulf by its imagination fashions for itself from the central fire a light, which stands connected with no principle and touches not the majesty of God, and which, if the name of God be violated in it, is extinguished, as is to be understood in the case of sorcery.

10. This expelled dragon or jaws of the hellish foundation is not the central fire of the eternal Nature, but a receptivity of self, an efflux from the fire. As smoke and fire are two things, and yet come from one origin; so is the dragon a thing of wrath, like smoke which arises from fire.

11. It is therefore wholly separated from God, just as smoke from fire, and yet receives power and strength from the central fire of the eternal Nature; for its life is rooted therein, but its will and desire resemble the smoke which arises from fire.

12. For its fire of nature in its creaturely (central) essence is burning; but in God's essence it forms a temperament with the central love-fire of the light. The cause of the fire is transformed into light; but in the throat of the dragon or jaws of the hellish foundation the properties in their working are manifest.

13. The hellish foundation and the heavenly foundation are to one another like day and night. They are near each other, yet neither comprehends the other, nor does one see the other in its essence. For what in God is a love-burning is in hell a wrath-burning.

14. This hellish gulf pours itself forth in some measure in many a region through the elements, especially in the earth, as also in the upper realm; whereupon pits of fire are discerned, now of great cold, and now of great heat; especially in vast solitudes and where there are chasms in the earth, wherein dwell damned spirits as well as damned souls of men; at which the evil spirits themselves are terrified, for it is the flames of hell.

15. The hellish foundation is at present not yet wholly revealed, and the devils have to await a greater

judgment. The sun and the water keep their kingdom concealed, so that it cannot be entirely manifested till the day of judgment. Only in the properties within themselves is it revealed. And therefore the last day fills the devils with terror.

16. Understand it aright. God in the foundation of hell is to be regarded as a nothing, for there he is unemanating according to his love. He assuredly is, but in himself only. To the hellish foundation, however, he is in respect of love a nothing.

17. So in like manner hell in God is a nothing. It assuredly is, but the light does not lay hold of it; they are to one another as death and life. Each lives and wills in itself, and the two together are as something and nothing.

18. In the light God is a something, and in hell he is a nothing. For the eternal Unity is a being and power only in the light, and lying is a being and power only in its own receptivity.

19. The devils stand therefore in great reproach, because they are so near God and yet cannot reach him; and that is also their source of anguish.

THE FOURTEENTH

AND

FIFTEENTH QUESTIONS

Q. 14. *What is the office of the devil in hell?*

Q. 15. *Had the foundation of hell a temporal beginning, or has it been from eternity? And how may it endure eternally, or not?*

Answer

1. The foundation of hell has been from eternity, yet not in a corresponding manifestation. For the wrath of God has existed from eternity, not indeed as wrath, not figurate or emanate, but as fire is hidden in wood or a stone till it be roused.

2. The rousing or kindling, or the open swallow of the dragon, had its beginning at the fall of Lucifer, as in a creature in which the self-will or the No turned itself away from the Yes.

3. But because this awakened ground has sprung from the eternal foundation, and has an eternal will, it cannot pass away; unless the whole creation were annulled, and the eternal Nature in self-receptiveness should become extinct. If that were to happen, then cognition and feeling, as also the kingdom of joy, would cease to exist.

4. Which cannot be. For there must be two eternal beginnings, one in another, in order that one

may be cognized and felt in the other, and that the holy angels and souls together with all the heavenly creatures may praise God and rejoice in the good, that they dwell not in the bad and have to be what is bad.

Printed in the United States
38265LVS00001B/121

9 781564 591463